The Law School Book

SUCCEEDING
AT LAW SCHOOL

The Law School Book

SUCCEEDING
AT LAW SCHOOL
SECOND EDITION

Allan C. Hutchinson
OSGOODE HALL LAW SCHOOL

IRWIN LAW

A Quicklaw Company

The Law School Book, second edition
© Irwin Law Inc., 2000

Published in 2000 by

Irwin Law Inc.
14 Duncan Street
Suite 206
Toronto, Ontario
M5H 3G8

www.irwinlaw.com

ISBN-13: 978-1-55221-045-1
ISBN-10: 1-55221-045-6

Library and Archives Canada Cataloguing in Publication

Hutchinson, Allan C.
    The law school book: succeeding at law school
2nd. ed.

Includes bibliographical references and index.
ISBN 1-55221-045-6

1. Law—Study and teaching—Canada. I. Title.

KE289.H88 2000   340'071'171   C00-931749-X
KF272.H88 2000

Cover and Interior Design: Sonya V. Thursby / Opus House Incorporated
Typesetting: Carolyn Sebestyen / Opus House Incorporated
Illustration: Linda Tae
Cover Photograph: J.A. Kraulis/Masterfile

The publisher acknowledges the financial support of the Government of Canada through the Book Publishing Industry Development Program (BPIDP) for its publishing activities.

We acknowledge the assistance of the OMDC Book Fund, an initiative of Ontario Media Development Corporation.

Printed and bound in Canada.

3 4 5   09 08

SUMMARY TABLE OF CONTENTS

DETAILED TABLE OF CONTENTS

PREFACE

In writing any book, certain assumptions have to be made about the likely audience, and this injunction is doubly applicable for this particular project. Although considerable risk is attached to such an ambition, this book has been written with three somewhat related groups of readers in mind:

- Those who are thinking of going to law school and want to know what it is about and how to get there. The early chapters try to give a good indication of what law school life is like, so that prospective students can make an informed decision about whether law and law school are for them.
- Those who have been accepted at law school and want to know how to succeed. Apart from the early chapter, the book aims to provide students with insights and tips on how to cope with the routines of law school life and how to succeed in becoming good law students and even better lawyers.
- Those who are studying law in an undergraduate course and want a general introduction to the law and its mysterious ways. Although parts of the book are directed more at the law school student, there is much throughout the book that will be helpful to those who want to get a basic orientation to law and go beyond the theoretical introductions for undergraduates.

No matter the group of readers, the ambition remains the same: to provide a readable and accessible introduction to law and its study. Although the book can be read in a conventional and sequential manner, it is also designed to allow readers to dip in and out as the topic and the mood take them. The hope is that, informed by this knowledge, readers will have a distinct advantage over some of their colleagues and competitors. While I do not claim that this book on its own will get students through law school, I do suggest that, by following its advice and recommendations, readers will be well served in their efforts to make their law experience a satisfying and successful time.

Although I have strong views about many of the topics discussed, I have tried to write a book that can be used by students and recommended by professors with different views from my own. While I have not completely submerged my ideas and opinions, I have striven to complete a text that is balanced and restrained. However, it will be clear in parts that my own slant on certain topics is far from the traditional. I trust that readers will be astute enough to recognize my views for what they are—arguments that are intended to open up a discussion, not to close one down.

The life of the law is sustained and made all the more exciting by the scope it allows for disagreement and debate. If there is a sin in writing books like this one, it is not the expression of particular ideas and partial understandings about law, but the suppression of such views in the false name of impartiality and objectivity. Law is about values, and it is incumbent upon lawyers, professors, and students to address those values and to come clean on the vantage point from which they view and assume such values.

It is impossible to write any book, let alone one like this, without a lot of help from several people. Many of them are former students and peers who, although few knew it, were the guinea pigs for some of the experiments that gave rise to my ideas and opinions on legal education; others are colleagues who have shaped my thinking about law; still others are co-workers who helped me to keep a sense of balance and organization in completing the book.

Some of these people deserve a formal mention. First and foremost is Pam Marshall who co-wrote the first edition of this book and was instrumental in its publication. Duncan Kennedy, Tim Roberts, and Robert Eagleson were generous enough to allow me to borrow directly their words and ideas. Talented and anonymous Osgoode and Toronto students wrote the memoranda, factums, and exam answers. Waleska Vernon updated all the tables and charts, originally compiled by Candice Feldberg and Tovit Schultz; and there is still the strong influence of Jim Smith and Simon Crawford who, along with Donna Gillespie, George Avraam, Susan Travers, Karin Edworthy, Brad Rafauli, Kurt Wildman, Barry Wadsworth, and Roberta Bald, contributed their views on student life. Last, but not least, I want to thank Bill Kaplan and Jeff Miller who continue to show great support for the project. Many thanks to one and all.

I want to end this preface on an optimistic and enthusiastic note; there is little worse than jaded and cynical professorial has-beens. Some depict law school as a harrowing experience and warn that above its entrance should be posted Dante's inscription over the portals of Hell—"Abandon all hope ye who enter here." I can only tell readers that, for all my carping and complaining about the law, lawyers and law schools, I continue to enjoy my time in its institutions and (mostly) with its inmates. Like life, law school is what you make of it. Go for it!

Allan C. Hutchinson
August, 2000

CHAPTER 1

So, You Want to Go to Law School?
The Inside Story

So, you think you want to go to law school? There are many reasons you might have for this conclusion — some conscious and reasonable, others less so. You might wish to go to law school because you want to change the world; you cannot bear the thought of starting work; you want to be rich and powerful; you do not know what else to do; you were rejected by medical school; you want to fulfil your child-hood dream; or your parents expect you to become a lawyer. But there are some facts and observations you should know about law school before you settle on any final decision. After all, it is a big commitment to embark on the road to law school and a legal career, one that is likely to have a profound effect not only on your future career but also on the way you look at and connect with the world. Accordingly, it is better to begin with your eyes wide open than to proceed on the basis of opti-mistic supposition and downright misinformation. Law school is not for everybody. Although you cannot really know whether it is for you without actually going there, you can at least become better acquainted with what to expect.

This opening chapter offers a glimpse at law school — its structure, courses, and mind-set. After debunking some of the major myths that have grown up around law school, there is a description of the basic set-up of the law school curriculum and courses; the intent here is to reassure potential applicants that law school, for bet-ter and for worse, is not all that it is claimed to be. There follows an overview of the admissions procedures that are employed at Canadian law schools, including infor-mation and ideas on the Law School Admission Test (LSAT), choice of pre-law pro-grams, discretionary admission policies, and how to choose a particular school. Next, there is a blunt assessment of the costs of going to law school and the thorny issue of working your way through law school. Throughout the chapter, the empha-sis is on providing a realistic account of the possibilities and prospects for getting into law school.

EXPLODING THE MYTHS

What are some of the main myths that have developed about law school? No doubt many misapprehensions are fuelled by law students and lawyers in order to intimi-date the potential or fledgling law student. Here are a few of the most notorious.

1

- *Law school is difficult.* While law school is not easy, it is by no means as difficult as myth would have it. Everyone who is admitted to law school — and many more besides — is fully capable not only of getting through law school but of doing well. The difficult part is getting in, not staying there. A law degree has much more to do with commitment and application than with innate genius. Students who are prepared to take their studies seriously and give them their best shot are assured of success. If you know what you are doing (and this book intends to tell you what you need to know), law school is not much more difficult than any other area of university study.

- *A law degree is a meal ticket for life.* If this myth ever was true, it is no longer a valid reason for going to law school. The market for law jobs and for legal services is competitive; good articling positions are in tight supply and, while it is better than it was a few years ago, the hire-back rate for articling students can still be discouraging (see chapter 10). Nevertheless, for those students who do want to become lawyers and are able to obtain suitable employment, the rewards remain relatively high. This rather mixed picture, however, has to be put in a realistic perspective. Although the market for lawyers may not be as uniformly buoyant as many outsiders think, it is probably no more demanding or challenging than any other, and there are many communities outside the large urban centres that need lawyers. Furthermore, a law degree still remains as good a degree as any to obtain if you are concerned about your future career prospects and earnings. In most non-specialized fields of business, an LL.B. outdoes a B.A. or a B.Sc.

- *Law school grades are notoriously low.* Although evaluation methods remained the same for many years, they have begun to change considerably in the last few years. The primary method of evaluation for all students in all years remains, for better or for worse, the 100 percent, two- to four-hour, final examination at the end of each course. Now, though, exams are more likely to be open book rather than closed book, and there will be reasonable opportunity to do alternative methods of assessments such as essays or assignments. Although these exams will demand that students supplement those skills that have got them this far (see chapter 9), all law schools operate a grading profile: students are judged against their classmates, and not some mythical standard. Grading profiles are as much a help as a harm, for it is assumed that most students who get to law school are capable of performing at a good level, and the profile is adjusted accordingly. More than half of law students leave law school with at least a B average. While this grade may not be as high as you want or expect, it will be sufficient to get you almost anywhere you want to go because it is the one that most law students obtain. As long as you do not set your sights too high, you will not be disappointed.

- *Law professors are a bunch of sadistic prima donnas.* Of course, some are: arrogance is not in short supply in law schools. But the majority are like any other bunch of academics — ordinary, if slightly eccentric and badly dressed people who do their jobs with varying degrees of competence and enthusiasm. One source of this myth is the dreaded "Socratic method" as personified by Professor Kingsfield in *The Paper Chase* film — a style of teaching that, whatever its original rationale and performance, has come to mean a savage cross-examination of selected students on assigned material. Recent years have seen the continuing decline (but not yet the disappearance) of this style of "guerrilla pedagogy" in favour of more relaxed and diverse teaching methods. Despite growing class sizes, the typical law student in any year will have the opportunity to participate in seminars, to choose whether to respond to questions thrown out to the class, and occasionally to work in small groups on certain topics or projects. However, it is still possible to encounter both the pure lecture format and the dreaded random call to respond to a professor's question (see chapter 4).

- *Law school is all theory and no practice.* A common complaint about law school, usually from older lawyers, is that it has lost touch with reality and is not teaching basic legal skills; it has become too much of a philosophical salon for metaphysical speculation or breeding ground for political radicals. Although it is true that legal education has become more reflective and concerned about the political and theoretical foundations of law, there has also been a parallel tendency to treat the acquisition of practical lawyering techniques more seriously. Basic courses, such as Civil Procedure, introduce a skills-based component to the curriculum. Many law schools now offer students the chance to take courses that have a practical focus, such as Trial Advocacy and Dispute Resolution. Moreover, some law schools are allowing students to take semester-long intensive programs, such as Poverty Law and Immigration, or Criminal Law, that require students to work in the field and that give them sound practical experience in important areas of law.

- *Taking undergraduate law courses gives you an edge.* The question of what students should study if they are to gain an edge in the competition for law school places or, once there, law school grades is much overrated. Admission procedures rarely differentiate among different courses taken; a grade in an arts course is no more valuable than one in the pure sciences. Although a few law schools do try to distinguish grades depending on the calibre of the university attended or the program completed, most law schools have no way to monitor such a process effectively or fairly and do not try — an A is an A is an A. The only genuine advice is to pick subjects in which you believe you will do best. Also, the temptation to choose undergraduate courses with an eye on law school grades ought to be resisted. Indeed, some law professors are of the opinion that taking general undergraduate courses in law can prove a disadvantage, because students tend to think they already know the area (when they do not) or they develop some mistaken ideas about the operation of law. Take the courses you want and let law school take care of itself if or when you get there.

- *"I want to be a criminal lawyer or litigator."* Some students arrive at law school with a definite idea of what kind of lawyer they want to be. This certainly can be troubling for those others who have no real idea what they want to do or why they are in law school. But the fact is that very few law students go on to do what they thought they would do. Occasionally, opportunities do not present themselves, but more often students change their mind once they realize the many different possibilities that exist. For all their high public profile, criminal law and litigation represent only a small part of what lawyers actually do. Keep your options open and take time to specialize — you have a whole career ahead of you.

WHAT LAW SCHOOL IS LIKE

Since most law students go to law school directly from undergraduate university studies, law school is not as different from other faculties as many students are led to believe or expect. The daily law school life consists of the usual round of classes, coffee, cramming, and conviviality. The atmosphere is a little more intense and competitive and classmates are slightly more dedicated and driven than in undergraduate days, but student life goes on much the same. Beneath the hype and the myth that pervade the early days of law school, it is an experience into which most people settle quickly and effectively. Let's face it, the hard part is getting into law school, not staying there. Apart from those few students who decide that law school is not for them, there are only a small number of students who law school decides are not for it. And that fact explodes the leading myth of law school: that it is difficult and only for the determined and brilliant few. Although it is not easy to be at the top of the law school class, it is by no means as difficult as many imagine to do well at law school and come out with a solid degree and education at the end of it.

The current format of legal education — three years in a university setting, followed by a law society–controlled articling process — began to assume its present shape more than fifty years ago. Despite numerous shifts in emphasis and orientation, the basic structure of the law degree remains much the same as it did then. Notwithstanding the move from an office-based apprenticeship to a university-based training, there has always been a tension between the idea and practice of the law school as a trade school and as an academic institution. This conflict is manifested most strongly in the clash of visions between the provincial law societies, which confer the privilege to practise law, and legal academics over what amounts to a good legal education: Is law school better conceived as a trade school or as an academic institution? While it is no doubt essential to know how to draft a will or to plead a case properly to be a competent lawyer, technical training will not equip a lawyer to deal with the difficult ethical problems and civic responsibilities that come with professional practice or judicial office (see chapters 2 and 10). Moreover, the whole framing of this debate assumes that all law students are destined to become practising lawyers. Whether chosen or imposed, an increasing number of students who enter law school make a decision, once there, not to become a member of the practising profession.

The uneasy compromise that has been struck between trade training and academic instruction explains the compulsory set of courses that makes up the first-year syllabus and, at some schools, courses in subsequent years as well. These compulsory courses cover many of the areas that both the law schools (although with less conviction than previously) and the law societies consider to be essential to the study of law — contracts, property, torts, criminal law, civil procedure, and constitutional law. These classes usually take place in large groups, although they are probably much smaller than some undergraduate classes. In recent years, most law schools have tried to ensure that students are in smaller, seminar-style courses for at least one of their classes. A compulsory component of legal research and writing has been incorporated into most first-year curriculums. Also, it has become commonplace for law schools to require that students take a first-year course that places their studies of substantive topics in a broader theoretical and social context. Combined with the different skills and techniques that students will be expected to absorb, this makes for a fairly hefty and diverse workload.

This same compromise between academe and the profession has also allowed the remarkable proliferation of non-traditional courses and seminars found in every law school calendar, with such titles as Law, Gender and Equality; Aboriginal Land Claims; Corporation as Criminal; Racism and Law; Bio-ethics and Law. This variety, though, can make each year's post-exam course selection period quite challenging. Students should expect to have to juggle their desire not to be caught short in the Bar Admission exams ("I've got to take Trusts, and Real Estate, and Taxation, and Family Law, and...") with the unexpected or interdisciplinary interests they might never again have the chance to indulge ("Well, I'll probably never get to use Aerospace Law, but...") or the passion they have newly found or refused to extinguish ("I don't care, I want to take the International Human Rights Law and Sports Law seminars"). As you make your choices, you should remain aware that each has a price: too solid an emphasis on only what you need to practise will deny you the best chance to examine some of the larger issues of your chosen field; but the scatter-gun approach without a plan of action will leave you with a lot to cover in the few months before the Bar exams. However, once in practice, there is rarely time or opportunity to think about the abstract issues that underpin and form the law. (A more in-depth account of the Bar Admission process and articling is found in chapter 10.)

As in most of the professional faculties, law school makes it easy to develop a sense of detachment from the larger world. Though part of the universities, law schools often stand apart — physically, socially, and intellectually. More than half the schools reside in separate and dedicated facilities. While law students have access to the main university library, the law libraries are distinct collections and are often housed separately. Some law schools have their own cafeteria, making it possible to connect only rarely with the general university community. Many law schools conduct their own intramural sports competitions. This insularity is partly a natural by-product of the setting combined with the intensity of the law student's course and reading load, and partly a shadow cast by the profession itself. This separateness can very easily convince law students that they are special, separate, and superior to the great unwashed. Although buying into this myth/stereotype remains a personal choice, students should get away from the faculty once in a while and take part in the wider life of the campus that they have travelled through on the way to class.

Once one moves beyond a fairly formal account of legal education, there is no one general introduction to the substance and style of law school that captures the likely experience of all law students. Law school suits the temperament of some students much more than others. Like the elephant in the fable of the seven blind men, law school can mean different things to different people. Because people enter with a wide range of often conflicting expectations and ambitions, there tends to be almost as many accounts of law school life as there are law students. However, while students react in more and less positive ways, there are certain challenges and situations that come with law school, and the way students respond to them will determine whether they are likely to be "happy campers." (Chapter 4 outlines these situations and suggests various coping strategies.)

GETTING THERE

In virtually every law school, the walls are covered with those curious antique photos of much earlier graduating classes. Take a good look at them: the faces there are extraordinarily homogeneous — white males in their early twenties, though look-ing older. The occasional white female of similar age pops up sometimes, but it is not until recently that a more diverse set of faces begins to appear. Even today, the student population remains dominated by certain groups and segments of society. But, with varying degrees of commitment and success, law schools are changing their admissions procedures to ensure that their student bodies approximate much more closely the general demographic make-up of the Canadian population. For too long, law schools have been the preserve of established groups. The advent of more inclusive admission policies reflects a belated recognition by law schools that a strong legal profession must be one that represents and serves all sectors of society. Slightly less than half of all law students are now women, and a small but growing percentage of the class will comprise people of colour, Aboriginal/First Nations stu-dents, the differently abled, and mature students (generally defined as people in their late twenties or older, and not entering directly from university education). Nevertheless, the basic requirements for successful admission to law school remain largely formal and traditional in scope and style — a combination of LSAT score and university grade point average (GPA).

THE DREADED LSAT

All applicants, without exception, must take the Law School Admission Test. It is a standardized half-day test consisting of three types of multiple-choice questions in five thirty-five-minute sections and one thirty-minute writing sample. The LSAT is a general aptitude evaluation that is intended to measure various analytical and intellectual abilities — to comprehend complex texts; to organize and synthesize large amounts of information; to draw inferences from arguments and facts; and to reason critically. It is administered four times each year, usually in February, June, October, and December, although increasing possibilities are soon to exist for a year-round testing on computer. You should plan to take the LSAT as much in advance of your desired entry into law school as possible, so you will not only have ample time to prepare, but will also have time to take the LSAT a second time — everyone can have an off-day, and studies suggest that most candidates who re-test improve slightly on their previous score. You can take the LSAT before you make a final deci-sion to apply to any particular law school.

Although the design and administration of the LSAT has improved significantly in the past few years, the criticisms of these kinds of tests are legend: they are uncon-nected to law, not Canadian, too abstract, and so on. There is little point in getting in a lather about such matters. If you want to go to law school, you have to do one. Because of its administrative efficiency, it still weighs heavily in the admissions process. Aware of the cultural limitations of the test and the lack of any proven link between test scoring and general success at law school, most law schools are much more leery about the use and relevance of the LSAT than they used to be; its results are not as final or determinative. The prevailing view in law schools is that, while very strong or very weak results on the LSAT indicate that the applicant is or is not likely to succeed on an LL.B., the LSAT is simply a convenient and uniform yardstick for comparing applicants from very different academic backgrounds and practical experiences.

Although the organizers of the LSAT claim that there is little need for preparation other than becoming familiar with the design and the demands of the test, it is wise to do some basic preparation. Almost all students claim that their test-scoring ability increased considerably with preparation and practice. The many LSAT aids on sale fall into two general kinds — short courses and self-help study guides. While the courses are expensive and, therefore, beyond many people's budget, the books offer good tips and suggestions. It all boils down to the fact that, once familiar with the different sorts of questions that the LSAT asks, you must have the self-discipline to do endless, timed sample tests. While most people can answer the questions given enough time, a major part of the test assesses your capacity to answer the questions quickly. Because the LSAT is a "right answers only" test, there is no penalty for wrong answers: this means that takers should, at a minimum, guess at all the answers — you have on average a 20 percent chance of the guesses being correct. As with all examinations, you should be organized in your preparation so that you are intellectually, psychologically, and physically at your best on the day of the test; rushing into the test after little sleep and without a meal is not a recipe for success. Also, law schools have different ways of dealing with the multiple test-taker (see table 1).

THE LAW SCHOOL END

Apart from the common admission requirement of the LSAT, law schools have begun to differ considerably on the use and weighting of other factors. For most schools, however, the bulk of successful applicants are determined by straight number-crunching — a statistical combination of LSAT score and academic GPA to give an overall average. In computing people's academic GPA, law schools tend not to go behind the grades as a general matter and inquire into the difficulty of the course or admission to such a program; all accredited schools are treated much the same, so that a B is a B is a B. However, in special circumstances, particular schools will go beyond the grades and take into account the larger educational context. Those who perform best on such a combined calculation will be the first to receive an offer of admission; further batches of offers will be sent out as final grades become available and up to the beginning of school, until each school has filled its available places. The final mix of students will vary from school to school, but most schools have a large contingent of students from their home province and, to a lesser extent, from their home town and university. The remainder of the student body will most likely be composed of students from almost any other province and a handful from foreign institutions. The number of educational institutions and disciplines likely to be represented is quite high. While the minimum educational requirement is evenly split between two and three years of post-secondary education, a majority of fellow students will hold at least one degree; more than a few might have a second or even a third degree.

Although most law students are still admitted by way of number-crunching, every law school has implemented some form of alternative admissions programs in order to reflect better the diversity of social, economic, ethnic, and cultural perspectives in Canadian society. Law schools vary in the reasons for and results of

Table 1 Admissions Data for Canadian Law Schools

Institution	Average LSAT	Average GPA	Educ. required	Treatment of multiple LSAT	Weight of LSAT (%)	Oldest accepted LSAT	Last test date for admiss.
University of Alberta	156	3.55	Min. 2 yrs undergrad	Averaged	LSAT $33\frac{1}{3}$ GPA $66\frac{2}{3}$	5 yrs	Dec.
University of British Columbia	161	78%	Min. 3 yrs undergrad	Averaged	LSAT 50 GPA 50	5 yrs	Feb.
University of Calgary	157	3.39	Min. 2 yrs undergrad	Averaged	N/A	5 yrs	Dec.
Dalhousie University	157	3.7	Min. 2 yrs undergrad	Highest Averaged	LSAT 40 GPA 60	June 1991	Feb.
University of Manitoba	156	3.66	Min. 2 yrs undergrad	Averaged, unless 8 pts. higher	LSAT 40 GPA 60	June 1991	Feb.
McGill University	159	80%	Min. 2 yrs undergrad	Averaged	Holistic	1992	Feb.
University of New Brunswick	158	3.5	Min. 3 yrs undergrad	Highest	LSAT 40 GPA 60	June 1991	Feb.
University of Ottawa	75%	80%	Min. 2 yrs undergrad	Highest	N/A	June 1995	Feb.
Queen's University	159	3.65	Min. 2 yrs undergrad	Averaged	LSAT 50 GPA 50	5 yrs	Dec.
University of Saskatchewan	156	78%	Min. 2 yrs undergrad	Averaged	LSAT 50 GPA 50	4 yrs	Feb.
University of Toronto	165	3.8	Min. 3 yrs undergrad	Averaged	N/A	3 yrs	Feb.
University of Victoria	88%	3.66	Min. 3 yrs undergrad	Highest	LSAT 30 GPA 70	June 1991	Feb.
University of Western Ontario	158	80%	Min. 2 yrs undergrad	Averaged	LSAT 50 GPA 50 (Averaged top 3 yrs)	June 1991	Feb.
University of Windsor	N/A	N/A	Min. 2 yrs undergrad	N/A	N/A	6 yrs	Dec.
Osgoode Hall Law School of York University	160	3.63	Min. 2 yrs undergrad	Highest	Equiv. to 1 yr of university	5 yrs	Feb.

[1]Special categories only
[1]Except regular

Notes: Many of these statistics vary slightly from year to year; therefore, it is advisable to obtain the calendar to any particular law school you are considering applying to, in order to have accurate and up-to-date information. Information up-to-date as of the 1999–2000 academic year. Some information may be more current.

Ref. letters	Pers. statem.	Applic. fee	Applic. deadline	# of applic.	Offers of admiss.	Size of 1st yr class	Full-time enrol.	Part-time program	Part-time enrol.
Yes	Yes	$60	Nov. 1	850	358	175	500	Yes	6
No	Yes[1]	Res. $44.50 Other $72.25	Feb. 1	1351	456	200	649	Yes	25
3	Yes	$60	Feb. 1	621	138	69	224	Yes	14
2	Yes	$60	March 1	860	287	156	452	Yes	10
Yes[1]	Yes	$50	Feb. 1	660	275	97	265	Yes	14
2	Yes	$60	Jan. 15	1021	240	154	574	Yes	24
2[1]	Yes	$50	March 1	699	164	80	240	N/A	N/A
2	No	$50	Nov. 1	1800	350	129	384	Yes	14
Yes[2]	Yes[2]	$50	Nov. 1	1785	568	157	465	Yes	20
Yes[1]	Yes[1]	$50	Feb. 1	690	234	110	304	Yes	27
No	Yes	$50	Nov. 1	1620	273	170	510	Yes	10
Names	Yes	$50	Feb. 1	964	230	104	380	Yes	12
2	No	$50	Nov. 1	1891	545	156	463	Yes	3
2	Yes	$50	Nov. 1	1462	381	150	438	Yes	5
2 rel	No	$50	Nov. 1	2146	711	279	876	Yes	6

Table 1 Admissions Data for Canadian Law Schools (cont'd)

Institution	Joint degree avail.	Grad. degree granted	# of courses offered	Required courses (years)	Special programs	Average age of 1st yr	% women students
University of Alberta	MBA/LLB	Yes	75–80	1, 2, & 3	Yes	26	54
University of British Columbia	MBA/LLB	Yes	182	1, 2, & 3	Yes	26	50
University of Calgary	MBA/LLB MED/LLB	Yes	68	1, 2, & 3	Yes	29	51
Dalhousie University	MBA/LLB MPA/LLB MLIS/LLB MHSA/LLB	Yes	90	1, 2, & 3	Yes	25	50
University of Manitoba	N/A	Yes	65	1, 2, & 3	Yes	27	50
McGill University	MBA/LLB MSW/LLB BCL/LLB	Yes	100	1, 2, & 3	Yes	25	52
University of New Brunswick	MBA/LLB	N/A	71	1, 2, & 3	Yes	25	51
University of Ottawa	MBA/LLB MA/LLB	Yes	95	1, 2, & 3	Yes	27	59
Queen's University	MA/LLB	Yes	75–80	1, 2, & 3	Yes	25	53
University of Saskatchewan	BA/LLB BComm/LLB BAdmin/LLB	Yes	90	1	Yes	26	48
University of Toronto	MA/LLB MBA/LLB MSW/LLB PhD/LLB	Yes	120	1	Yes	26	52
University of Victoria	MPA/LLB MBA/LLB MA/LLB	N/A	70–75	1, 2, & 3	Yes	29	59
University of Western Ontario	MBA/LLB	N/A	89	1, 2, & 3	Yes	24	50
University of Windsor	MBA/LLB	No	59	1, 2, or 3	Yes	N/A	55
Osgoode Hall Law School of York University	MBA/LLB MES/LLB MPA/LLB	Yes	105	1	Yes	25	53

% visible minorities	National or prov.	Prov. rep.	F/time faculty	P/time faculty	% faculty women	Volumes in library	Compu. stations	F/time tuition ($)	P/time tuition ($)
N/A	85% Alta.	7	26	60	35	350,000	22	4300	2150
N/A	(40% out of province).	7	37	87	50	280,000	21	3418	1709
N/A	N	4	17	27	45	170,000	21	4600	365 per course
N/A	Spaces for NS, PEI, NFLD, NWT, & Yukon	10	36	42	44	252,000	50	5983	188 per credit
N/A	About 70% Man.	5	21	41	24	282,000	25	5000	2500
13	N	9	34	36	26	167,000	20	Res 2668 4468	1500
N/A	N (50% out of province).	9	20	9	28	130,000	10	3620	N/A
20	N	9	28	46	50	200,000	25	4412	150 per credit
N/A	N	8	30	42	36	160,000	24	5400	per course
12	N, slight pref. for res. of Sask., NFLD, NWT, & Yukon	12	20	25	31	165,000	15	3488	per course
22.5	N	10	52	40	29	237,000	28	8760	4402
20	N	8	26	33	24	412,941	27	3300	per course
N/A	N	10	28	39	24	250,000	59	5400	per credit
N/A	N	8	24	18	21	185,200	39	4886	2294
N/A	N	8	47	54	32	480,000	50	8660	4300

such initiatives, but there is a general commitment to remedy the previously skewed demographics of law school admissions; this change has introduced an enriching diversity of voices, experience, and opinion to the classroom. Every applicant, except for those intending to study in French at Ottawa or at Moncton, must write the LSAT, but consideration is also given to a number of factors, including life/work experience, systemic barriers to access, age, First Nation status, personal difficulties, and achievement in other fields (see table 1). Many schools ask students to submit a biographical statement and references, so that a more balanced and informed assessment of an applicant's file can be made. If you are eligible for admission under these programs, you should take this request seriously, because it will usually be the only information that the school's admission committee (often comprising staff, faculty, and student members) will have. Be honest and candid — committees are alert to attempts by candidates to inflate or sugarcoat their life's achievements or challenges.

Mature students are encouraged to apply, and around 10 percent of all law school admissions are set aside for them. These applicants usually fall into two main groups:

- Those who have had no university education but are over twenty-five (most are considerably older) and have a number of years of work experience. Some people in this group are intimidated by the thought of applying to law school, but many law schools are committed to providing genuine possibilities for admission and have introduced serious programs to support such applicants. An assessment of their files will be based on a rounded evaluation of their overall life experience. If you are such a mature applicant, it is a good idea to take a couple of undergraduate courses so that you get a feel for university studies and can reassure the law school that you are serious about your application.

- Those who have had some university education but whose grades are insufficient to get them into law school. Provided they have worked for a number of years and have gone on to some success, the law schools will give their applications serious consideration. If you are such a mature applicant, you will have to demonstrate that your achievements in the last few years have more than made up for your (immature) undergraduate performance.

In both cases, the law school will place great weight on your biographical statement; often it will be the only information and writing sample that the law school will have. So you should work hard at developing a strong and cogent statement. While your LSAT performance will be taken into account, it will be treated in a more liberal manner than the regular applicants'. Also, although it is still quite rare, some schools invite candidates for interviews in person or by phone; such contact provides an occasion to demonstrate that you have the academic and personal qualities to make a success of law school. Mature applicants should be confident in their plans; they have much to offer the law school and the student body. Nevertheless, you should realize that law school will require a full-time commitment and that you must have a realistic plan in place to meet the financial, family, and personal demands that law school will place upon you.

How do students decide which is the best law school for them? Of course, for many applicants, this will be less a matter of choice and more a fact of circumstance — location, cost, or acceptance. The quality of Canadian law schools, in contrast to those in the United States, is reasonably uniform. In spite of efforts by *Maclean's* and other publications, there is no accepted league table of law schools. A more important set of distinctions is that:

- there are sixteen common law schools in eight provinces (Nfld, PEI, NWT, and Yukon do not have law schools);
- there are two common law schools that offer an LL.B. program in French (Ottawa and Moncton);
- there is one Quebec school that offers a common law degree in English (McGill); and
- there are three schools that offer a fourth year providing a joint common law/civil law degree (Ottawa, Osgoode, and McGill).

Each school will of course put its best foot forward and emphasize its strengths; all will attempt to sound the biggest or smallest, the most cosy or the most cosmopolitan, the most connected to the financial district or the corridors of political power, the most modern or most traditional. Although there are reasons to prefer one school over another, each of Canada's sixteen common law schools offers a remarkably similar form and substance of legal education. While some law schools are now introducing half-time studies, all schools offer a program of three intense years of full-time academic study. The first year consists of a set of mandatory "core" courses; the second and third years involve either a mix of required and optional courses or a free selection from a wide range of courses and seminars. Each school incorporates legal research, writing, and "mooting" components (see chapter 8) into either first or subsequent years. Although it is possible to follow a strictly traditional mainstream law degree, each school currently offers a broader or a narrower range of alternatives — joint degrees, part-time study, and intensive programs in a clinical setting or in a particular aspect of the law. In choosing which school(s) to apply to, your main tool should be the printed calendar for each school, the Website, and the comparative chart in table 1; the table is based primarily on data available for 1999–00, and many of the figures refer to regular, non-discretionary admissions. These two sources will provide you with a sufficient amount of relevant detail about each school. Of course, you should not hesitate to contact the schools themselves; most have a variety of outreach initiatives and will welcome your inquiries.

Remember the old adage — "If at first you don't succeed, try again." Although there are limits to how often you should try, you need not be deterred by an initial rejection. Most law schools do not hold it against students that they did not get in first time around or that they got a poor first LSAT score. There are many ways to improve your record and to boost your chances the second time around. You should not refrain from taking a long, hard, and dispassionate look at your credentials. There is little to be gained from railing at the admission officers; law schools do not succumb to the impassioned or affronted plea for admission. However, you ought not to be down on yourself if you fail to make the admissions cut; it is not a general assessment of your talent as a person or as a student. Many people who do not secure a place at law school would do well at law school; it is simply that there are too many other people ahead of them in the queue.

PAYING YOUR WAY

For many aspiring law students, it is not so much the likely intellectual challenge of law school that is cooling their ambition as the significant costs that are associated with a law school education. Most students have already shouldered a sizeable debt load to get through university, and the prospect of adding to it is scary. In the past couple of years, the costs of a legal education have begun to grow alarmingly, particularly in some schools. However, that does not mean that a person of humble means should or need not apply. Law school is full of students who, by hook or by crook, are making ends meet for the three-year tour of duty. Government grants or loans are relied upon by many, and a good number of students have learned to tighten their belts and rely on their partner's income or family resources. Also, as an effort to off-set the effects of increased fees, many law schools have beefed-up the funds available for bursaries. Other students hold part-time jobs on weekends or in the evenings. Although law schools tend to discourage students from working in term-time, most are realistic enough to accept that many students have little choice and that the curriculum, at least in the second and/or third year, is not so demanding that a student would be unable to work part-time. Remember that many of the costs are distributed over the year, during which time you can apply for assistance or search for supplemental income. The basic costs of being at law school are approximately as follows:

- *The cost of application.* The general fee for LSAT registration is $120, the cost of an LSAT preparation course can be anything from $300 to $1000, expenses in attending the LSAT test amount to about $50, application fees are generally around $50 per application, and sundries such as postage and telephone costs add up to $50. These expenses amount to about $1000 on average. The Ontario schools have standardized the application procedure by requiring students to make a common application through the Guelph Centre.

- *The cost of school.* Tuition fees are the main cost of law school. They vary much less than in the United States, but they do vary from school to school. In the current economic situation, there will be increasing variability among fees in different provinces, depending on how they are coping with government cut-backs and budgeting policies. The federal government has made significant changes to the way it funds education, changes that allow the provinces to deal separately with education funding. Tuition fees will probably increase further and annually during the next few years. A safe bet for cost of books in any one year is about $1250. Law books are expensive: a median price for a single text is likely to be over $70, and casebooks (cerlox-bound photocopied compilations of cases and articles) come in at about 10 cents per printed page and can vary from $20 to $50. You may save by not buying new books; there are usually used book sales at the beginning of each term. But you should be careful in buying used books: law books date quickly and new editions come out every couple of years. A cheaper, but out-of-date coursebook is one of the most expensive purchases you could ever make. Either way, you will likely fall into one of the main vices of law students — excessive and frenzied photocopying. This indulgence will quickly eat up the change from $1250 by year end. Also, law schools are becoming increasingly computerized and, while it is by no means obligatory, ready access to a modest computer is obviously desirable.

- *The cost of living.* The most variable factor will be the living expenses in the city where your school is located — living in downtown Toronto is not the same as living in Saskatoon. Rather than trust the soon-out-of-date figures provided in law school and LSAT materials, get out and do some research on living costs where you are thinking of going to school. If you are not planning to live on campus (where that option is available), check out housing and transit costs; some schools are far outside the downtown core. However, remember that you would have to live anyway, so do not exaggerate the costs of being at law school; make a comparative and sensible assessment.

These are the core money considerations. Be sure to count on whatever level of (dis)comfort you feel you want or can endure. Like everything else, you will be better able to cope if you are informed and organized. On a more general note, the relative cost of legal education in Canada will depend on who you talk to — it is either prohibitively expensive (thus still precluding all but the well-heeled) or a real bargain (compared with US$25,000 tuition per year for Harvard or $10,000 per year for private school fees in Canada). There is, however, only one way the costs will go — and that is up; by what magnitude and how quickly will be determined by political and economic factors beyond the scope of this introduction. Interestingly, many of the factors that will influence the price of a legal education are in the hands of politicians who are or were themselves members of the traditional legal establishment and who benefited from low-cost, accessible, and publicly funded education.

Financial sources are available to help defray or delay the costs of completing law school. There are three traditional sources of support. Each province, in addition to the federal government has some form of student loan (or possibly even grant) programs: funds are ever more limited, so it is best to apply early and to be persistent in reviewing or appealing the scheme's assessment of your needs. As I said, most law schools offer bursaries. Based on declared and documented financial need, these grants are administered by the individual faculties of law and/or the parent university. They are awarded after the school year has begun, so you will need to look into the individual university's policy regarding deferral of fees, emergency loans, and other assistance. There are never enough of these grants to go around, and their amount can vary from enough to cover full tuition for the year to much more common contributions of between $500 and $2000 towards your costs. Also, there are a small number of substantial scholarships, which are usually given for superior academic achievement and/or other extracurricular accomplishment; a few are restricted to certain designated groups, such as children of veterans or residents of particular regions.

Although not considered to be part of the traditional sources of financial aid for law students, there are also private enterprise 'education' loans. With the worsening of the economy and the consequent shrinkage of government aid to students, several Canadian banks have advertised "student loans" programs. Whether these loans are short-lived experiments or an indication of the long-term future remains to be seen. The market for such bank loans does exist, particularly since government programs have increasingly restrictive criteria. However, a general note of caution is warranted: since these student loans are in effect bank loans like any other, this avenue should be left until every other possibility (including appeals to any kindly family member) has been explored. A law degree no longer equates with a guaranteed place on easy street (if it ever did), and borrowers should ponder the heavy weight of a bank loan that they will have to shoulder on graduation.

GETTING PREPARED

So, you made it into law school, but what happens then? If you are like most law students, you will spend the summer working to scrape together as much money as you can before Labour Day or, if you are one of the lucky ones, you will take time to relax and enjoy your remaining months of freedom. Obviously, it will be best if you can have all your basic living arrangements and support system in place before term starts; it does not help you adjust to law school life if you spend the first few days running around town looking for accommodation or furniture. Other than that, there is nothing special you need to do. Indeed, it is preferable to avoid focusing or obsessing too much on the coming months. In particular, you should not bother to read the books you have been assigned, as few professors follow the table of contents and, more importantly, you are more likely to be intimidated than reassured by this effort at early preparation. If you do feel the irresistible temptation to do something, you can familiarize yourself with the physical and social environment of the law school by visiting the campus, touring the library, and speaking to the few students (mainly research assistants) who will be around.

CHAPTER 2

Let's Get Jurisprudential:
The Study of Law

Seeing that the laws are excerpted out of the middle of moral and natural philosophy, how should these fools have understood it, that have, by God, studied less in philosophy than my mule. RABELAIS

Now that you know how to get into law school, what will you be doing when you get there? This is a straightforward question that invites a straightforward answer. However, apart from the fact that you will be attending classes, reading law books, and taking exams, there is little else that can be said with any great confidence or certainty about your time at law school. What amounts to legal education, let alone a good legal education, is something that varies from school to school, from class to class, and from professor to professor. The whole notion of what it is that law schools should be doing and how they do it is a matter of continuing debate and, at times, considerable antagonism. Law schools are not only an intellectual arena within which legal education takes place but also the site where the contest over what law and legal education should be about is at its most fierce. Because of this dual function, the best approach in introducing you to legal education seems to be to incorporate the theoretical disagreements over what amounts to a good legal education into the practical experience of legal education itself.

Accordingly, before acquainting you with some of the phenomena and personalities you will encounter at law school and some of the techniques and manoeuvres you will need to succeed, it is important to get a handle on the larger historical and educational context within which your likely day-to-day experience at law school has taken shape and significance. In this way, you might better be able to make sense of the expectations that are placed on you and to live up to them in a more effective manner. For some, this stuff will be of interest in and of itself — a fascinating challenge that naturally whets their intellectual appetite; for others, it will seem an unnecessary diversion that strays from their central reason for being at law school. To the latter group, I can only say that you should be prepared to take this material seriously, even from the position of your own focused agenda. Let's face it, an awareness of the theoretical and educational context of your legal education can hardly hinder your success in that legal education — you study better if you know what it is and why you are being asked to study in the way you are.

So, let's start at that most trite and challenging of questions: If you are to study law, what is it you are studying? *What is law?* After trying to make some sense of that inquiry, I will explore the tension that has energized law schools in their efforts to develop an appropriate curriculum and modus operandi: *Is law school about training lawyers or educating people about law?* Finally, as a result of the inconclusiveness of the debate around these two burning issues, I will canvass some of the major intellectual perspectives that inform and guide the teaching of law in law schools today: *How do we and how should we think about law and its study?*

A BRIEF TOUR OF JURISPRUDENCE

Countless generations of jurists have expended vast intellectual energies in seeking to answer the question: *What is law?* The question is exquisitely deceptive in its brevity and simplicity because the difficulties it raises and the answers it invites tend to be extremely prolix and complex. The elusive nature of the project can be gauged by the plethora of solutions that have been proposed. The traditional approach has been to try to arrive at a definition that covers all eventualities at any given time and in any given place. More recently, the focus of jurisprudential attention has become both narrower and broader: narrower in that attention has been concentrated on the performance of the judicial role in a liberal democracy, and broader in that resort has been had to a wide variety of interdisciplinary inquiries.

WHAT IS THIS THING CALLED LAW?

Traditional jurists have searched for an all-embracing answer to the question, *What is law?* They sought a definition that could embrace the writings of Grotius and the Canadian Constitution, that might shelter both a regulation of the European Community and the taboos of a New Guinea tribe, and that might include the customary laws of First Nations and the unwritten protocols of the Internet. Such definitions are intended to connect those elements that ought to be connected and to separate those elements that ought to be separated.

Many jurists presented their definition of law as the crowning achievement of their entire life's work. Often arrived at by torturous and torrid argument, some of the more popular contributions included:

Law is a system of rules.
Law is the will of God.
Law is the command of the sovereign.
Law is patriarchy writ large.
Law is what the courts say it is.
Law is a marketing resource for lawyers.
Law is a system of racial and ethnic subordination.
Law is an attempt to achieve justice.
Law is a tool of social engineering.
Law is a weapon of class warfare.

While each of these definitions says something about law and, in the broad sense, contributes to the fund of legal knowledge, none of them can be said to have struck upon the final and unchallengeable essence of law. Each contribution is guilty of some distortion, exaggeration, or omission. Happily, modern jurists have not proved so gullible and naive. It is now generally recognized that absolute definitions are unattainable and that such an enterprise is futile. Any view of law is influenced by the observers' vantage point and by their own understanding of what they are look-ing for. As Roscoe Pound, a famous American jurist, pithily noted, "our conception of the problem to which our discourse is addressed shapes both." So any answer to the question *What is law?* will depend on who wants to know, why they want to know, and who they ask.

The main insight to note about law is that it is not so much a thing as it is a process or a practice; it is as alive as the lawyers who use it and as active as the peo-ple who are affected by it. Law is not simply what is found in law books, statutes, or law reports: it is everywhere — at work, at home, at play, at school. It is much more than a set of orders backed by threats; it provides the stage, props, and partial script for life's drama. Law plays a part in everything we do, who we are and can be, what is ours and is not ours. It pervades people's lives and, as cultural anthropolo-gist Clifford Geertz has put it, it is "a way of imagining the real." But although law is everywhere, it is not omnipotent — it does not do all that it claims to do, and it often does the opposite of what it was intended to do. There is a gap between "law in books" and "law in action." If you want to know what goes on in any particular segment of social life, the body of rules and regulations will provide, at best, an incomplete source. For example, to understand the way in which the criminal process works, it is much more instructive to visit a police station or a local court than to read about the governing legal framework. Law is as much to be found in the warm flow of daily living as in the cool stacks of law libraries.

WORRYING ABOUT JUDGES

Much jurisprudential scholarship has found its focus in describing and justifying the problematic role of the judiciary within a liberal democracy; although judges exercise great power, the courts are an unelected and unaccountable institution lacking any basic democratic mandate. The traditional response to this dilemma has been to posit adjudication as an objective and rationally bounded process of rule application. As such, there remains a very real commitment to the idea that a just compromise of competing political interests can be effected through a resort to law's logic, that the rational discourse of law can transcend the rhetoric of vulgar politi-cal debate: lawyers and judges can engage in politics in a distinctly legal and legitimately democratic way. However, a strong and persistent critique argues that no distinctive mode of legal reasoning exists to be contrasted with political dialogue. Law is simply politics dressed in different garb; it neither operates in a historical vac-uum nor exists independently of ideological struggles in society. The history of legal thought has followed a general path that has tried to negotiate the pushes and pulls of these traditional and critical traditions around the notion that law is an objective and determinate process of reasoning.

On one side is *formalism*. Developing around the mid-nineteenth century, this approach conceived of law as a closed body of determinate rules that could be applied in a quasi-scientific way through the special techniques of legal reasoning; gaps and incoherences were the fault of its erstwhile expositors, not the legal system itself. Law's validity derived from its formal pedigree, not its substantive content. However, while formalism did not give primary weight to the moral content of law, it did provide a moral defence of the amoral view of law-as-rules as best suited to the institutional demands of a powerful judiciary in a democratic age. In such an account of law, the role of the lawyers was largely uncomplicated and technical. By divorcing adjudication from the political sphere of ideological decision-making, the exercise of judicial power is made to seem less an infringement on democratic values and practice.

This classical mode of formalism held sway until the early decades of the twentieth century and fuels much of the self-understanding of lawyers as non-political and professional operatives. Although many jurists are more critical of present judicial performance, they still cling to the belief that adjudication, suitably reformed and purified, can be carried out in conformity with the dictates of liberal democracy — "the right argument will always win the day." They have fashioned a formalist account of law that goes beyond the discredited classical vision of law-as-mechanical-algorithm and attempts to colonize a middle ground between a naive faith in the dispositive power of rules and an unsettling fear that judges might only be ideologues at large. As Ronald Dworkin puts it, "law ... is deeply and thoroughly political ... [b]ut not a matter of personal or partisan politics." Accordingly, while these jurists have acknowledged an intimate and crucial relationship between law and political morality, they have continued to insist that judges can engage that morality in a distinctly legal and professional way. Formalists have sampled and used the insights of other disciplines to craft a more sophisticated and compelling account of formalism.

On the other side of the jurisprudential debate is *non-formalism*. These critics have gone by many names and many intellectual faiths. Apart from their rejection of formalism, they differ considerably among and between themselves. Largely drawing their inspiration from the American legal realists of the 1920s and 1930s, they seek to demonstrate that the appeal of an objective, impartial system of legal thought is illusory; the power of formal rationality is suspect and the precedential force of the law is easily manipulable. The formal categories of law and legal reasoning are not as reliable as claimed and tend to gloss over law's inconsistencies and incoherences; principles of fairness and equity are more sites than solutions for addressing problems. The realist Fred Rodell, writing of the formalistic tendency to regard the American Constitution as a source of explicit commands capable of direct implementation by a professional judiciary, had the opinion that "the alleged logic of constitutional law is equally amorphous, equally unconvincing, equally silly whether the decisions the court is handing down are 'bad,' 'progressive' or 'reactionary,' 'liberal' or 'unliberal.' "

However, the thrust of realist scholarship was essentially negative and iconoclastic; it lacked any unifying thread or positive political program. The more recent work of the non-formalists has made a much clearer and sustained connection between law and politics. While some of its many strands have been around for a long time, they have in recent years combined with new deconstructive trends to form a powerful, if eclectic, challenge to law's traditional image of itself. The major energies of the non-formalists are directed towards undermining any and all claims about the worth or viability of the formalist project: law is not so much a rational enterprise as a vast exercise in rationalization. Each of these critiques, to a greater or a lesser extent, seeks to drive home the flawed nature of the formalist project and its tendency to allow class, gendered, and racial elites, in different ways and at different times, to set the terms on which others are to lead their lives. While these critics take a slightly different tack in exposing the ideological structure and sources of the law, they are unified in their efforts to theorize in the service of a progressive critique to benefit the disadvantaged and disenfranchised in society.

SCHOLARS OR TECHNICIANS?

It should come as little surprise to learn that legal education has been strongly affected by these debates around the question, "What is law?" Although mediated by other institutional forces and transformations such as the general increase in tertiary education, changing demographics, and expansion of the legal profession, the development of legal education has largely tracked these theoretical engagements. Indeed, the history of Canadian legal education is a story that moves from law office to university classroom, and from practising principal to academic professor; it is only recently that the training of lawyers has been part of university education.

IN THE BEGINNING

The training of lawyers has a long and illustrious pedigree that harks back to the aristocratic aspirations and affectations of the legal profession. In the thirteenth century, the English Inns of Court were community colleges at which members studied, lived, worked, ate, and prayed. Modelled on old trade guilds and pre-dating university legal education, students would be tutelaged in legal crafts and professional lore. As Sir John Fortescue described them in his fabled *De Laudibus Legum Angliae*, the Inns were not so much Law Colleges as Schools for English Gentlemen. As with so much else, Upper Canada imperfectly followed this English tradition. By the end of the nineteenth century there were no elite ranks of Canadian faculties of law. With few exceptions, legal training remained firmly under the direction and in the hands of the legal profession. Late in the century, in some provinces, a short and rudimentary program of lectures and classes, taught mostly by practitioners, was introduced; the tenor and substance of these courses was decidedly practical, and the transmission of "black letter" law and procedure was its *raison d'être*. Even today, legal education is more English than American; it is vocational and practice-based rather than academic and intellectual. As such, the continuing history of Canadian legal education still consists of an attempt to bend an archaic institution to the demands of the late twentieth century.

University law schools began to appear in the early years of the twentieth century. They were small and modest affairs, with entry to the profession strictly and jealously controlled by the profession's governing bodies. Some attempts to introduce a more academic and reflective approach to legal education were made, but the orientation of legal training was professional and practical. It was only after the Second World War that university law schools began to carve an academic niche for themselves and to oblige the law societies to take them seriously as (semi-) independent centres of learning at which students were required to study law as a scholarly discipline as much as a professional rite of passage. Nevertheless, even as the law schools have taken an increasingly academic course, they are still very aware of the demands of the practising bar and the desires of students to keep law schools "relevant and real." Although the law school curriculum is not subject to formal approval by law societies, the existence of the post-degree professional admission courses exerts considerable pull on both the law schools' curricular offerings and pedagogical approach and the students' educational expectations, professional ambitions, and areas of study.

This tradition affected the self-image and the confidence of law schools in plotting what they thought was an appropriate model and challenging experience for legal education. From early in the century to the 1950s, survival and subservience to professional goals was the order of the day. However, as university law schools began to establish themselves and a more academically trained professoriate began to take shape (growing from about forty in 1950 to more than six hundred today), the thrust and content of legal education also began to change. The study of law began to become more intellectual and rigorous; and an expository tradition of didactic learning gave way to a more varied and engaged style that took a critical approach to law and its study.

FROM HERE ON IN

Today, the self-image of the law school is less of a vocational halfway house and more of a professional and humanistic centre of learning. Originally based on the almost exclusive and uncritical mastery of legal doctrine, in the sense of the legal rules and principles that make discrete subject areas, the changes have been twofold: introduce students to basic legal practical skills, such as client advocacy and dispute resolution techniques, and to encourage students to place these skills and legal doctrines in a broader and more critical context. In so doing, the hope is that students will be better prepared as lawyers and as citizens to operate in an increasingly complex and demanding world; they would begin to see themselves as active practitioners in law and society as much as passive technicians of the law.

Against such a historical backdrop of always competing and often contradictory answers to the question, "What is law?" it ought not to come as a surprise to students that law schools remain unsure about their own basic mission and *raison d'être*. As they have progressed in their sophistication and sweep, law schools have not only struggled to come to terms with the most fundamental issues about the meaning of law, but have agonized over the relation between legal education as a training for legal practice and as a liberal arts program: Is it supposed to be producing technicians or scholars, or some judicious combination of the two? On the one hand, there is the image of law schools that produce technical experts with specialized knowledge who pride themselves on their no- nonsense competence to do the job, unhindered by abstract considerations; functionality is the test of knowledge, not insight. On the other hand, there is a competing image that celebrates the creation of wise and enlightened decision-makers who are educated to be judicious in judgment and who cherish the rigour of intellectual discipline, the width of critical learning, and the wisdom of human experience.

Some argue that the professional training of lawyers tends to be undermined by the academic advancement of law students. Others contend that a false dichotomy is posited between the scholarly and the technical images of legal education: the better technicians are those who understand and appreciate the larger context and setting of their craft, and the most useful scholars are those who understand the practical working and the doings of the law. There is much truth to this view. Surely the most effective technician is one who can ally it to a richer and more encompassing vision of human society. If law students learn only the extant legal rules without any contextual framework of broader understanding, they will be ill equipped to respond to novel situations, to appreciate the implications of changes in the legal rules, and to grasp the possibilities and parameters of their professional roles. If you aspire to be more than a hack or a shyster (as you presumably do), the best practical training you can have is one that sees that technical knowledge and practical skills are a necessary but not sufficient condition of a good legal education: the sociopolitical context of the origin and effects of technical knowledge is an invaluable and essential dimension of that proficiency. Good technicians know not only how to, but also when to and why to. Such ideas cannot be left to chance, but must be taught in as thorough a way as the technical knowledge itself. If lawyers are not to be involved in some way in such matters, then who is?

Of course, in attempting to produce scholarly technicians (or is it technical scholars?), the real danger is that law schools will fail miserably on all counts and will turn out graduates who are neither competent technicians nor able scholars. Whatever their success, law schools are committed to maintaining a style and a substance of legal education that straddles a variety of objectives: to receive academic respectability and kudos; to offer a constructive critique of the operation of the law in society; and to train future members of the legal profession, which is itself riven with conflicting aspirations as big business and as a social service. The days of a core faith in a basic orthodoxy and a shared mission for legal education are well passed; pluralism and eclecticism are the order of the day. Today, law schools are more vibrant, challenging, diverse, and demanding than ever before. The incorporation of the continuing debate over the purposes, process, and priorities of what amounts to a "good" legal education into the core curriculum has led to a more serious and fruitful academic enterprise, even if it is a more confused one.

TODAY'S THINKING ABOUT LAW

The debates and disagreements that swirl around the law school concerning the definition of law and the best way to study law continue. Some law schools have now incorporated a formal dimension to the first-year curriculum that introduces and addresses the major intellectual currents on the jurisprudential scene. However, consistent with the rest of legal education, there is still a catch-as-catch-can attitude to the appreciation and understanding of the different intellectual perspectives that pervade the teaching of law. I will present a series of "snapshots" that captures the central thrust of these perspectives. Each of them has obvious implications not only for the way we think about law but also for the way we organize and engage in legal education.

MAKING THE BEST OF IT

There are four main perspectives — *positivism*, *natural law*, *law and economics*, and *law and literature* — that take an optimistic view of law and of legal education's chances of redeeming their potential to be a professional force for good in society.

Positivism

The most traditional attempt to revive the flagging fortunes of formalism has been made by the positivists. As a more normative and pluralist brand of analytical philosophy, its jurisprudential adherents, like Leslie Green and Wil Waluchow, maintain that it is still possible to defend an account of law and adjudication in which law and morality are kept separate, that rules are the heart and soul of the legal process, and that adjudication has an inescapable element of choice. The leading positivist is the late H.L.A. Hart. He depicts law as a functional and sophisticated system of two kinds of rules: obligation-imposing primary rules that comprise the bulk of substantive legal doctrine, such as criminal and contract law; and authority-conferring secondary rules that distribute institutional power and jurisdiction, between legislatures and courts, for example, over the creation and enforcement of the primary rules. Against this analytical backdrop Hart developed a suggestive account of adjudication; it was a description of what occurs, even if what is described is evaluative in substance.

Presenting a reasoned and reasonable account of modern judging, he unashamedly sought to inhabit a middle ground between the realist "nightmare" in which judges always make the law, and the formalist "noble dream" in which judges never make it. Hart's patented jurisprudential formula for a legal good night's sleep took rule-application to be at the heart of the judicial task. In fulfilling their duties, judges have to call on a variety of analytical skills and reasoning techniques: they act inductively when they extract rules from a line of past cases, and they act deductively when they apply the inductively extracted rule to the case in point. However, because legal language is open textured, there are so-called hard cases. In these cases, they act politically when the inductively extracted rule or its deductive application is uncertain or difficult; they try as best they can to analogize from the values and principles underlying the rest of the rules. In this unpretentious account of judging, indeterminacy is something that pervades the judicial task, but it is always relative, marginal, and not to be exaggerated. Accordingly, Hart-like judges are not a bunch of mindless automatons, Delphic oracles, well-meaning simpletons, rampant legislators or cynical manipulators; they struggle to do justice in a way that respects rules without becoming enslaved to them.

A contending group of positivists maintain that Hart went too soft on the important distinction between law and its moral basis. They see his account of judging as not so much a triumphant compromise but a misjudged sell-out: Hart was a radical in traditionalists' clothing who had reneged on the democratic compact by letting the political cat out of the legal bag. However, rather than salvage the legal enterprise by mixing in more morality, these arch-positivists seek to redeem law's democratic legitimacy by purifying it of any moral entanglements at all. Such a hard variety of positivism treats law exclusively as a matter of social fact, and not a moral ideal. While not everything judges say or do is law, their application of legal rules not only can but must be free of moralizing; to do more (or less) would be improper, unjudicial, and undemocratic. This is not so much an amoral stance as a moral position that defends a formalism of strictly rule-bound adjudication as the most morally defensible account of law and adjudication in a constitutional democracy. It is a vision of judging that celebrates the systemic virtues of regularity, predictability, and certainty over the concern with substantive justice in particular instances. At their most extreme, these jurists and judges maintain that "there are times when even a bad rule is better than no rule at all."

Natural Law

The positivist effort to rehabilitate formalism from the realist assault was taken by many to compound the problem, not resolve it. Nevertheless, critics and defenders alike have retained Hart's central article of positivist faith — namely, that rules are the basic currency of legal transactions and that they have a core meaning that can deal with and resolve most situations. Even anti-positivistic jurists like Ronald Dworkin accept that there are frequent occasions on which a rule "applies itself," and pragmatic theorists like Richard Posner embrace the idea that the skill to apply rules in a creative way and to make that application persuasive to others is the hallmark of the good lawyer and judge. However, the great majority of jurists have sought to envelop an understanding of law and adjudication in a larger and more expansive moral universe. Although Hart was accurate in observing that rules were open textured and that their application did not exhaust the judicial function, these neo-naturalist jurists argue that he failed to appreciate the extent to which the law consists of more than rules. Behind and within the rules is a political morality that guides and constrains judges when the application of rules is unclear or undesirable. As David Beatty and Brian Slattery insist, law is about values and politics, but not in any idiosyncratic or ideological way.

For the natural lawyer, the primary task of theorists and judges is to detect and cultivate the sociopolitical principles that breathe life into the dry bones of legal rules. Different groups claim that this task has been achieved in different ways:

- the legal process is a subtle economic game in which the invisible hand of the market shapes and wields legal rules in the best approximation of economic efficiency;
- legal doctrine is a morality play in which individual rights struggle with collective interests over the soul of constitutional justice;
- law is always in the process of making itself pure in the historical elaboration of law's immanent rationality; and
- the courts represent a privileged site for the forging of truly republican values and public virtues.

In spite of their obvious differences, these conflicting naturalist trends unite in their shared and enduring formalistic belief that there must be a clear and defensible line between valid adjudication and ideological disputation; legal reasoning is a detached and determinate enterprise that can generate correct and predictable answers to social disputes in a way that marks it off, in a non-trivial and meaningful way, from open-ended political wrangling. While immersed in politics and history, law is self-sufficient and not entirely reducible to anything else. Without such protection, the fear is that the Rule of Law will be subverted and that democratic governance will succumb to the tyranny of special-interest groups. Moreover, without adequate determinacy in legal discourse, judicial arbitrariness will become the order of the day, and adjudication will collapse into a series of ad hoc and unprincipled encounters.

Dworkin is the leading contemporary neo-naturalist; he has elevated formalism to a fine art by asking lawyers to construct the most compelling interpretation of law in terms of its internal coherence and political morality. In this way, law and adjudication are claimed to satisfy the Rule of Law by meeting the democratic demand for judicial objectivity and the popular need for political justice. While some rail that an activist judiciary is antithetical to democratic governance, Dworkin argues that, if judges are to fulfil their democratic responsibilities under the Rule of Law, they must make political decisions, albeit not personal or partisan ones. For Dworkin, judges are political actors whose power is limited by a legal system's history and liberal character. The state does not give them a blank cheque on which to write in the political currency of their choice; they must interpret the extant legal materials in their best light as a theory of political morality. The judge breathes political vitality into the lifeless words of legal texts by applying the twin tests of "formal fit" and "substantive justice." Any interpretation must be able to demonstrate some plausible connection with society's legal history. This requirement obliges the judge to develop a scheme of rights that a just state would establish and enforce. While this task can be only provisionally and partially performed, the conscious striving for such a perfected theory is the hallmark of naturalist adjudication.

Dworkin and other naturalists concede that this account of law might well exact a price in the development of a communitarian spirit, but they insist that members of a genuine political community are governed by a common set of principles that are constitutive of social justice. Anxious to deflect charges of being insufficiently democratic, Dworkin reminds his readers and would-be critics that the Rule of Law "is the parent and guardian of democracy and enriches democracy by adding an independent forum of principle where justice is in the end a matter of individual right, and not independently a matter of the public good." He casts the courts as the central constitutional institution through which the citizenry can debate, articulate, and implement its collective standards for social justice. In elevating legal conversation to a privileged form of democratic discourse, Dworkin has persuaded many *Charter*-inspired Canadian judges, jurists, and lawyers to subscribe to a natural law theory of adjudication. Nevertheless, the naturalists have not swept all before them.

Law and Economics

In 1897 a prescient Oliver Wendell Holmes Jr observed that "for the rational study of the law, the black-letter man may be the man of the present, but the man of the future is the man of statistics and the master of economics." He has been proven right in more ways than one — economics has become the holy grail of much contemporary scholarship, and men have remained its main exponents. Initially concerned with economic sectors of law (i.e., competition law and personal damages assessment) law-and-economics scholarship began to apply its concepts and arguments to other non-market areas of law, like crime and discrimination law. Its adherents, like Michael Trebilcock, now attempt to explain or critique law in terms of an economic logic; it is based on viewing law as a series of incentives and disincentives to influence the behavioural choices of people who are viewed as rational and self-interested maximizers of society's scarce resources. As a mode of positive analysis, it evaluates the empirical impact of different legal rules as price-setting devices in terms of their allocative efficiency and distributive justice. More controversially, as a mode of normative analysis, it judges whether any particular change in legal doctrine will increase economic efficiency either because it makes someone better off without making anyone worse off (Pareto efficiency) or because it will generate sufficient gains to pay off the losers (hypothetically) and still leave gains for the winners (Kaldor-Hicks efficiency).

Not surprisingly, law-and-economic scholarship has found the most fertile ground for its analysis in the private law doctrines of property, contract, and tort law. So, for instance:

- Beginning from a preference for voluntary market-based exchange over collective state-initiated management, these scholars have sought to enhance the functioning of contract law by developing legal rules that encourage cooperation rather than defection or opportunism (remedies); that reduce the transaction costs (e.g., negotiation and information-production) in making agreements (implied terms); that discourage carelessness and detrimental reliance (mistake and misrepresentation); and that authorize appropriate excuses for non-performance of contractual obligations (breach rules).

- Similarly, in tort law, the law-and-economics scholar is interested in the extent to which legal rules (standard of care, defences, damages, etc.) work to minimize the sum of expected accident costs and avoidance costs so as to ensure that there is an optimal level of investment, but not overinvestment in safety precautions.

Of course, there have been many criticisms of the law-and-economics approach to law: it is reductionist in its insistence in viewing all social conduct in terms of market behaviour; it manages, by giving everything a monetary value, to overvalue and undervalue much of human interaction; its leading concepts (voluntariness, transaction costs, etc.) are theoretically vague and practically indeterminate; it is ethically bankrupt in that it takes all personal preferences at face value and refuses to distinguish among them; it is self-serving in that it treats all personal preferences as independent of the social or market system in which they are generated and satisfied; it ignores the distinction between willingness to pay and ability to pay; and it celebrates individual autonomy over communal attachment. Nevertheless, law-and-economics scholarship does focus attention on the important economic function of legal rules and obliges lawyers to attend to the instrumental consequences of different legal regimes and reforms. Perhaps more than most theories of law, its fatal flaw is that it overreaches itself and, instead of being content with offering a partial insight into the operation of law and society, it claims to provide a total and hegemonic account of law. As such, it reveals itself as an ideology as much as a philosophical theory.

Law and Literature

In the past decade, the jurisprudential community has begun to treat the problems of law as language more seriously. Unconvinced by the attractions of philosophy and economics, some theorists, like Brian Langille, have turned to literary studies. In the same way as their legal counterparts, literary theorists are concerned to locate meaning in the encounter between reader and author through a textual medium. In seeking to enrich legal study by reference to literary study, there have been two kinds of approach — the humanistic and the hermeneutical:

- The humanistic approach compares law and literature as discursive efforts to give meaning to life's experience. As acts of writing and reading, law and literature help to create a humanistic discourse through which people engage in the vital task of cultural enhancement. Scholars like James Boyd White contend that adjudication is not simply about the professional weighing of competing precedents, but is an important activity through which society and individuals define both themselves and the world they inhabit.

- The hermeneutical approach is more interested in using literary theory to establish a workable and authoritative theory of interpretation that will allow for creative use of legal texts as well as limit the range of meanings that can be legitimately attributed to such texts. For instance, Dworkin has suggested that law can be profitably thought of as a continuing "chain novel" in which judges are free to add a new chapter as long as they commit to developing the earlier chapters of the novel as a whole.

Having involved themselves in literary theory, jurists got more than they bargained for. Far from facilitating the process to fix law with a determinate meaning, the literary diversion has highlighted the futility of jurisprudence's attempt to fix legal meaning and has added further problems for good measure. As many literary-theorists-turned-legal-theorists have emphasized, the literary enterprise is a strange place to look for reassurance about the possibility of hermeneutical certainty; good literature tends to be celebrated for its richness of interpretive possibilities, not its capacity to generate a limited range of meaning. Literary theorists like Stanley Fish have reminded lawyers that to ask about meaning is to ask about everything; there is no formal place or process that can ground legal interpretation such that the debate about law's meaning and substance can proceed in a neutral or a non-ideological way. Also, critics have pointed out the extent to which law-and-literature scholars ignore the sociopolitical contexts of language, literature, and law; they maintain that literature, like law, is written and read in a historical context of elite political interests and is beholden to a partial vision of human identity and social interaction.

GETTING CRITICAL

There are four main perspectives — *Marxism, feminism, critical race theory*, and *postmodernism* — that take a pessimistic view of law and legal education's chances of redeeming their potential to be a professional force for good in society.

Marxism

Few political critiques have been as misunderstood and as pilloried as Marxism. Although there is a common set of features that mark a political theory as "Marxist," there is little agreement on what amounts to a Marxist theory of law. Like the law-and-economics scholars, Marxists prioritize the "economic" as the most useful explanatory category, although they take a radically opposed stand on its operation and effect. Traditional Marxist accounts emphasize several important claims:

- Marxism is primarily an account of history that seeks to understand social arrangements like law and culture as manifestations of the material struggle in and through history. History is driven by the economic relations that exist among classes, relations that are exploitative and antagonistic; they determine that the benefits of production are owned by employers, not workers.

- As a superstructural phenomenon, law is understood to be an institutional process that responds to and reflects the social base of prevailing economic structures and interests. In this way, law is not so much a neutral or independent site for the resolution of disputes as a social resource to maintain class inequalities and social domination.

- The legal process and its personnel operate both as a coercive weapon (the threat or imposition of criminal sanctions and civil damages) and an ideological medium (the manufacture of legitimating explanations to gloss over the contradictions and false necessity of the status quo). As members of the elite, judges hold values and make decisions that are beneficial or, at least, acceptable to that elite.

Modern legal Marxists like Judy Fudge and Harry Glasbeek accept that the scientific paraphernalia of traditional Marxist theories cannot be fully justified. Although economic relations are claimed to give rise to legal relations, the fact is that, as property relations, economic relations are always constituted by legal relations; economic relations are situated in historical context, which is defined by its social and legal form. Instead, they accept that there is a more dynamic and organic link among economic, social, and legal relations. They do insist, however, that the prevailing economic interests and relations do causally constrain the kind of legal rules and forms that can exist. Although there is little need for every detail of the law to reflect dominant economic claims, the basic structure of the legal system must facilitate the prevailing interests; a capitalist system requires the general regimes of property and contract, but can tolerate a range of rules on restrictive covenants in property law or offer and acceptance in contract law. Accordingly, there is and can be a certain "relative" degree of legal autonomy from the status quo; Marxists are not obliged to explain all judicial decisions in terms of the economic demands of capitalist logic. Indeed, in order to claim the support of the under-classes, a legal system must occasionally and consistently hold the upper classes to its general norms of expected behaviour; a flourishing and formally fair scheme of law is a way to turn might into right.

Marxists tend to be formalistic in construing law; they view the development and application of rules as proceeding in a determinate and fixed way. Moreover, they remain extremely categoric and static in their accounts of social interaction and historical development. As the grand theory of explanation, historical materialism is hard pressed to reduce the manifold operations of society or law to one overarching and enduring historical dynamic. Although holding on to much of their class analysis of contemporary society, many Marxists no longer, if indeed they ever did, hanker after some future communist utopia in which humankind will be redeemed by a collectivist combine. Breaking down the polarized thinking that oscillates between more/less state intervention and more/less market freedom, these scholars emphasize the need for a society that takes an unrelentingly democratic stance on the exercise and distribution of power; they are prepared to explore all kinds of processes and institutions that enhance the extent to which people participate in and control the terms and conditions of their own lives. As part of this political program, some legal Marxists are prepared to encourage the use of constitutional litigation strategies to challenge the social establishment; others view such lapses as more likely to underwrite rather than undermine the present undemocratic play of power.

Feminism

There are probably as many feminist approaches to law as there are women lawyers and jurists. Nonetheless, the centrepiece of feminism is obviously women's experience and the fact that law is a thoroughly gendered process and institution. Women's inequality is ignored, and is experienced as ordinary and natural by most men and also by many women. Legal rules operate to blind society to the harm that women suffer; physical violence against women is trivialized by criminal law's male viewpoint in sexual assault, and the economic oppression of women is exacerbated by family law's solicitude for men's interests. Also, legal rules tend to downgrade the need for women to have control over their reproductive lives; the legal system is complicit in the government's failure to provide suitable health care, maternity leave, and child care for women. Early feminists sought to criticize and improve the law in terms of its capacity and willingness to ensure that men and women have the same rights; the elimination of bias and the establishment of gender neutrality was the goal. However, the problems with such a "sameness" strategy became apparent: courts held that the state's refusal to respect pregnant women's claims for maternity leave was not discrimination since non-pregnant persons were both male and female. Shifting tack, many feminists, like Brenda Cossman and Susan Boyd, began to highlight the physical and socially constructed differences in gender and to argue that such differences ought to be fully accommodated in a legal system devoted to equality.

However, for many scholars, feminism is not only about the obvious exclusion of women from legal entitlements and participation, but how the law's vaunted rationality and impartiality is a front for patriarchy; the move has been from seeing law as a functional tool of male power to understanding it as male ideology. Radical feminists like Catharine MacKinnon contend that law's neutrality is only the reflected "objectivity" of male experience and that it works as a device to subjugate women. As a form of discourse, law's categories and concepts help to construct the idea and experience of "women" and, for MacKinnon, the feminist challenge is to confront the relations of domination and oppression that are institutionalized by law. By consciousness-raising, women should work to re-craft existing legal categories entirely, rather than simply neutralize or extend them; a whole new perspective on legal decision-making, facts, and reasoning had to be nurtured in which more nuanced and contextualized standards and practices responded to women's lived experience.

In recent years, feminism has been assailed by male (and some female) theorists who insist that it has allowed its political zeal to contaminate and undercut its theoretical salience by overstating the extent to which law is a scourge of oppression as well as a forum for transformation. It has also been challenged by Aboriginal and differently abled women, lesbians, and women of colour who criticize the essentialism of much feminism. Such scholars, like Marlee Kline, argue that the category of women is diverse and multiple; it is intersected by considerations of race, sexuality, and class, and cannot be reduced to the political interests and social identities of white, heterosexual, and middle-class women. At the heart of this critique is the observation that all women do not experience oppression in the same way and, therefore, that women must be prepared to develop a whole slate of dynamic and different strategies to analyze and alter their social condition and their legal persona. The ambition is to open up the law to voices that have previously been ignored or silenced. The hope is that, with the advent of more women lawyers and judges, it might be possible to advance the cause of equality and to improve society for everyone.

Critical Race Theory

Despite protestations to the contrary, many people contend that North America can still be viewed as a deeply racist society. Although the expression of openly racist attitudes is on the decline, the distribution of power and privilege is still predominantly effected along racial and ethnic lines. In the broader legal community, the theoretical commitment to a multicultural society is undermined by the practical effects of discrimination that marginalize the role of visible minorities. The idealism of equality rhetoric is hard to reconcile with the reality of inequality in terms of job opportunities, housing, health, education, and other important indicators. A developing body of literature is devoted to addressing the racist practices that engulf society and to working towards substantial change. However, the claim is not that this discriminatory behaviour has gone on outside the purview of the law, but that it has been institutionalized and legitimated through law; a prime example is Canada's treatment of Aboriginal peoples. Whether it is the criminal justice process or the immigration system that is being examined, the form, substance, and attitudes of the law have been shaped by the demands of a white elite against the interests of a large ethnic under class.

As well as describing the historical experience and social plight of visible minorities, scholars have begun to offer a much deeper and richer account of the way law has been used to poison and perpetuate unequal relations between white persons and people of colour. Critics like Patricia Williams and Patricia Monture have argued that legal discourse forecloses the involvement of "outsiders" and, in imposing an alien language and dominating culture, refuses to give a voice or a place to the permanent "others" in society. In particular, law helps to construct and sanction a set of values and social identities that entrench the status quo; it is a primary device through which reality and the channels for change are structured and controlled. By way of prescription, it is proposed that there must be not only a transformation of the rules and institutions that permit racism but also a profound revision in the way that law promotes and neutralizes very partial sets of values and ideas. As with feminism, however, there is strong division over the role to be played by litigation and the courts in any strategy of change. The question remains, Is law capable of becoming a small part of the solution and not only a large part of the problem?

Postmodernism

As strong a grip as formalism has on the constitutional and legal mind, a critical strain exists in political and jurisprudential thought that rejects such an account and adheres to an avowedly non-formalist account of law and adjudication. Drawing on a broad strain of postmodern theory and comprising academics of different political stripes, this specialty tends to be referred to collectively as "Critical Legal Studies." This disparate group which originally included feminists, critical race theorists, and Marxists once existed as an activist organization, but now tends to function as an exclusively intellectual trend. Postmodernists tend to distrust large-scale theories of all kinds, including some feminist and Marxist offerings, that claim to offer one simple, totalizing, and formalized account of law and its development; they seek to disrupt and unsettle the bases on which closed and stable schemes of meaning and authority are supposedly grounded. Traditional jurisprudence has simply effected a shift from black-letter law to black-letter theory. Law is never simply there; it is always political in the sense that what counts as the law has to be argued for and defended politically. Nevertheless, most critical scholars are committed to challenging law's role as an oppressive and dominant force in the service of the status quo. They consider legal education (in its pedagogy, content, faculty, attitude, and evaluative methods) to be all about, as Duncan Kennedy puts it, "training for hierarchy." Despite its monumental efforts to hide the fact, law school is a profoundly political place, perhaps no more so than when it is intent on insisting that it is not at all political. Although students are correct to believe that they are at a great feast, they tend to forget that they are the dinner, not the diners.

Rather than view the completion of the formalist project as a noble dream, critical scholars like Joel Bakan and Richard Devlin (and myself) see it more as a nightmare from which people must be awakened. The charge is that philosophical revelation is a poorly disguised style of political advocacy and that the law's inner purpose is the reflection of lawyers' instrumental preferences. Rational discourse does not exist in any pure form, but is thoroughly beholden to its ideological context. As such, law and rights talk are not so much a rational enterprise as a vast exercise in rationalization. As psychiatrists create "a monologue of reason about madness," lawyers tend to establish a sham discourse of reason about the contingent confusion of political and social life. Legal doctrine is nothing more than the well-intentioned but self-righteous opinions of a professional elite that can have no claim to constitutional priority over democratic deliberation. Any claim that judges are being held back from a frenzy of arbitrariness only by rules' restraining power is unrealistic, and it does scant credit to the integrity and efforts of most judges. In short, law is politics.

Some critical legal scholars have gone so far as to suggest that, without some plausible account of determinate rule-following, there will be an official anarchy in which rules will count for nothing or simply be used as *ex post* rationalizations for *ex ante* decisions. If appointed to the bench, these self-proclaimed nihilists would adopt a "currently fashionable theory" of adjudication and then use it to advance the progressive cause. Other critical scholars argue that this approach fails to take the legal enterprise seriously and that judges are both more and less constrained by rules than any of the positivists, naturalists, and nihilists think. They are more constrained in the sense that they cannot get completely outside rules and exercise an entirely free choice, and less constrained in the sense that they are not obliged to reach any particular decision as the result of a commitment to resolve disputes through rule application. The meaning of a law and its application never simply is — it is something to be argued for or with, and not something to be argued from. Law is a special kind of activity or game that is defined by rules and roles; one where the nature and effect of those rules and roles are themselves always in play. When properly understood, the critical claim is not that "anything goes," but that "anything might go."

NO THEORY, PLEASE; WE'RE LAWYERS

You might be thinking that all these categories sound, at best, fascinating and, at worst, frightening. Do I really need to understand all this theoretical stuff? Surely I can avoid most of this? Do I really need to know the difference between wealth maximization and historical materialism, and between patriarchy and postmodernism to get through law school? The answer is, as you will learn is true for most questions in law school, yes and no. If you want simply to get through — survive rather than succeed — you can skirt these issues and remain largely ignorant of the theoretical underpinnings of law. But if you want to do well at law school, a nodding acquaintance with the basic arguments around and in legal theory can turn out to be one of the best practical moves you ever made. By understanding the larger intellectual pool within which lawyers and professors swim and thrive, you will be able to grasp the broader significance of particular styles of reasoning and rules. Such knowledge can only work to your advantage in the competitive maelstrom of law school.

Furthermore, by giving legal theory a chance, you might actually enjoy it. Beware of those students and teachers who try to persuade you that there is simply law and its traditional study, with a series of new theoretical approaches as fancy variations on the basic theme. This approach is simply wrong, a defensive anti-intellectualism of the worst kind. To teach or to talk about law, everyone has to have some understanding of what law is, along with a theory (however rudimentary) about its conceptual identity and functional operation. The only difference between those who claim not to have such a theory and those who do is that the latter know what theirs is and the former do not (or, what is worse, they are being disingenuous or dishonest). A denial of legal theory's existence or relevance is as wrongheaded as those who insist on treating law as only a theoretical phenomenon. As an early American sceptic, Karl Llewellyn, put it, "technique without ideals is a menace; ideals without technique are a mess."

As we move into the second millennium, the recondite world of legal theory will continue to remain dominated by the tension between the formalists and the antiformalists. Can law maintain its prestige and power as a (semi-)autonomous discipline and practice in an increasingly sceptical world, or must it be comprehended as an irreducibly political process with little independent legitimacy or appeal? This dynamic will energize not only the development of the law but also the substance, performance, and experience of legal education. Most of the time, it will be the silent but very real source of the positions and postures that animate legal study. Occasionally, however, that tension will make its presence felt in a loud and disruptive voice. Either way, you will be better prepared to meet its challenge and take a stance if you understand that it is there, and if you have some sense of its theoretical pedigree.

FURTHER READINGS

Devlin, R. *Canadian Perspectives on Legal Theory.* Toronto: Emond Montgomery Publications, 1991.

Dworkin, R. *Law's Empire.* Cambridge, Mass.: Harvard University Press, 1986.

Fish, S. Doing *What Comes Naturally.* Durham, N.C.: Duke University Press, 1989.

Frug, M.J. *Postmodern Legal Feminism.* New York: Routledge, 1994.

Hutchinson, A. *It's All in the Game: A Non-Foundationalist Account of Law and Adjudication.* Durham, N.C.: Duke University Press, 2000.

Kairys, D, ed. *The Politics of Law: A Progressive Critique*, 3rd ed. New York: Pantheon Books, 1997.

Kennedy, D. *A Critique of Adjudication fin de siècle.* Cambridge, Mass.: Harvard University Press, 1997.

Law and Learning: A Report to the Social Sciences and Humanities Research Council of Canada [The Arthurs Report]. Ottawa: Social Sciences and Humanities Research Council, 1983.

MacKinnon, C. *Feminism Unmodified: Discourses on Life and Law.* Cambridge, Mass.: Harvard University Press, 1987.

Posner, R. *The Economics of Justice.* Cambridge, Mass.: Harvard University Press, 1983.

Posner, R. *The Problems of Jurisprudence.* Cambridge, Mass.: Harvard University Press, 1990.

Twining, W. *Blackstone's Tower: The English Law School.* London: Stevens and Sons, 1994.

White, J.B. *The Legal Imagination.* Boston: Little, Brown, 1973.

Williams, P. *The Alchemy of Race and Rights.* Cambridge, Mass.: Harvard University Press, 1991.

CHAPTER 3

This Crazy Little Thing Called "Law": Legal Materials and Institutions

Law is a dynamic and social force, but its formal existence can be traced to a variety of sources. These are the raw materials of the law that make up the basic phenomenon of "law." They will be the basic working resources that you will need to learn and become familiar with, if you are to make any progress in understanding law. However, you will make a serious mistake if you understand these sources as lifeless and dry forms; these products and processes of the law are human creations and, as such, are organic substances in a state of constant flux. The sources may be constant, but their outpourings are volatile and varied. Also, as Dickens put it in *Bleak House*, courts are "the foggiest and muddiest of places," and law students ought not to be surprised that the task of identifying and understanding the basic resources of the law is not as straightforward or as clear as they might like it to be. This chapter maps the essential features of the legal topography that students must learn to negotiate in their efforts to come to grips with legal study: the constitution, the common law, legislation, and customs and values.

THE CONSTITUTION

Many people wrongly assume that Canada has had a constitution only since 1982. However, Canada has had a formal constitution since its creation in 1867 by the British North America Act and, even before, there were legal instruments stretching back to the first colonial settlements that established a Canadian territory. Of course, none of this traditional history tends to recognize that Aboriginal nations had constitutions that can be traced back for hundreds of years. Although the *British North America Act* was a statute of the British government, it formed the basis of Canada's constitution until the repatriation of the constitution in 1982. At this time, the name of the *British North America Act* was changed to the *Constitution Act, 1867* (but its content remained unchanged), and the *Constitution Act, 1982*, added, among other things, the *Charter of Rights and Freedoms* to Canada's constitution. These constitutional measures place very definite, if unclear, constraints on what the federal government and its provincial counterparts can and cannot do. As such, the doctrine of legislative supremacy has always had a special and attenuated significance in Canada.

Up to 1982, the constitution divided powers between the federal and the provincial governments, but did not restrict what they could do or enact within their authorized area of action. For example, whereas the federal government had power to legislate on criminal law, the provinces had power to regulate property and civil rights: the difficulty has been to fathom the relation between various powers in a society that is very different from that of 1867. Since 1982, the *Charter* has also placed limits on the kind of action that any particular government or legislature can take; Canadians have a constitutionally guaranteed freedom of communication and the right to life, liberty, and security of the person that government cannot infringe. For instance, if a government wished to introduce legislative measures to control smoking or tobacco advertising, the only question that used to be asked was whether that particular government had the authority to act. Now, once the issue of jurisdiction is resolved, the question has to be asked whether any government can take such steps for fear of infringing the rights and freedoms of Canadian citizens and/or corporations. Contemporary constitutional law is as much about the substantive content of government action as it is about its formal source in the federal system.

Yet it would be entirely mistaken to portray the constitution as an official collection of dry texts. It is important to stress that the constitution is not a single written document or even a set of written documents. The constitution is not a fixed or static document; it is an involving practice and way of life. In the time-honoured phrase of Lord Sankey, "the constitution is a living tree capable of growth and expansion within its natural limits." It should not be forgotten that a constitution is constitutive in that it provides a way in which a society can imagine and form itself. Neither a one-time event nor a purely practical act of political will, the constitution is a tradition that is alive, one that is only imperfectly captured by the various legal texts that lawyers talk about as the constitution. As one pair of constitutional commentators put it, "the constitution is not concise, legalistic and static, rather it is voluminous, flexible and evolving." It also comprises a variety of unwritten customs and conventions. These traditions include a mix of political matters that strike to the heart of Canada's situation, including the appointment of the prime minister, the prime minister's role on authority, and the role and function of the cabinet. In an early *Charter* decision, then Chief Justice Dickson left little doubt that the constitution and its judicial interpretation is as much about substantive values as it is about formal documents:

> A constitution . . . is drafted with an eye to the future. Its function is to provide a continuing framework for the legitimate exercise of governmental power and, when joined by a Bill or a *Charter of Rights*, for the unremitting protection of individual rights and liberties. Once enacted, its provisions cannot easily be repealed or amended. It must, therefore, be capable of growth and development over time to meet new social, political and historical realities often unimagined by its framers. The judiciary is the guardian of the constitution and must, in interpreting its provisions, bear these considerations in mind. . . .
>
> The Court must be guided by the values and principles essential to a free and democratic society which I believe embody, to name but a few, respect for the inherent dignity of the human person, commitment to social justice and equality, accom-

modation of a wide variety of beliefs, respect for cultural and group identity, and faith in social and political institutions which enhance the participation of individuals and groups in society. [*Hunter*, [1984] 2 S.C.R. 145]

Canada's basic constitutional documents can now only be changed through special amendment procedures that require the substantial consent of provincial and federal governments. However, like any written text, the constitution does not speak for itself, but has to be interpreted and spoken for. This is the task of the courts. While most of the wording of the *Constitution Act, 1867*, has not changed in more than 125 years, the meaning and effect of its provisions on the division of provincial and federal powers have gone through a process of continual re-definition. Consequently, the constitution also consists of the many judicial cases that have sought to interpret and apply constitutional arguments to changing social and political circumstances. Indeed, the substantive differences between the formal acts of amending the constitution and interpreting it are difficult to pin down. A plausible argument can be made for the fact that the constitution is amended every time it is judicially reinterpreted.

A good example of the power of judicial interpretation is the case of *Sparrow*, [1990] 1 S.C.R. 1075, in which the courts had to interpret the meaning and effect of section 35 of the *Constitution Act, 1982*, which reads that "existing aboriginal rights . . . are hereby recognised and affirmed." This section is outside the *Charter of Rights* and so is not governed by the limiting force of section 1 of the *Charter*, which states that all the rights and freedoms in the *Charter* are "subject only to such reasonable limits prescribed by law as can be demonstrably justified in a free and democratic society." Nevertheless, the Supreme Court held that, although the text of section 35 has no mention of reasonable limits, the federal government has the continuing general power to impose reasonable restrictions on the exercise of any rights protected under section 35. If this is interpretation, it is difficult to imagine in what substantive, as opposed to formal, ways an amendment of the constitution would differ from it.

The constitution has been described as "a mirror which reflects the soul of the nation." As you begin to study constitutional law, many will likely think that the whole constitutional process of judicial interpretation is more smoke than mirrors; it bears strong testimony to Oliver Wendell Holmes Jr's quip that "lawyers spend too much time shovelling smoke." Constitutional law is a baffling mish-mash of texts, customs, conventions, ideals, and cases that defy the ordering instincts of most informed lawyers; it is a historical and political tour-de-force of Canadians trying to come to terms with who they are and who they want to be. However, one thing is certain: whatever the constitution does and does not say, it is the major and leading source of Canadian law that trumps all other pieces or practices of law-making.

THE COMMON LAW

Derived from England, Canadian law is part of the common law tradition: both as a source of law and in the practice of law. As a source of law, common law refers to the vast body of judicial decisions that has developed over time; judges decide present disputes by reference to past decisions, and also establish rules for future controversies. Dating back to England of the eleventh century, it originally referred to the customary rules that were adopted by itinerant judges as they sought to develop a "common" law for the resolution of disputes throughout the country. These cases do not so much offer interpretations of the law — the reasons given by judges for their decisions are the law. In this sense, although decisions are now reported extensively, common law is often thought of as unwritten law; it is not collected or contained in any one authoritative code. Large parts of the subjects that you study in the first year, such as Contract and Tort, are made up of common law decisions.

Common law can best be appreciated in contrast to legislation and civil law. As we will see, legislation is an enactment by Parliament, a provincial legislature, or a city hall that stipulates certain rules and principles that must be interpreted and followed by the courts. Under the doctrine of legislative supremacy, legislation is superior to the common law and, in any conflict between legislation and the common law, legislation will prevail. However, common law has a historical pedigree that means that judge-made law forms the backdrop against which the enactment and the interpretation of legislation take place. Also, as a source of law and a practice of law, the common law is to be distinguished from the civil law that dominates in Quebec. Deriving from Roman law, civil law comprises a written code or codes of general provisions that combine to form an authoritative and complete statement of the law. While codes obviously require interpretation, those decisions are not themselves of binding authority in the way that the common law is binding.

The depiction of the common law as a practice of law-making is as important as the body of legal decisions it produces. It is the distinguishing characteristic of the Canadian legal process. Common law is understood as much as an intellectual mind-set to law-making as a technical practice, and lawyers have transformed a natural tendency to use past performance as a guide to future conduct into an institutional imperative. By way of the doctrine of *stare decisis* (see later), the common law method insists that past decisions are not only to be considered by future decision-makers but are to be followed and treated as binding. One way to understand this process is to imagine the body of legal decisions as being the product of a continuing and sprawling "chain-novel" exercise. Judges approach the task of giving reasons for judgment in particular cases as if they had been asked to read the many chapters of earlier judgments that have already been written and to contribute a chapter of their own that in some significant way continues the story of the common law. While this process places judges under certain constraints, it also leaves them, like the creative writer, with considerable leeway to interpret what has gone before and to add a few twists and turns of their own. Law is to be found in the unfolding struggle between the openings of decisional freedom and the closings of precedential constraint.

Although the common law method may be seen as giving extraordinary powers to judges, it is defended as providing citizens with a necessary check against the exercise of arbitrary judicial authority in deciding cases, and as supplying people with a predictable baseline against which to organize their own affairs. However, like most matters, the theory of what is supposed to or is said to happen is not always congruent with what actually does happen. The challenge for the courts in a rapidly changing world has been to operate the system of precedent wisely so that the need for stability is balanced against the demand for progress: the courts must not allow certainty to eclipse justice. The success of such an undertaking cannot be judged in technical terms alone, but calls upon the discourse of ideals and ideology.

With the establishment of a thorough system for reporting court decisions accurately, an elaborate body of rules and principles has been developed by the courts around the functioning of this doctrine of precedent. The basic operating premise is that "like cases are to be treated alike," so that the reported reasons for deciding a case are binding on inferior courts in deciding later cases that involve fact situations that are similar. The force of a precedent, therefore, is determined by the authority of the deciding court, the ruling in the case, and its subsequent history. In order to understand how this practice works, three essential topics need to be clarified — the system of case reporting, the hierarchy of the courts, and the ruling in cases.

CASE REPORTING

In the early days of the common law in the thirteenth and fourteenth centuries, the reporting of judgments was done by word of mouth. However, as both the court system and the methods of reporting became more sophisticated, law reports became a reliable source of legal information for the common lawyer. Today, the problem is not so much a dearth of law reports as a surfeit of them; it seems that almost all decisions appear in some set of law reports or other. Although the advent of official reports is relatively recent, law libraries and databases are full of law reports that are organized in a variety of ways — by court, by region, and by subject matter. Although preference should be given to the official reports where available, reliance on the commercial reports is widely accepted. A list of some of the leading modern Canadian, English, and American reports you will find in your early encounters with the common law, along with the conventional forms of citation, can be found in chapter 7.

At an early stage in law reporting, conventions developed about the way that different cases and judgments were to be cited. Many professors place great stock on students' capacity to cite cases in the appropriate style; others are more concerned with your ability to identify and apply the ruling of the case. Much is made of the correct placing of the comma between the name of the case and the citation, and of the use of square brackets or round parentheses around the date of the case. A rule of thumb is that the comma goes after the date if the date is not a necessary part of the citation, and that the date is placed in parentheses if the date is not a necessary part of the citation. The correct style of citations for the decision of the Supreme Court of Canada in *Horsley* v. *MacLaren* would be:

Horsley v. *MacLaren*, [1972] S.C.R. 441.
Horsley v. *MacLaren* (1972), 22 D.L.R. (3d) 545 (S.C.C.).

These citations mean that the judgment of the Supreme Court will be found in the volume for 1972 of the Supreme Court Reports commencing at page 441, and in volume 22 of the Third Series of the Dominion Law Reports commencing at page 545. Whereas the former citation includes the date and identity of court and, therefore, need not be separately included, the latter does not and, therefore, the date and the identity of the court have to be included. In some instances, the method of citation can become complicated. Accordingly, it is best to obtain or access a citation guide, such as the *Canadian Guide to Uniform Legal Citation* or the *Harvard Blue Book*; your law school should advise you which to follow.

When you do locate the case in the law reports (for a more detailed introduction to legal research, see chapter 7), you should first read the case to determine the players, the venue, and the outcome: you can worry about the reasons for the decision later. You will find that most reports follow a similar format: names of parties and status; date of decision; identity of court and judges; catchwords; headnote; cases, statutes and authorities cited; nature of proceedings and counsel; reasons for judgment; and the disposition. In the report of *Horsley v. MacLaren*, the following examples illustrate the abbreviated version of the format:

> Astrid Horsley and Richard J. Horsley, Lawrence A. Horsley, Michael A. Horsley, all infants by their next friend Thomas Robertson *(Plaintiffs) Appellants;*
> and
> Kenneth W. MacLaren and the ship "Ogopogo," and Richard J. Jones *(Defendants) Respondents.*

As well as giving the names of the parties to the action, the report also gives their status. In this case, the action was initiated by the plaintiff (the individual who commenced the proceedings), who later appealed against an adverse decision and became the appellant; the case was brought against the defendant, who was initially successful and became the respondent in the plaintiff's later appeal. Because three of the plaintiffs/appellants are children, their action has to be brought in their names by "their next friend," a legal term for an adult relative or guardian. Also, when the case is cited, it will usually be shortened to *Horsley v. MacLaren*.

> 1971: May 5, 6; 1971: October 5.

This information indicates the dates of the hearing before the Supreme Court and the date that the judgment was handed down.

> Present: Judson, Ritchie, Hall, Spence and Laskin JJ.

> ON APPEAL FROM THE COURT OF APPEAL FOR ONTARIO

The first line tells you that only five of the Supreme Court's complement of nine sat on the case — an unusual number, as the court usually sits as a full court, so there must have been a reason for the other four judges not to be present (illness, conflict of interest, other official duties, etc.). However, the only formal requirement is that, in any case from Quebec, at least one of the Quebec judges must be present.

> Negligence — Invited guest on cabin cruiser accidentally falling overboard — Duty of owner-operator to attempt rescue — Another invited guest diving into water in

attempt to effect rescue — Dying from shock sustained on contact with icy water — Whether owner-operator negligent in rescue attempt — Whether liable for death of second passenger.

These catchwords give a point-form summary of the principal issues, concepts, and doctrines dealt with in the case. In commercial reports, the summary is often done in such a way as to tie in with the various research tools that exist (see chapter 7).

M, an invited guest on a cabin cruiser, which was owned and was being operated by the respondent K, accidentally fell overboard. In the course of rescue operations, another invited guest, H, dived into the water to help him. The effort was without avail. The rescuer was pulled from the water by others on board, could not be resuscitated and was later pronounced dead. The body of the rescuee was never recovered.

K was first alerted to M's fall when the body was only about a boat-length and a half behind him. Instead of following the recommended method of effecting a rescue, i.e., to circle and bring the boat bow on towards the body, he reversed, after putting the engines momentarily in neutral, and backed up to within four or five feet of the body, where he shut off the engines. M, who had been in the water for approximately two minutes, was apparently unconscious and attempts to rescue him with a pike pole and a life-belt were unsuccessful. The boat having begun to drift away, K restarted the engines and again backed towards M. Three or four minutes had now passed since the fall overboard, and it was then that H dived into the water from the stern, coming up about ten feet from M. The latter was seen to fall forward, face and head in the water, and another passenger, J, jumped in, one foot away, to hold up his head but M disappeared beneath the boat. J's husband grabbed the boat controls which K yielded, swung the boat around bow on, and approached J on the starboard side where she was pulled in. K then resumed control and went forward towards H who was then also pulled in but in unconscious condition. Attempts at resuscitation failed. Medical evidence established that H died from shock sustained on contact with the icy water.

Two fatal accident actions were brought against K for the benefit of the widows and dependants of the two deceased. H's family succeeded at the trial but their claim was dismissed on appeal, and they then sought restoration by this Court of the favourable trial judgment. The other claim failed at trial and was not pursued farther.

Held (Hall and Laskin JJ. dissenting): The appeal should be dismissed.

Per Curiam: There was a duty on the part of the respondent K in his capacity as a host and as the owner and operator of the cabin cruiser to do the best he could to effect the rescue of M.

Per Judson, Ritchie and Spence JJ.: There was no suggestion that there was any negligence in the rescue of H and for K to be held liable to the appellants it was necessary that such liability stem from a finding that the situation of peril brought about by M falling into the water was thereafter, within the next three or four minutes, so aggravated by the negligence of K in attempting his rescue as to induce H to risk his life by diving in after him. Although the procedure followed by K was not the most highly recommended one, the evidence did not justify a finding that any fault of his induced H to risk his life by diving as he did. If K erred in backing instead of turning the cruiser and proceeding "bow on," the error was one of judgment and not negligence, and in the circumstances ought to be excused.

Per Hall and Laskin JJ., *dissenting.* The view that K had been merely guilty of an error of judgment was not accepted. This was not a case where K had failed to execute the required manoeuvre properly, but rather one where he had not followed the method of rescue which, on the uncontradicted evidence, was the proper one to employ in an emergency, and there was no external reason for his failure to do so. This breach of duty to M could properly be regarded as prompting H to attempt a rescue. He was not wanton or foolhardy and his action was not unforeseeable. In the concern of the occasion, and having regard to K's breach of duty, H could not be charged with contributory negligence in acting as he did.

[*Vanvalkenburg* v. *Northern Navigation Co.* (1913), 30 O.L.R. 142, overruled; *Videan* v. *British Transport Commission*, [1963] 2 Q.B. 650, referred to.]

This summary provides a succinct statement of the facts, the parties to the action, and the history of the case to date. Along with the summary of the reasons for judgment, this information is called the headnote. Although students are often advised to ignore headnotes or to treat them with suspicion, they are an excellent resource to begin your reading or research; they prepare you for the more complicated and less structured judgments to follow and, in some circumstances, will let you decide whether the case is actually worth reading or not. As one of the most illustrious of English jurists, H.L.A. Hart, said, "the head-note is usually correct enough" for deciding what a particular case is authority for.

APPEAL from a judgment of the Court of Appeal for Ontario [1970] 2 O.R. 487, 11 D.L.R (3d) 277 allowing an appeal from a judgment of Lacourciere J. Appeal dismissed, Hall and Laskin JJ. Dissenting.

W.R. Maxwell and *S.M. Malach*, for the plaintiffs, appellants.

B.L. Eastman and *J.A.B. Macdonald*, for the defendants, respondents.

This information provides a more formal reference to the decisions in the courts below and the disposition in the Supreme Court. It also lists the names of counsel who argued the case before the Supreme Court. In some English reports, this section is followed by a summary of counsels' arguments to the court.

The judgment of Judson, Ritchie and Spence JJ. was delivered by

RITCHIE J. — I have had the opportunity of reading the reasons for judgment of my brother Laskin and I agree with him that the case of *Vanvalkenburg* v. *Northern Navigation Co.* (1913), 30 O.L.R. 142, 19 D.L.R. 649 should no longer be considered as good law and . . . .

. . . . warning to remain in the cockpit or cabin plays no part in my reasoning. For all these reasons I would dismiss this appeal with costs.

The judgment of Hall and Laskin JJ. was delivered by

LASKIN J. *(dissenting)* — On a cool evening in early May, 1966 an invited guest on board a cabin cruiser which was on its way to its home port, Oakville, from Port Credit . . . .

....Subject to this, I would allow the appeal, set aside the judgment of the Ontario Court of Appeal and restore the judgment of the trial judge but vary the damages to take account of the limitation of liability. On this basis, the appellants are entitled to judgment for $663,128.42, which should be appropriated to the widow and children on the proportions fixed by the trial judge. The appellants are entitled to costs here and in the Court of Appeal as well as to costs of the trial.

These arguments are the reasons for judgment and make up the major part of the report. In this decision the court split over the appropriate way to dispose of the issue, so there is a majority and a minority judgment. Also, in some cases, there may be more than one judgment in the majority or the minority; this division of opinion makes the vital exercise of extracting the precise ruling of the case (see later) even more difficult and tends to lessen the precedential force of the decision as compared, for instance, with a decision in which the judges are unanimous and give only one judgment.

Appeal dismissed with costs, HALL and LASKIN JJ. dissenting.
Solicitors for the plaintiffs, appellants: Levinter, Dryden, Bliss, Maxwell, Levitt & Hart, Toronto.
Solicitors for the defendant, respondent, Kenneth W. MacLaren: Du Vernet, Carruthers, Beard & Eastman, Toronto.

This is the Court's final and formal order disposing of the case. An important phrase is "with costs." It is commonplace at the end of the decision for the court to direct who has to pay the costs of bringing the case or appeal; these costs can be very large, as they include not only the fees paid to the courts to file documents and the like, which are relatively small, but also the fees charged by the lawyers in the case. The usual rule is that the loser will have to pay the costs of the winner, an amount that usually comes to two-thirds or three-quarters of the actual costs incurred by the winning party. Obviously, this provision is a considerable burden, as losers will have to pay their own costs as well. You will deal with the economics of litigation in Civil Procedure, a compulsory course at most law schools.

THE HIERARCHY OF COURTS

Having located a case, the next step is to determine the level of court that made the decision. There is a very definite hierarchy to the Canadian court system. The basic rule for the purposes of precedent is that a later court will only be bound by decisions of earlier courts that hold a superior position in the judicial hierarchy. Decisions of courts of lower or equivalent standing are not without force, but their effect is more persuasive than binding. In a similar way, Canadian courts extend precedential privileges to the decisions of other jurisdictions; the precedents of the British House of Lords and the American Supreme Court, for example, are looked to for advice and inspiration.

The court structure is very detailed and complicated: you will cover it in a course on Legal Process and/or Civil Procedure. However, while it varies from province to province, the basic hierarchy can be easily charted for the purposes of precedent (see figure 1).

Figure 1 Canadian Court Structure

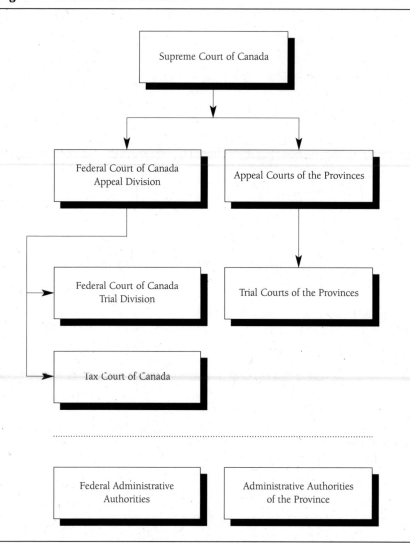

Although decisions of the Supreme Court of Canada are binding on all lower courts, the Supreme Court does not consider itself bound by its own decisions. However, it will overrule itself only when it is absolutely necessary. Unanimous decisions are obviously of more value (or more difficult to get around) than split decisions. A growing tendency is for many, if not all, of the judges to write opinions, even if they concur with the actual disposition of the case; these statements are called concurring judgments. Also, although the decisions of one province are not binding on the courts of another province, they are treated with respect. Since administrative tribunals are not courts, their decisions must be looked at in that light. Tribunals are created to interpret and enforce specific statutes. Their power and authority comes from the enabling statute. In this way, their decisions are relevant only to the particular case and the administrative body. However, such decisions are significant within the particular jurisdiction. The Ontario Labour Relations Board will use decisions from its previously decided cases to assist it, but these decisions would rarely be cited in a judicial forum.

THE RULING

Up to now, the doctrine of precedent has been quite mechanical and easy to follow; it simply involves becoming familiar with the reporting of cases and the hierarchical organization of the courts. However, the next two steps — extracting a decision's ruling and the techniques of avoidance — are much less simple to explain and grasp. They require the development of sophisticated analytical skills and go to the very heart of the common law method. As primary components of the lawyering craft, these skills will be fully acquired only with substantial practice; they cannot be taught or learnt in abstraction. As with so much in law, the skill of extracting a ruling from a case is always a matter of context — the material to be analysed and the purpose of the analysis. The astute student is one who recognizes that the task of locating the ruling in a judgment and making a compelling case for its recognition cannot be carried out mechanically or acquired by rote learning; a case never stands for only one ruling that is the same for all purposes at all times. Accordingly, it is necessary to nurture one's sense of judgment, creative imagination, and talent for persuasion if one is to become an accomplished lawyer. The good lawyer is someone who not only knows the basic techniques of lawyering, but also is able to deploy them with style and flair.

Nevertheless, there are certain basic instructions that can be conveyed and comprehended about the task of extracting rulings from decisions. The most basic lesson is the distinction between the *ratio decidendi* and the *obiter dicta*. There has been much ink spilt and more than a little nonsense talked about the drawing of this admittedly important distinction. While it is often depicted as a kind of scientific procedure that can be performed with cold logic and objective rigour, it is much more an art that is not defined exclusively by its logical quality or achievement. As most law professors and commentators are wont to remind students, if only to forget it themselves, "the life of the law is not logic, but experience." This observation starkly and correctly suggests that the good lawyer is one who knows that law is a human and warm-blooded pursuit that draws on much more than the cold tools of the logician; it requires a good measure of judgment about values, purposes, and equity.

In fathoming the operation of precedent, it is important to understand that it is not all the reasons that go to make up the judgment that are binding on later and lower courts. Rather, a distinction can be made:

- The *ratio decidendi* or *rationes decidendi* (literally, the reason(s) for the decision) are the explicit or implicit legal reason(s) used by the judge to decide the particular factual dispute before her or him and, without which, the decision would be incomplete or deficient. To fix upon the *ratio*, it is necessary to distil the decision down to its bare legal and factual essentials.

- Everything else is *obiter dicta* (literally, "words by the way"); they are reasons and ideas expressed by the judge that are not essential to the actual decision made. Although they do not have the same precedential pull as the ratio, they should be accorded some argumentative respect; they possess some persuasive authority whose strength will depend on the precise issue and the uttering court or judge.

Of course, the drawing of a distinction between *ratio* and *obiter* is a process that is not guaranteed to reach an obvious or shared consensus among different legal analysts. Moreover, this task is compounded by the fact that not only will there likely be more than a single reason in each case, but there will often be more than one judgment in each case. Accordingly, despite the technical sounding terms, the distinction between *ratio* and *obiter* should not be expected to be drawn or reached simply or straightforwardly: it is the stuff of legal debate.

In order to ensure that the common law does not grind to a halt and begin to slide into irrelevance and injustice under the weight of its own backward-looking mind-set, the courts have developed a number of techniques that allow them to avoid the binding force of precedent. In a manner of speaking, institutional necessity has been the parent of judicial invention. Some of the more important and acknowledged devices that courts use to circumvent inconvenient or undesirable precedents include:

- the court that rendered the earlier decision was not a superior court;
- the precedent was given per incuriam; this explanation means that insufficient care had been taken to consider binding statutory or judicial authority. An example is the admonition of the Court of Appeal by the Supreme Court of Canada in the *Horsley* case.
- the precedent has been subsequently overruled or doubted in other cases;
- the precedent was based on a faulty interpretation of earlier cases;
- the scope of the precedent is unclear;
- the precedent can be distinguished;
- social conditions have changed; and
- the precedent has been criticized by academic commentators; this reasoning may be wishful thinking by academics, but judges seem to be citing scholarly books and articles more often to justify their decisions and arguments generally.

It is vital to remember that no case has a ruling waiting to be discovered; rulings are not so much found as created. Of course, you are not free to claim that a judgment stands for just any ruling or to ignore it at whim, but you are by no means as constrained as you might think. Legal analysis never takes place in a substantive vacuum; it is always situated within a particular context of circumstances and objectives. Except in the occasional classroom, it is never reasonable to ask what a case does or does not stand for in isolation. As a practical activity, legal analysis is concerned with how one situation or judgment relates to another situation or judgment; there is a very pragmatic and focused reason for asking what is the ruling of any particular decision. The common law method makes sense only when understood as a way of solving discrete disputes, not as a general process of intellectual reflection. In isolating the ruling of a decision or a set of judgments, you ought not to drive yourself to distraction by viewing yourself as an explorer in search of some sunken treasure. Instead, you would do better to heed the slightly cryptic but wonderfully sage wisdom of a scientist: "The footsteps that we will find on the shores of the future will be our own."

Consequently, the ruling of a decision is to be identified and understood relative to the purpose or purposes for which that identification is being done. One way to grasp this relationship is to think of a judgment as an answer whose precise meaning and scope will change depending on the question that is asked: the nature of the question that is posed will influence the nature of the answer as well as its perceived persuasiveness. For instance, in the famous case of *Donoghue* v. *Stevenson*, the question for the court was whether a ginger beer manufacturer could be liable to someone who became ill after drinking some ginger beer with a dead snail in it, but who had had the drink bought for them. It is entirely ridiculous to contend that the House of Lords' judgment gives rise to any one overriding *ratio* or ruling. Depending on the context in which the inquiry is made, the leading judgment of Lord Atkin can be convincingly and legitimately analysed to produce a vast array of rulings: What does it tell us about the responsibility of builders, accountants, parents, municipalities, and so on? What does it tell us about liability for omissions or failure to act? What does it tell us about recovery for loss of profits? The answer to each of these answers will emphasize a different facet of the judgment and suggest a slightly different shading of meaning. For instance, even in a most general way, Lord Atkin's judgment can be (and has been) not unreasonably interpreted to support a range of rulings that run from "Scottish manufacturers in the late 1920s of opaque bottles of ginger beer are expected to check that dead snails are not left in them" through "all persons who make goods or offer services to the public must ensure that they are fit for their intended purpose" to "everyone should act with due care in their interactions with others." An extended account of how this process of legal analysis works is the subject of chapter 5.

LEGISLATION

The distinguishing feature of twentieth-century legal history has been the shift from common law to statutes as the major source of law. While the common law tradition of deciding cases is arguably still the major characteristic of the legal process, the common law as a source of law has been relegated to a secondary position in terms of size and significance. Notwithstanding this state of affairs, the dominant attitude of lawyers is that the common law comprises a taught tradition of ideals, methods, doctrines, and principles into which legislation from without is added. It is a tradition in which the act of judging, not administering, holds the chief place. Statutory enactments are treated as temporary blights on the legal landscape. Whereas the common law is portrayed as a vast and intricate landscape, carved out with enduring patience and insight over time, statutes are treated as unsightly man-made structures, accommodating transient economic and political interest groups, that disturb the natural beauty and harmony of the common law. The supremacy of legislative intervention is begrudgingly acknowledged, but never fully accepted. The failure to appreciate fully or act upon the statutorification of the law has meant that the accelerator of legislative change has always been affected by the brake of judicial tradition.

THE LAW-MAKING PROCESS

Although the federal and provincial legislatures are most conspicuous as venues for political wrangling, they are the nation's main source of law, and their output is

Figure 2 The Process of Law-making in Canada

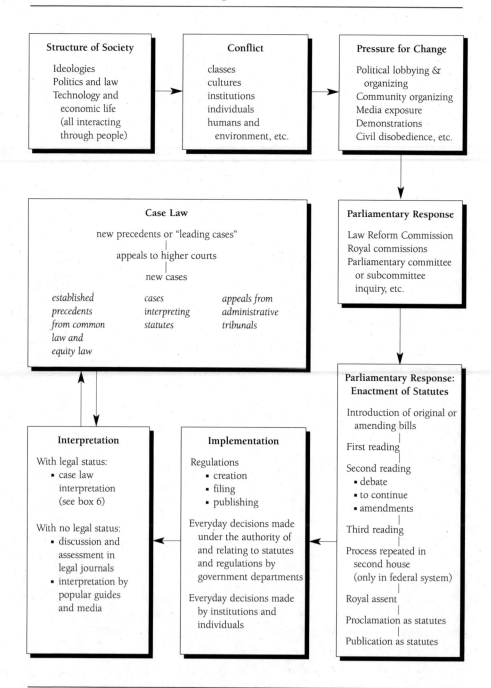

SOURCE: Tim Roberts, *Taking the Law into Your Own Hands: A Guide to Legal Research,* 2nd ed. (Vancouver: Liberal Services Programs, 1984)

prodigious. They do not debate or enact every detail of the government's legislative policy; that is done in committee. The reasons for enacting statutes are varied and complex: legislative proposals are dominated by the government of the day and have gone through a considerable process of consultation and lobbying before they are formally drafted as legislation. In an important sense, statutes tend to be remedial in character in that they respond to an existing state of affairs and regulate it in accordance with prevailing views. The course of law-making is rarely smooth; proposed legislation can be defeated at various stages of the process and for different reasons. The actual procedures that are used today are British in style and are similar in the federal Parliament and from province to province. Figure 2 offers an accessible and dynamic, though tidy, appreciation of the factors, processes, and institutions that go into law-making.

Because much of their time is taken up with political (and partisan) debate, federal and provincial legislatures also authorize other agencies and bodies to legislate subordinately on their behalf. This delegated legislation comprises the greater part of legislation, and the formulating bodies are able to deal in a much less partisan manner with legislative proposals. Since they are staffed by experts, they can appreciate better than politicians the ramifications of particular policies, and are more suitable for deciding on appropriate regulations. Accordingly, while Parliament might lay out some general policy guidelines in the enabling legislation that brings the delegated body into existence or confers powers on an existing authority, it will be for that agency to convert those general policies into workable details. A good example is the setting up of various marketing boards that are empowered to enact rules for the production and sale of goods and foodstuffs, such as wheat and eggs.

The law-making process through legislative enactment has been severely criticized. An account of these failings is beyond the scope of this book, but there are two general matters that warrant further comment: remedial efficacy and complexity:

- Lawyers too often confuse the passing of legislation with the resolution of the problem addressed. There is many a slip between enactment and implementation; situations abound in which legislation has been turned to very different and occasionally opposite effect than that intended or supposed by the legislators; tax statutes are a good example. Although legislation is enacted with judicial interpretation in mind, the courts have the last say. Courts are not the only entities or institutions to be involved in the interpretation of statutes. This activity is carried out by a whole range of individuals, including ordinary people, the police, bureaucrats, and agencies.

- The drafting of legislation is considered by many to have plumbed new depths of unintelligibility; statutory enactments are often written in a clotted and archaic style that defies lay understanding. Yet there is no reasonable excuse for the more convoluted instances of this affected approach (see chapter 6). However, the detail of modern legislation is often a response to ingenious lawyers' efforts to undercut and neutralize the effect of legislation on their clients. Again, the example of tax statutes is revealing; lawyers complain about their complexity, but conveniently forget that their own efforts to read them in contorted and highly original ways are a contributing cause of statutes' complexity. While the resort to "plain English" is to be strongly encouraged, it ought not to be forgotten, for instance, that no one complains that computers are complicated and should be made in such a way that everyone understands them. Sometimes, the subject matter of legislation is simply complicated.

STATUTORY INTERPRETATION

In an age of statutes, the judicial struggle to enforce or enfeeble statutes is at the heart of the legal and judicial process. Although the nature of the various obligations and responsibilities imposed on the different arms of government has varied considerably, the friction between statute and common law has been constant and pivotal. Even though the courts accept that legislatures have institutional priority over them, it is not the words of the statute that are law, but the courts, particular exposition of those words: legislatures make the law, but judges say what it means. Consequently, statutory interpretation is a battleground not only for litigants but also for the institutions of government. In theory and in contrast to the common law's inductive approach, statutory interpretation should be more deductive in method, as it involves the application of a canonical statement of the law to the particular facts of discrete disputes. However, both systems turn out to be much the same in practice; the judicial struggle with late twentieth-century legislation continues to be fought with the age-old weapons of the common law.

In the name of democratic legitimacy, unelected judges attempt to follow the directives of their elected colleagues in government; they do not stand in judgment on the wisdom of the statute or, at least, they are not supposed to. Most forms of statutory interpretation are archaeological in method and ambition: they seek to discover and apply the original legislative intent. All judicial approaches rely on some larger understanding of what amounts to justification and legitimacy in a liberal democracy (see chapter 2). Following the age-old tradition of the English courts, the Canadian courts still claim to use three basic methods of statutory interpretation. Whereas the first two confine themselves to the text of the statute, the third looks to the legislature's purpose(s) in enacting the particular legislation. These approaches are:

- *The literal rule.* Courts follow the plain and ordinary meaning of the statute's words as understood at the time of the enactment, without concerning themselves with the social impact or desirability of their decision. In interpreting literally a statutory provision that "no vehicles are allowed in the park," a judge might decide that an ambulance or a bicycle is a vehicle and that a horse or an airplane is not. In light of the increasing sophistication of legislation, the complexity of modern society, and the general scepticism about there being "literal meanings," this approach has lost judicial favour.
- *The golden rule.* Courts will strive to follow the plain and ordinary meaning of the statute's words, though if necessary they will construe the statute's words in such a way as to avoid absurdity or injustice. In assessing "absurdity" or "injustice," courts will be guided by the larger context of the overall statute. In interpreting the rule that "no vehicles are allowed in the park," a judge might decide that it is absurd to treat an ambulance as a vehicle and an airplane as not.
- *The mischief rule.* Courts will strive to interpret the statute's words in light of the legislature's purpose for enacting the legislation such that the mischief to be addressed

is effectively remedied. In interpreting the rule that "no vehicles are allowed in the park," a judge might conclude that, as the purpose of the enactment was to permit people to relax or play in the park without worrying about their safety, the use of skateboards and roller-blades falls within the spirit of the prohibition.

While the first two approaches are not without their judicial and academic champions, it is the third approach that is most predominant. Although no longer tied to the search for the mischief to be remedied, the basic thrust of most statutory interpretations is the judicial effort to fulfil legislative expectations, at least as understood by the courts. Indeed, all three approaches have tended to fuse together. As one Canadian authority observes, "first it was the spirit and not the letter, then the letter and not the spirit, and now the spirit and the letter." However, the received view in Canada remains that courts cannot use legislative debates to elicit that intent; it is to be gleaned from the overall text and structure of the statute. If this rule ever had any validity, it is difficult to find a convincing contemporary rationale. The reporting of parliamentary debates is no longer deficient, and they are available almost immediately online. Although this evidence is by no means exhaustive or clear, it seems to be a resource to which the courts should be permitted access. Nevertheless, the introduction of such resources in evidence will not bring to an end the problems of statutory interpretation. It is as likely to provide simply one more resource to be (mis)interpreted in the pursuit of the statutory meaning. Even the conservative House of Lords has begun to permit resort to evidence of legislative intent approach (see *Papp* v. *Hart*, [1993] A.C. 593).

Even if courts were correct in their assumption that this approach would best fulfil their democratic mandate, it is by no means clear that it is possible to generate a finding of what a large group of legislators would have wanted over time, after circumstances have changed, and in unanticipated disputes; the identification of past intentions, particularly of collective entities, remains doggedly resistant to present interpretation. Legislators rarely have a specific or exact intention in mind across a range of potential future disputes. The courts are obliged to engage in the most speculative of "what if" investigations — if legislators had thought about this problem, which they did not, how would they most likely have answered the problem. This approach also assumes that legislators would want their general intention to bind future and specific inquiries. It is simply naive to believe that the legislature is filled with politicians who are a reasonable group of people engaged in pursuing reasonable goals reasonably and say what they mean. In hard cases, it is difficult to imagine how an imagined refinement of purpose can yield determinate answers. Any purpose or objective that is consistently attributable to legislatures is likely to be so general that it will be of little help in specific circumstances. In short, as the American critic Robert Post concluded, the judicial attempt to locate legislative intent is "frequently historically uncertain, practically indeterminate, politically repugnant, and conceptually incoherent." Also, it is by no means obvious that democracy is best served by giving effect to the presumed views of older politicians and values; substantive justice demands much more than the slavish adherence by courts to the formal words of statutes.

In this effort to apply and interpret statutory provisions effectively and consistently, the courts have developed a series of maxims and presumptions that are intended to reduce the leeway for errant interpretation. These guidelines include:

- *ejusdem generis* — of the same kind or class;
- *expressio unius est exclusio alterius* — the inclusion of one is to the exclusion of another;
- *noscitur a sociis* — it is understood by the company it keeps;
- *generalia specialibus non derogant* — general provisions do not detract from particular ones;
- *pari materia* — similar statutes are to be treated similarly;
- penal and tax statutes are to be narrowly construed;
- statutes are to be interpreted to preserve their constitutionality;
- words and phrases are to be construed in the context of whole statute;
- statutes are not assumed to derogate from the common law; and
- statutes are not to be given retroactive effect.

Despite the rhetoric, therefore, the methodology of statutory interpretation does not limit the courts in what they can and cannot do. Although presented by the judges as a kind of constitutional compact in which they play junior partner to the legislature's dominant lead, the judicial interpretation of legislation is in practice better understood as judges paying lip-service to the formal arrangement in order to preserve and disguise the reality of the compact — legislators say what the law is, but judges say what it means. In most parts of the law, statutory interpretation is not simply a backward-looking exercise. Although interpretation is framed in terms of text and intentions, statutory interpretation is forward-looking in that it is often concerned as much with the facts, equities, and consequences of cases as with the nature of the statutory resources and the legislative mind-sets themselves. In so many ways, statutory interpretation goes on in much the same way that the common law method provides. It is dynamic, evolving, and value-laden. Although reluctant to admit it, the courts recognize that interpretation is not simply an effort to recreate past meanings. Instead, it is an attempt, as with the common law generally, to use the past to decide present issues in light of future concerns. Judges have little option but to engage in policy-making. Indeed, this approach might accord better with a democratic account of adjudication in the sense that the task of the court might be, like other government agencies and tribunals, to shape policy in such a way that it best serves a broad set of public values. As one of Canada's great jurists, John Willis, stated in 1938, "a court invokes whichever of the rules produces a result that satisfies its sense of justice in the case before it."

CUSTOMS AND VALUES

Apart from the more formal resources of law, the law is energized by reliance on customary and communal norms of behaviour. Law is not only a top-down enterprise but also a bottom-up exercise. As I said in the introduction to constitutional law, the task of deciding on the meaning of constitutional rules draws heavily on prevailing values and normative commitments in Canadian society. Indeed, while traditional sources of law are no longer as prominent, there are vast tracts of the law that have arisen organically from mercantile or administrative practices. They developed independently of the courts in their force and effect; it was only later that they received official recognition. Customs were accepted as having legal authority if they were continuous, certain, reasonable, and followed. The common law method is the crystallization of such a process and disposition. You will find that the courts rely extensively on custom in the area of civil obligations. For instance, in determining whether a professional or a manufacturer has acted reasonably, the courts have developed rules that make explicit reference to the accepted custom and usage in particular areas of expertise. Whereas conformity with general practice will usually rebuff an allegation of negligence, failure to adopt the common custom will indicate a want of care (see *Kauffman* v. *T.T.C.*, [1960] S.C.R. 251).

Encouraged by the advent of the *Charter of Rights and Freedoms*, Canadian courts have become much more open in the way and extent to which they incorporate arguments of policy into their judgments. In almost all cases, judges will justify their particular decision by reference to some consideration about its social, political, or institutional consequences (see chapter 5). It is not so much rules that decide cases, but whatever set of ideas and values that courts accept and follow that is law. Indeed, some judges have gone so far as to suggest that it might be better to forgo resort to particular rules and instead deal directly with policy matters. In a torts case, Lord Denning said:

> At bottom I think the question of recovering economic loss is one of policy. Whenever the courts draw a line to mark out the bounds of duty, they do it as a matter of policy so as to limit the responsibility of the defendant. Whenever the courts set bounds to the damages recoverable — saying that they are, or are not, too remote — they do it as a matter of policy so as to limit the liability of the defendant. . . .
>
> The more I think about these cases, the more difficult I find it to put each into its proper pigeon-hole. Sometimes I say: "There was no duty." In others I say: "The damage was too remote." So much so that I think the time has come to discard those tests which have proved to be elusive. It seems to me better to consider the particular relationship in hand, and see whether or not, as a matter of policy, economic loss should be recoverable. [*Spartan Steel*, [1973] Q.B. 27 (C.A.).]

However, behind this apparently expansive or, some might say, cavalier attitude to policy, there often remains a very "black-letter" approach to decision-making — policy arguments are marshalled and used in a quite formalistic manner such that the instrumentalist nature of policy analysis is marginalized or lost. Judges tend to cite policy arguments in much the same way that they cite legal precedents; a potentially dynamic source of decision-making is reduced to a static mode of reasoning (see chapters 2 and 5). At bottom, the resort to policy is part of the attempt by most lawyers and judges to make good on the basic understanding that, in the final count, law is a matter of justice. Of course, this does not make for certainty or predictability, but it does place the emphasis where it should be. Ultimately, because law is about values, it is always important to ask not only what those values are, but also whose values they are and whose interests they benefit.

FURTHER READINGS

Arthurs, H.W. *Without Law*. Toronto: University of Toronto Press, 1985.

Bale, G. "Parliamentary Debates and Statutory Interpretation: Switching on the Light or Rummaging in the Ashcans of the Legislative Process" (1995) 74 Can. Bar Rev. 1.

Cross, R. *Precedent in English Law*. Oxford: Clarendon Press, 1977.

Eskridge, W. *Dynamic Statutory Interpretations*. Cambridge, Mass.: Harvard University Press, 1994.

Funston, E. & E. Meehan. *Canada's Constitutional Law in a Nutshell*. Toronto: Thomson Canada, 1994.

Hogg, P. *Constitutional Law of Canada*, 3rd ed. Toronto: Carswell, 1992.

Kwaw, E. *The Guide to Legal Analysis, Legal Methodology and Legal Writing*. Toronto: Emond Montgomery, 1992.

Levy, E. *An Introduction to Legal Reasoning*. Chicago: University of Chicago Press, 1949.

Twining, W. & D. Miers. *How to Do Things with Rules*, 4th ed. London: Weidenfeld and Nicolson, 1999.

Waddams, S.M. *Introduction to the Study of Law*, 4th ed. Toronto: Carswell, 1995.

Willis, J. "Statutory Interpretation in a Nutshell" (1938), 16 Can. Bar Rev. 16.

CHAPTER 4

Get a Real Life:
Living Through Law School

Most law students believe that you can either go to law school or have a life — being in law school and having a life seems oxymoronic. It is true that law school can be a gruelling experience that brings out the competitive drive in placid students and induces alienation in affable students: even the camaraderie can be contrived and superficial. However, it need not be like that. Within certain limits, it is possible to be a law student and have a real life; you can have a successful law school career without withdrawing from life as you previously knew it or making your life nothing but being a law student. Moreover, many students make lifelong friends at law school and, like it or not, your student peers will be your professional colleagues for the rest of your life. While law school life is different and will change some of your habits and attitudes, it need not all be for the worse. If you are aware of the stresses and strains that the law school will have upon your expectations and values, you will be prepared to resist them or to harness them in your desire to become both a better lawyer and a better person. Contrary to popular myth, you can have a life, be a good person, and be a law student.

Law tends to be a world unto itself and law schools are its branch plants. The nature of the work, the privilege and power that lawyers (and law students) hold, and the natural arrogance of many lawyers (and law students) contribute to the public perception that lawyers are a breed apart: they are smart, they are articulate, they are confident, and they are intimidating. Obviously, this apartness does not translate into a flood of public approbation; lawyers are often thought to be clever rather than smart, and glib rather than good. Many people (mis)quote Shakespeare's Dick on the topic of lawyers: "the first thing we do, let's kill all the lawyers." Lawyers are the butt of more jokes than almost any other group. Indeed, a measure of lawyers' perverseness is that many seem to take great delight at their depiction as money-grubbing reptiles who would shop their grandmother for a fast buck. All this talk fuels the myth and mystique that surrounds the legal profession; it reinforces the idea that to be a real lawyer, one has to be a thoroughly egotistical and nasty piece of work or, at least, to develop such a professional persona.

This stereotype is nonsense and most certainly need not be the case. Because some lawyers cultivate an image that emphasizes their aggressive, hard-headed, and ruthless attitude to law and life, there is no reason to believe that all lawyers must be like that. And it definitely does not mean that you have to ape such attitudes and behaviour if you are to become a good lawyer. Quite the contrary. It is not necessary to be a bastard to become a good lawyer. Because you managed to get to law school, you might be smart; you might be articulate; you might be ambitious; and you might be tempted to take on airs and graces. But your status as a law student makes you into no better a person than anyone else. Least of all does it give you a licence to act in an obnoxious or arrogant manner. The message is simple and to the point — GET OVER IT. You can do well at law school without being a jerk; without being arrogant; without being aggressive; and without becoming someone that you would not like. And, believe it or not, you can be a good lawyer without those traits as well. In fact, anything that makes you a better person can also make you a better lawyer. But I do not intend to feed you pollyanna tales about law school life or the life of lawyers. It is a tough life, and law does seem to have more than its fair share of jerks; it is up to you to decide whether you will join the herd or whether you will resist in the name of something better.

But I am getting ahead of myself. You need to know how to get through law school, and how you can have a real life at the same time. After dispelling some of the main myths that swirl around the law school, I focus on the realities of law school life and develop some strategies to deal with its day-to-day challenges — stress, study groups, summaries, classes, professors, and politics. So, armed with this book and a healthy dose of scepticism, you can learn not only how to survive at law school, but also how to thrive.

THE MYTHS

You will hear many myths about law school. Some of them have already been mentioned in chapter 1 as they relate to the decision to go to law school, but there are several more that should be identified. What follows are the more pervasive and debilitating myths; there are many more that you will discover as you go through law school. A sense of humour, a sense of priorities, and a social life are your best weapons and defences against such attitudes:

- *Everyone is doing better, understanding more, and getting better marks than I am.* Never believe a law student who brags about marks, unless you see a transcript. As much a comment on their situation as on themselves, law students are notorious for exaggerating their performance; it is part of the machismo that seduces and threatens many of them. Everyone has heard stories about the law student who never or rarely goes to class, gets a great summary, and aces the exam — but none of this is true. Avoid letting your whole self-esteem rest on your own or others' performance at law school.

- *Students who are related to a lawyer have an advantage.* Unless the relative is giving up a job to tutor the student, this "advantage" is not all that it is cracked up to be. Lawyers who graduated years ago are not well placed to understand or respond to the challenges of a modern legal education. Being from a lawyering family may give students connections for interviews, but it will not make them into good lawyers. Who you know may get you in the door, but it will rarely keep you there unless you have the smarts to go with it.

- *Students who ask the most questions and speak the most in class do the best.* There is no correlation between those students who talk most and those who get the best grades: it is as likely to be the ones never heard from in class as much as the ones always talking who do the best. You should participate in class at a level and with a regularity with which you are comfortable and which contributes to your own sense of achievement.

- *There are certain courses I must take to pass the bar admission course.* All law students should take the courses in which they are most interested, because they are likely to do better in those courses. If you have no interest in Real Estate Law and plan never to practise in real estate, you need not take a course in it. The Bar Admission Course should not be your goal; the exams are relatively easy, and very few students fail. Success at law school should be your first priority. If you do that, the general skills that you will have had to master will ensure that you will pass the Bar Admission Course with little difficulty. Whereas law school examinations are something to excel at, bar admission exams are simply to be passed, unless you crave the pleasure of winning some prizes and having them awarded to you in front of everyone else at the Call to the Bar.

- *If you become a lawyer, you will get rich.* Unless you have been in a cave for the past few years, you should be aware that the market for lawyers is tough and competitive, although there is always a niche for energetic lawyers. Unfortunately, many talented graduating law students cannot find articling positions immediately, and some lawyers who have been called to the bar are working in jobs far removed from the courts — some for the better and some for the worse. The fact that the job market is tough out there (see chapter 10) provides even more reason why you should not only do the best you can at law school, but also develop other complementary skills and interests that will give you an edge in the job market. Nevertheless, armed with a law degree, you are at least as well placed as other recent graduates in the job market.

- *Law professors are a bunch of sadistic prima donnas.* As with most of these myths, there is some truth to this one. Some professors are arrogant, aggressive, and delight in humiliating students. Most, however, do not. Law professors can be funny, boring, annoying, friendly, stand-offish, approachable, fair, patronizing. In short, most of the things that most people can be. You will not like them all. But, if you are lucky, you will connect with one or two who will engage you in intelligent and spirited debate and make your law school experience a memorable one. And, surprisingly, it is often the professor with whom you do not agree who turns out to be the strongest influence. You will learn much more from someone who challenges you and makes you examine your thinking on certain subjects than from one who simply spoon-feeds you or confirms your prejudices. For advice on how to deal with the truly objectionable professor, see the later section in this chapter.

- *I do not need to learn how to do research.* Some law students seem to believe that lawyers have clerks and articling students to do research, so there is little need to make the effort to know your way around the law library or the databases. This attitude is a big mistake. First and foremost, your legal research skills will have a definite bearing on your law school grades. Second, if you get through law school, you will likely be an articling student some day and will need to know how to find your way around a library or database. Also, even though there are many senior lawyers who brag about never entering the library in their firms, it may take you more than a few years to get to that point. Learn your way around the library and the web early and save yourself time, trouble, and embarrassment later (see chapter 7).

- *You cannot work and go to law school.* This myth was surely started by young students who were lucky enough to be supported by their family. However, many law students do not have parents who are able or willing to support them through law school. In addition, many law students are parents themselves. The changing face of law school has meant that many mature students are entering law school with families, mortgages, and lives to support. For these students, working is not an option — it is a necessity. Obviously, it is not ideal to have to be working long hours during term time, but it can be done. The best advice would be to put yourself in the most advantageous position for the first year by saving as much as you can and by cutting back as much as possible in first term, at least until you get the hang of things. Once you have figured out how much time your studies need, you can adjust your work schedule accordingly. This assumes that you have a flexible job situation — something that may not be possible for everyone. However, if at all possible, those who must work should try to keep as much flexibility in their job as possible so they can cut back at exam time and increase at slacker times.

- *I owe law school nothing.* Apart from the obvious fees that they owe the law school, some students think that law school is all about taking and not about giving. This is a personal choice, but it is not a happy one. Law students are an extremely privileged group of people. No matter where you came from or where you end up, getting a law degree will likely mean your chances of succeeding in the world are increased many-fold. This opportunity should not be wasted. You should get as much as you can from your law school experience, but you should also put back: the two, of course, are not unrelated. Volunteer for the Legal Aid Clinic, go to local high schools to talk about law as a career, tutor other students, work on student council, and organize social events. You do not have to be the Ken-and-Barbie or Oscar-the-Grouch of law school. Also, there are many ways that you can give back to the law school after you graduate: donate to your alumni association, mentor law students, and offer to speak at Articling Day or Law Day. Being a lawyer is a public service profession.

A DOSE OF REALITY

The best sources of information on how to survive your first year at law school are those people who have done it; drawing on their experience is an obvious strategy for those who are about to do it. To give some "street cred" to the following insights, I have canvassed a diverse group of students — men, women, people of colour, mature students, workers, and critics — for their thoughts and advice; their words are spread throughout the chapter. What follows is a taste of law school life from the first-hand accounts of these real law school survivors and thrivers. Of course, they are the views of certain students only and, like the myths, should be taken with a large shaker of salt. But they do represent the "inside story" and it would be foolish to dismiss them out of hand; they might help you take a less intense and obsessive attitude to the process. In many ways, you will realize that law school is very like "high school for adults." And, as with high school, you too can emerge at the graduating end of law school with a personality, a life, and — this is the difference — a career.

COPING WITH STRESS

So Who Is the Enemy Anyway? Make a note of situations and people that drive you crazy — then try to avoid them.

Dog eat Dog you'll be told, and there's more pit bulls than Chihuahuas out there . . . and if you believe what they say, then you're bound to find the odd rottweiler. Undeniably, law school is competitive, and some students are more competitive than others. But it doesn't follow that the more competitive students will get the summer jobs that lead to articling jobs that translate into a corner office at Big, Better & Best.

There's a tremendous period of fright that most students go through — a defensive feeling created by being, for once, among a group of A-grade students. And the environment may agitate the problem, being graded on a curve, being reminded of the limited number of summer jobs, being encouraged to be adversarial. The upshot of all this is a suspicion that everyone's got some edge, some insight, some contact in the field that you don't have. And the truth of the matter is that a good 98 percent of these people "on the inside" think the same as you.

There is a lawyer topology, long entrenched in our culture, that perpetuates the suspicion that behind every advocate is a diabolical and shadowy manipulator. As law students we tend to suspect that among us are the pupae of these creatures, still premature but just as predatory. O.K. . . . here's the short straw . . . there's more healthy collaboration, group comradeship than there is selfishness and aggression.

Sleep some, eat some, play some, and work some every day — not having fun will make you crazy, not doing work will make you fail, and not sleeping or eating will kill you. None of these is good.

Read non-law stuff whenever you can or you may stop enjoying reading altogether.

Don't be afraid to ask for help. Don't be embarrassed if you don't understand something. If you knew everything you wouldn't have to go to law school. Professors and fellow students will be more willing to help. All you have to do is ask.

Try not to compare yourself with others in your class. The people who talk all the time do not necessarily know anything more than you do.

For most law students, all the academics and social aspects of law school don't fall into place right away; don't be surprised and don't be alarmed. The language, along with the methods of evaluation, may be foreign, but the impact of these and other features can be ameliorated if you do not expect to be comfortable instantly.

Stress is an inevitable by-product of the competitive nature of law school and law students. Some will thrive in the hothouse atmosphere; others will wilt. Either way, you need to find ways of coping so that this atmosphere does not prevent you from performing at your best or getting the most out of law school. One of the best ways to deal with stress is to use it to your advantage. Stress is not always a bad thing. If it forces you to read before class, prepare well in advance for exams, and generally keep up with the work, you will likely have removed most of the reasons for experiencing the negative aspects of stress. Getting behind will produce the most stress — so don't. Remember that the hardest part is getting there; once you are in, the real pressure is off. Make a concerted effort to combat competition and resist the temptation to go with the flow. The failure rate at law school is exceptionally small; you need to work hard at failing to succeed or being asked to leave. Also, most students leave law school with an overall B average. Do your best, but don't sweat it.

KEEPING SOCIAL

Do not miss orientation week; the upper-year students you meet will be an important source of information.

Get involved in extracurricular activities — most firms do not concentrate solely on marks.

Do not study all the time; take time to enjoy the rest of your life.

Have fun, because law school offers more than just an education — you'll have lots of work to do once these three years are over.

Subject to your academic responsibilities, don't give up your passions for playing sports or music just because you are in law school. Many schools provide outlets for these interests and manage to make allowances for your academic demands.

You might feel isolated if you miss out on or are late for Orientation activities, especially the initial ones. Relax and enjoy your law school experience. It will be something that will be with you for the rest of your life. Eventually the confusion that you may experience the first week or two will disappear.

Do not be intimidated by younger students if you are an older than average student. They can be wonderfully supportive. They are respectful and offer academic support. Many of the younger students are away from home, their families, and friends. They will often come to older students for advice about personal problems. A kind and caring response goes a long way.

Any athlete will tell you that it's important to stretch before you do your thing — whatever that thing is — because if you don't, you are bound to overextend yourself and damage parts that you would rather not know that you own. When you get to law school, the same advice applies. It's like a game show: Do you take what is behind door number one, two, or three, or do you take what's in the box? Too many first-year students try to take them all — to join the paper, the journal, the environmental law club, the young aristocrats club and they overextend themselves. Without fail, they find themselves dropping clubs and commitments and backing out of a whole lot of what seemed like good ideas. The solution is pre-activity stretch. Commit to one or two activities with the goal of devoting enough time to each that people know who you are and what you can do. The thinner you spread the caviar, the less you'll taste it. If you handle volunteering for the community legal aid program and you have extra time, then stretch a little more and take on an intramural sport. Do it this way and you'll be doing cartwheels when the crunch hits.

It is essential that you make plans to get away from law school at regular intervals and maintain some kind of social life. This is true for many reasons — retaining your sanity, allowing you to recharge your batteries, and keeping in touch with "real life." Spending all your days and nights in the law school and around other law students is not the best way to deal with stress. Try to keep up your outside interests — sport, movies, politics, and so on. Find a group of like-minded friends – an important hedge against stress, provided you do not fall in with some of the more hyper-competitive souls at law school and exacerbate matters. You will establish friendships at law school that will delight you or dog you throughout your professional and personal life. There is always safety, support, and "something special" in being part of a friendly study group. All work and no play make lawyers into a duller bunch than they already might be.

STUDY GROUPS

These groups, if composed of members who have similar work ethics and attitudes, can be very successful in both personal and academic terms. Smaller groups work much better than large groups. A good idea for putting together a study group is to look for students who have different subject strengths or who have different areas of interest.

Try to find someone you feel comfortable with to study together. It is helpful to talk about the material to make it more clear in your mind.

Develop a study group. We know that first-year students think they are heroes and can do everything themselves, but there are just not enough hours in the day.

Study groups can be a great boon to any law student. Their main purpose and activity is to generate summaries, to allow for discussion, and to share the work-load. But you should remember that they will be a support for your work: you ought not to abandon the task of covering all the material yourself. After all, it is you who will be sitting the examination; the study group does not sit the examination collectively. Also, as you are likely to spend a lot of time with these few people, you should make sure that you pick or are picked wisely. Your study group should be made up of like-minded people — nit-pickers should stick with other nit-pickers; more relaxed studiers are better to hang out with other laid-back individuals, and vice-versa. On the other hand, there is nothing wrong with a good mix of people and personalities. But, regardless of the make-up of the group, you should lay down some ground rules. Everyone must be committed to doing the work prior to getting together. It is unfair to the rest of the group if members come to the study session unprepared and waste everyone else's time getting up to speed. However, the group should not be so rigid in its operating rules that it cannot make allowances for members who have acceptable justifications or excuses.

Study groups can be arranged in many ways. Some groups organize weekly or more frequent get-togethers at which there is a specific topic that is prepared for discussion; others divide the work between the members, and each member is responsible for a certain topic; and still others get together only in the weeks leading up to exams to review class material and practise answering exam questions. Whatever your particular type of group, be sure that it is one that fits you: too many students end up in a group that has poor group dynamics and that, of course, can translate into poor results. The optimum number is probably four-to-six people. While loyalty to the group is important, there is little point in remaining in a study group that is causing you more pain than pleasure. In such circumstances, it is better to study on your own or to join another group.

PERSONAL LIFE

Develop a support system. Make friends with other students. Often their problems are your problems. Like the *Star Trek* crew, take comfort from knowing that you are not alone.

Employ the "park it principle". Many students are involved in a litany of relationships. They are parents, children, partners, caregivers, siblings, and friends. Relationships can drain much-needed energy, and energy is vital to your success in law school. Learn to park your personal problems at the front door and return to them at a later time. Not easy, but necessary.

Relationships are put through tremendous strain by the demands of law school. If you are a parent and your children are old enough to understand what you are doing, sit down with them well before you start school and discuss with them the changes that are about to occur. In fact, if they are more than six, you should talk about the idea of going to law school long before it becomes a reality. They need to know that this is something very important that you are doing and that you will be counting on them to be as helpful as their age will allow. Older children should be told that you will need their support and understanding. You will be the best judge of what your children will need to be told. But do not make the mistake of downplaying the significance of what you are doing. Children deserve to be aware that you will not be as available as you might have been in the past. You should warn them that you will need to spend a good deal of time away from home and that often, when you are at home, you may be preoccupied with your work or need to be left alone to study. Although there are times when your responsibilities will give you little choice, you should take your children to school. Most professors have little problem with kids in their class (unless they carry on excessively — the kids, that is), but it is best and polite to inquire first.

Even if you are not a parent, you will likely have significant relationships, and these people deserve similar information and concern. Law school is not only time-demanding, but it can also effect changes in your attitudes and values. These changes can be very troubling or threatening to those close to you. Remind the important people in your life that you will likely be preoccupied, stressed, tired, and generally difficult to be around at times. Ask for their help and forgiveness before you need it. And do not forget to reward them for their kindness, patience, and concern. At periods in the year when the workload is lighter, be sure to spend time with those people who put up with you when you are at your most unlovable. You will be a lesser person if you operate on the assumption that everyone exists to serve your needs. You have obligations to others, and they are entitled to expect that you are supportive, attentive, and accommodating to their needs. However, even if you survive and grow in law school, you should not assume that all relationships will do so. It is a fact of law school life that as many relationships are made at law school as are unmade.

Define success in your law school career in ways that include rather than exclude your family and/or personal relationships. It is important that you do not set yourself up for professional success and personal failure; a good professional life is not half as good if you do not have a personal life. Law school is a phase of your life. While it will result in important changes (mostly positive, one hopes), it should not come to define your life. You will not be able to do everything. Your life was probably fairly hectic before you went to law school and it is not likely to get any more placid. So you must learn to prioritize: this is a skill that will benefit you in every facet and stage of your life. Be rigorous with yourself and recognize that you will have to let some things slide a little — you should do this while you will still have a choice or otherwise circumstances will make decisions for you. Also, although you need to devote quality time to being with your family, you must also try to make time for yourself. For some, this will be the same thing, but for others it will not. If you neglect yourself, the cost will be high: you can postpone payment, but not for too long. Also, the more that you are able to share about law school will help your family or partners realize that it is not so different than most other educational institutions and workplaces. However, try not to spend all your time away from law school talking about law school; it is important to remember that those you live with have a life too.

POLITICS AND PROFESSORS

Despite differences in politics, professors may be extremely clear in their presentation and willing to assist you in understanding course content. At the same time, a professor whose politics you have deemed akin to your own may have a personal knack for giving students an inferiority complex.

Know what's going on, but beware of getting overinvolved in law school "politics." Ignorance is not bliss when it comes to being cognizant of the political climate of your school. At the same time, "overinvolvement" (something you must honestly define for yourself) that leads to preoccupation could have an adverse effect on your academic success and overall enjoyment of your law school experience.

Don't prejudge the racial environment of the law school. It will take some time to see where things stand with regard to race relations.

Understand that law school is not just about learning rules and law. Policy is very important and a first-year law student must be able to ascertain the difference between policy and law.

Limit your presumptions about professors as being "progressive" or "conservative"; quite often you can be pleasantly and unpleasantly surprised.

Visit your professors. It can be useful to visit them in the weeks before the exam. However, be warned that professors want to face specific questions, not blanket concerns about what the exam may include. If your course has a participation grade, do not cut your own throat by revealing your ignorance during the appointment. The last thing you want to do is to have your professor recall your dim-witted questions (constituting clear evidence of your non-participation) when she is contemplating a malleable aspect of your grade. But be sure to make yourself known to your professors.

Like most people, law professors come in many shapes and sizes. You should not forget that your professors were once students themselves and that they probably drink in pubs, endure difficult personal relationships, and have bad habits. They are, beneath some of the bullshit, people just like you. But when it comes to class and teaching style, there are three main types. Each of them is an exaggeration and overly negative, although less than a caricature.

- *The note-dependent lecturer.* These professors come to class with a written text that they proceed to read to the class. There is little or no opportunity for interruption by way of questions, comments, or discussion. This type of professor is comfortable with, but helpless without, a written script. Distract them at your peril. Some students enjoy this kind of teaching. For them, spoon-feeding means they do not need to think or read before the class. At exam time, little more is expected of them than a regurgitation of the information. For other students, this kind of class is excruciatingly boring and tremendously frustrating. For any student interested in the intricacies of the issues and eager to discuss them, this type of professor should be taken in small doses in the upper years. The compulsory nature of first year denies you the opportunity to avoid these professors, but if you are unhappily saddled with one, you can at least take comfort in the knowledge that you now know what is in store in the future.

- *The free-wheeling performer.* These professors breeze confidently into class with few, if any, notes. They throw out ideas and comments, challenging everyone in the class. There is no chance to sleep or daydream. Students are compelled to listen, whether they want to or not. This type of professor can be the most stimulating, but at the same time the most frustrating. They are often engaging, skilful, actor wannabes, who enjoy teaching, are well read, and know their subject inside and out. However, they may give the traditional, lecture-seeking student the sinking feeling that they are not being taught the law. These professors enjoy healthy and spirited discussion, encourage debate, and foster an environment of questioning and scepticism. For many students, even those who do not agree with the particular perspective presented, these professors are the ones who can make law school exciting and inspiring. One way for traditional lecture-seekers to cope with this kind of professor is to seek them out privately, where they will be less animated and will likely be willing to deal with specific issues in a more focused and straightforward way.

- *The arrogant, student-loathing professor.* If you are lucky, you will be spared the dubious experience of a class with this type of professor. They still exist, however, and you should be aware that you may run into one. Usually male, they think that, if only the students would go away, they would be able to get on with their important work. These professors can delight in embarrassing, humiliating, and generally showing up students who get in their way. These are the same professors who often use the "Socratic" method of classroom teaching. If you are caught in class unprepared, take the Disraeli line — "Never Apologize; Never Explain." The professor may persist in going after a student who admits to being unprepared, but in most cases will back off. Of course, the best defence for these types is to be well prepared, but no one can be on top of the game every day. Remember that no matter what happens, everyone else in the class will be so grateful they were not chosen that they will feel at least some sympathy for your position. Nevertheless, there are the perverse few students who will thrive on this combative experience of classroom-as-battlefield; they will view this experience as a much-needed rigour that is missing in the boredom of the note-dependent lecturer and the entertainment of the free-wheeling performer.

Of course, it is much too simple (and too negative) to put all professors in these three categories. Many professors will be a combination of these styles. In first year, you will have little choice in your professor, but you will gain knowledge about the styles and individuals you like or those you want to avoid. You can use this information in your upper years. In addition, you should gather more information from other students about the professors they have had. In many law schools, student evaluations of professors are compiled and distributed to the student body. An important caveat about these student evaluations is that often it is the most disgruntled students who delight in filling them out, while those students who are pleased do not bother. Canvassing friends or acquaintances who have had classes with certain professors may be more useful. However, make sure you find out how the student did in that professor's class. Often, students' opinions of the professor have a habit of going up and down with the grade they received.

It should be stressed that students ought not to feel that they are at the mercy of professors who act in a totally unprofessional or unacceptable way. This behaviour can involve a whole range of conduct, from bullying, through making sexist, racist, homophobic, or other offensive remarks, to outright harassment. Such conduct should not and need not be tolerated. In recent years, law schools, and the university at large, have become much more serious about discouraging and disciplining such behaviour; there are procedures and processes in place that allow students to make complaints, without retaliation. If possible, it is best when a few people who experienced the situation get together and speak to the professor directly or, where this is not viable, report the professor and the specifics of the situation to the appropriate person (often an associate or assistant dean) in the law school. This is not an easy thing to do, but unacceptable behaviour should not be allowed to continue. As a group, students have more power than they think and, even individually, they can effect a considerable change in faculty-student dynamics.

BEING A CLASS ACT

Attend all your classes. Many of us learn more from vocal instruction. Class participation, whether in the form of passive listening or asking questions, often clarifies issues that have not been clear in the readings.

Go to class even if you do not get all of the readings done beforehand.

The most important and most ignored advice that you will get about classes is — GO. An hour of class can be worth a day of reading.

Of course, it would be unrealistic to imagine that every student will attend every class and read every part of the assigned materials before the class. However, whatever your strategy in undergraduate courses, you run a considerable risk if you do not attend the majority of law classes. The style and approach to classes by professors is usually very different; readings are assigned before class, professors do not tend to read out notes, and students are expected to contribute to class discussion. At the beginning of law school, many students leave class full of ideas and arguments, but with very little in the way of notes — a cause of certain anxiety. Few students attempt to write down everything a professor says and can later be faced with sheets of rambling observations and questions. What you must do is develop an integrated way of preparing for class, engaging in class discussion, taking notes, and following through after class. This process may sound an onerous undertaking, but, once you get into the swing of things, you will use your time much more efficiently and effectively.

In most classes, the professor will provide you with an outline of the material to be covered and a schedule of readings that are expected to be done before class. Most professors assume that you will have read the material, but not that you have necessarily understood it: the purpose of the class is not to read the material for you, but to help you understand it and to put it in a larger context of questions and concerns. You are expected to be a joint participant in the learning experience; the onus is on you to ensure that you have grasped the main points and arguments. Do not be afraid to ask questions. While it is better to query during the class, most professors are available immediately after class to answer questions. Also, the law school usually requires that faculty make themselves available to students at set times or office hours throughout the term.

Preparing for class and attending class will take up much of your time at law school, and it is important that you maximize the opportunities to turn those obligations into a thorough and focused mode of studying. As regards reading before class, you should keep a few suggestions in mind:

- *Try to read the assigned materials as often as possible.* Reading before class makes class time more useful in that you will spend less time figuring out what the cases are about and more learning why certain cases are important. Pre-class reading should be more than skimming, but less than exhaustive (and exhausting).

- *Make notes before class.* You will find that you cannot possibly take part in class and write down everything the professor says. Therefore, if you have a basic set of notes beforehand, you will be able to concentrate on taking more specific and sophisticated notes rather than scrambling to stay with the class. Some students brief cases before class, but this is not always a good idea — you are briefing the case before you know whether you really understand it and you may find when you get to class that the professor thinks the case is useless, or that it is about something entirely different from what you thought. Therefore, if you are going to brief cases as a way to learn, do so after class when you have the benefit of the professor's input (see chapter 6).

- *Identify problems and formulate questions.* Reading before class lets you identify conflicts in the cases that you will want or need explaining in class. It helps you figure out what you do not understand, and alerts you to the kind of question you might want to ask or the answers that you might want to hear in class.

Having prepared for class, you will now be ready to get the most out of the class itself. While you will probably be able to think of many better or more enjoyable things that you could be doing, you should bear in mind the following reasons why you should go to class:

- Learning with and from others is easier and more enjoyable than doing so in a vacuum.

- You will likely get something from each class; even the most boring professors can say something useful, or someone will ask a question or raise an issue that you had not thought of.

- Professors will mention aspects of the case that they think are important and that you may have overlooked or not placed much importance on. Remember that, for the purpose of the evaluation, what the professor thinks important is important. However, many professors do have open minds and are interested in fresh ideas.

- Attending class will force you to keep up with the reading. Even if you do not get time to read everything, go to class anyway. Staying on top of the work is essential. Do not fool yourself into thinking that you can catch up later; you most likely will not. Understanding a term's worth of work will take a term — there are no easy As.

- Classes will give you insight into the examinations. In class, professors will cover the areas, principles, and ideas that they think are important or interesting. Make special note of what is stressed in class, and study those areas more completely. What the professors say at the beginning and the end of class is often what they think is most important, and therefore most likely to be on the exam.

- Questions and hypothetical cases in class often serve as the basis for exam questions. Make note of these items during class and use them in preparing for exams.

- If you do miss a class, you will have to rely on the notes from another student. It is, of course, important to ask someone in whom you have confidence, preferably a member of your study group. Do not make the mistake of merely photocopying the notes, but read them and use them to make your own notes. It may be worthwhile to get more than one person's notes to compare what was said.

- Reviewing another student's notes is better than going to see the professor. If you have missed the class for a good reason (illness, or family emergency), the professor will most likely be willing to go over the material you missed. If you go to the professor for help, make sure you have read the material so that you can ask reasonably intelligent questions. However, most professors will be unreceptive to the student who has no genuine excuse, and will not be amused if you expect them to cover what you have been too lazy to read.

- You can ask questions. Do not be afraid of looking stupid. If you have done the reading, tried to understand it, listened in class, and still do not get it, the likelihood is that others are confused as well and that they will be glad you asked for clarification. However, every class has one or two arrogant show-offs who use questions to demonstrate to everyone else how smart they think they are. If you do take this route, expect your classmates to be thoroughly alienated, and the professor to put you in your place.

- You can ask relevant and pithy questions. Do not ask questions about material from a different class and do not apologize for asking the question. At the polar extreme from the show-offs are the hesitant or self-effacing students; they start off their question with "I'm sorry, I know this is not a good question, but ..." or "I'm probably wrong, but ..." Better to avoid this apologetic or self-diminishing preamble and get to the point — objectionable professors will only use this cue to their advantage and your disadvantage.

- Be prepared for the professor to turn your question back on you. Attempt the answer, again without apologizing. If you have read the material, you will likely know more than you think you do. Do not be afraid of making a fool of yourself — often there is no right answer, and that may be exactly why you are confused.

- Do not skip classes that are given by guest lecturers. The professor will not take kindly to a half-empty class. Some students make the mistake of thinking that these classes are not part of the real class work. Professors will often put questions on their exam that relate to what the guest talked about.

MAKING SUMMARIES

Forget last-minute cram studying. This practice has the usefulness of condoms in the Vatican.

Do a nightly review of your class notes. Your ability to recall lectures during the exam period will be greatly improved if you have set time aside during the term for review. Some do it nightly; others weekly. Some students do half-term review during which they summarize their notes for the first half of the term, review them, and then confront the professor with any loose ends. This allows them to progress to the second half of the term satisfied that they have a head start on exam preparation.

Ask your professor for an example of an A-grade exam answer or a grading sheet. Some professors may say that to do so is impractical, but many professors are willing to oblige. The advantage to looking over such an answer is that you can get a feel for what the professor values in an answer. Some professors insist that students cite the jurisdiction and weight of certain judgments. Other professors are concerned not so much with the relevant cases as with the relevant legal tests and language. Still others stress using very simple, concise arguments that are not burdened with legalese. Professors can be very particular. Learn to cater to certain teaching techniques. A teacher who spoon-feeds the readings in class will often expect much more on an examination than one who lectures on the premise that the students have read the course material.

Don't just get summaries from others; know how to make them so they are effective for you when it comes time to write exams. Find out how upper-year students have gone about constructing summaries. Utilize the techniques taught for writing research memos in building a summary. Use other people's summaries wisely, but not as a substitute for preparing your own. The best summary in the world is not as helpful as going over the material yourself. Work with a course summary when preparing for exams. Getting ones from previous years is valuable, but the preparation of your own is an invaluable studying experience.

After you have done the reading and gone to class, what do you do with all this information? You need to synthesize it, organize it, and compile it into a usable form that can be taken into an open-book exam. In short, you need to make a summary. Soon after you enter first year, you will begin to hear about summaries. Classmates will tell you they have scored an A summary — a sure winner. All you need do, they say, is copy the summary and you, too, can succeed at exams without going to class, without doing the reading, and without much studying. It all sounds too good to be true. And, of course, it is.

The purpose of summaries is obvious by their name — to summarize the course content. However, it cannot be stressed enough that the benefit of a summary is not in holding it or owning it, but in actually making it. Recent summaries made by former students in your professor's classes can be useful when you are putting together your summary. But they should not be used as an excuse for not making your own summary. They can be a helpful resource in that they allow you to check on your own note-taking. As you compile your summary, compare your notes on specific issues with those in other summaries. If they conflict, reread the legal materials on point, check your textbook, and get clarification from others in the class. If you are still unsure, you should ask the professor to go over the point with you.

In a perfect world, law students would review their daily class notes and make daily summaries. Then, every week, these daily summaries would be put together into weekly review notes. If this was done each day, each week, and each month, when exam studying time arrives, you would be fully prepared; your summary would already be done and you would need only review it. However, most law students do not live in this perfect world; like most people, they inhabit the less-than-perfect world of too-little-time-to-do-too-many-things. However, most students will do most of the reading, go to most of their classes, and, in the two or three weeks leading up to exams, stress out because they are attempting to prepare decent summaries in too little time.

Despair not — realistic planning and organization is the key to success in summary-making and exam-taking. As long as you give yourself sufficient time to go over all your notes, categorize them into subject areas, review the cases, and refer to any other summaries you have obtained, you will be fine. If you have four exams to write, you should allow at least one week per course. You should start your summaries at least four weeks before your first exam, but start earlier if you have not kept up with the reading and have a lot of catching up to do. No one can tell you how long your summary should be; only you can decide that. It should be long enough to cover in a concise but useful way the contents of the course, but it should not be so long and unwieldy that you cannot find what you need in the exam. In putting together your summary:

- Remember that you will not have time during the exam to read your summary.
- Do not include extensive case briefs in your summary.
- Include one or two word-triggers that will remind you what the case stands for.
- Remember that the most important part of your summary is a usable index.
- Use coloured tab-dividers to separate subject areas.
- Do not merely copy your class notes.
- Look at how other people have put together their summaries.
- Use ideas that work for you.
- Anticipate essay questions and include sample outlines of answers.

You should start your summary by identifying the main issues of the course. Often the syllabus of the course will provide a starting point for highlighting the issues. After you have a list of the issues, outline the rules/principles of law that go with those issues; cite the most relevant and leading cases; and finally include any comments on point made by your professor. Do not forget to include opposite points of view and any exceptions to specific legal principles. The index should give you a number of ways to access the information contained in your summary — by cases, by issues, or by keywords. As you read an exam question, you might recognize a familiar fact pattern that reminds you of a case that was covered in class, but you cannot identify the issue. With a well-indexed summary, you can scan your case list and, once identified, you will have a cross-reference to the section in your summary that deals with that issue. It is trite but nonetheless true that you will get out of your summary only what you take the time and effort to put in.

As regards using the summary in an exam (see chapter 9), the important thing to remember is that your summary is a tool. It will work for you only if you know your way around it and have compiled it in an organized manner: going into an exam with someone else's summary that you have barely glanced at is a sure recipe for disaster. After deciding which questions you will answer, go to your summary and remind yourself of the important principles and rules that apply to your problem. If you have prepared your summary properly, it will cross-reference to case law and other sub-issues that apply. If you have really done your work, you will have outlined an answer that fits the specific type of problem asked.

CONCLUSION

As a great jurist might have said, "The life of the law student is not logical, but it is an experience." Few people look back on law school as not being memorable; they might not have loved it or even liked it, but it will have left its memories and marks. Try not to be the victim of your own choices and instead become their beneficiary. You make your present into a better past for the future if you at least give law school a fair crack. All the usual rules about life apply doubly for law school — work hard, play hard, and take what comes. Although not always entirely true, law school is as good or as bad as you make it. Enter with reasonable expectations, throw yourself into it with enthusiasm, and you have a good chance of leaving it with satisfaction. Law school ought to be something to be enjoyed, not endured, and something to be remembered, not forgotten.

CHAPTER 5
Making Moves:
Legal Reasoning

It seems that whole libraries, or at least large tracts of them, have been written about the mysterious concept and practice of legal reasoning. Although there has been much toing-and-froing around the matter, the common wisdom still prevails that, as Chief Justice Coke (said "Cook") put it in the seventeenth century, there is an "artificial Reason and Judgment of Law which requires long Study and Experience before a Man can attain to the Cognizance of it." Law has its own special form of reasoning that distinguishes it in some important way from other disciplines and from other forms of reasoning (economic, scientific, logical, political, or sociological). However, like all reasoning, legal reasoning is a process of argumentation by which it is possible to infer or move from one already accepted proposition to another that has yet to be accepted. As a normative exercise, it is not an empirical matter of truth or falsity: it is about persuasion and being convinced about the validity of any such reasoning manoeuvre. Accordingly, reasoning is less a demonstration of logical necessity and more a practice of human justification.

As central as it is to the whole legal enterprise, the precise identity or nature of legal reasoning still remains elusive; it defies simple classification or easy analysis. As with much else in law, there is a fiery debate over how special or different law's reasoning is. As I tried to explain in chapter 2, some authorities contend that there is a meaningful and distinct identity to law's mode and deployment of reasoning, while others argue that, shorn of its legal nomenclature and dressing, it is simply a general and non-specific style of reasoning that lawyers and courts have colonized and become particularly adept at. Of course, legal reasoning is distinctive to the extent that it works on a particular set of materials (e.g., cases and statutes), is framed in a professional jargon (e.g., *stare decisis* and *obiter dicta*), and is engaged in by a restricted community of professionals (e.g., lawyers and judges). Nevertheless, the claim often made is that legal reasoning not only is special in its formal attributes but also is capable of providing "one right answer." The competing viewpoints are captured by the traditional Edward Levy and the critical Duncan Kennedy:

> The contrast between logic and the actual legal method is a disservice to both. Legal reasoning has a logic of its own. Its structure fits it to give meaning to ambiguity and to test constantly whether the society has come to see new differences or similarities.

Social theories and other changes in society will be relevant when the ambiguity has to be resolved for a particular case. Nor can it be said that the result of such a method is too uncertain to compel. The compulsion of the law is clear; the explanation is that the area of doubt is constantly set forth. The probable area of expansion or contraction is foreshadowed as the system works. This is the only kind of system which will work when people do not agree completely.

Teachers teach nonsense when they persuade students that legal reasoning is distinct, as a *method of reaching correct results*, from ethical and political discourse in general (i.e., from policy analysis). It is true that there is a distinctive lawyers' body of knowledge of the rules in force. It is true that there are distinctive lawyers' argumentative techniques for spotting gaps, conflicts, and ambiguities in the rules, for arguing broad and narrow holdings of cases, and for generating pro and con policy arguments. But these are only argumentative techniques. There is never a correct legal solution that is other than the correct ethical and political solution to that legal problem. Put another way, everything taught, except the formal rules themselves and the argumentative techniques for manipulating them, is policy and nothing more.

In putting together this chapter, I will try to remain largely agnostic. I take the line that, if law does have its own special form of reasoning, it is to be found in its peculiar blending and borrowing of other more stereotypical modes of reasoning (e.g., inductive, deductive, analogical, and syllogistic); it is not in the creation of any unique or unusual style of reasoning. Consequently, the aim of this chapter is to give you an account of legal reasoning as a practical skill that involves a limited repertoire of argumentative manoeuvres. I intend to scotch the common conceit of law professors that legal reasoning can only be learned by immersion and by trial and error — a hazing rite of passage into the professional world of law. After introducing the craft-like nature of legal reasoning, I will reduce these operative techniques to a generalized typology of customary legal arguments and reasoning formats. Whether this process adds up to a special or distinct "legal" way of reasoning about or around problems that gives rise to "one right answer" is for you to decide. Legal reasoning may have a limited number of moves, but the main question is whether these moves are limiting in the sense of placing limits on what can be done with them.

A CRAFTY APPROACH

You would do well to remember that legal reasoning is primarily a practical activity. Contrary to much of the hype, it is not some abstract and arcane meditation on legal intelligence: it bears more resemblance to architecture than it does to mathematics. Like most practical skills, it is acquired by the experience of doing it and is handed down from practitioner to practitioner: it is about "knowing the ropes." Legal reasoning is not a formulaic application but a functional engagement; it is not a philosophical reflection but a practical activity; it is not a logical operation but an exercise in operational logic. However, although it is primarily an activity, it does not mean that it does not have a basic structure, nor that there are no basic guidelines to follow. Although he is talking about Canadian constitutional cases, Brian Slattery's comments are equally applicable to legal reasoning generally:

Deciding constitutional cases is a practical art, just like playing baseball, raising children, writing short stories, cooking a good meal, diagnosing an illness or governing your country. Good constitutional decisions are made, not by logical deductions from explicit constitutional standards, but by tapping one's tacit knowledge of the practical workings of the constitutional system and its implicit values and principles, which the explicit standards only partially and palely reflect. To attempt to use these standards as the sole basis of decision will be like trying to learn driving from the provisions of the Highway Traffic Act. … The indeterminacy of general constitutional standards is a reflection of the fact constitutional decision-making is a highly concrete and contextual art that requires experience and skill and more than a little wisdom.

Legal reasoning comprises a repertoire of arguments that combine to sustain a culture of legal reasoning. Too often, law students are led to believe that law is an interlocking body of rules, principles, policies, and standards and that their primary task is to commit them to memory. But this idea is mistaken. It is far too static an understanding of law and the students' challenge: it fails to capture the dynamic quality and experience of the law and its practical development. Being a good law student and a good lawyer is not so much about knowing the rules as it is about using those rules effectively. And this is where legal reasoning becomes so important. The key is to remember that what you are really learning is not so much the content matter of particular subject areas or courses (although that is not unimportant), but the technical form and method of argument they exhibit; legal doctrine is the residual product of the argumentative process. However, again, the learning of these reasoning devices is not an end itself, but merely a prelude to nurturing the practical skill to use them effectively and routinely in legal argument.

Viewed in this way, law and legal reasoning is a practice of rhetoric — the ability to deploy these argumentative resources in an effort to persuade. The different techniques of legal reasoning are to be treated not so much as rules, but as moves in a game. Indeed, it can be useful to think of the legal craft as an experimental game in which its defining rules are always in play. In this vibrant and ever-changing game, there are a limited number of moves to be made, but they can be made in a bewildering combination and to unexpected effect. For every argument, there is a counterargument: they are not so much solutions to problems as probes into finding a solution. Legal reasoning is about justification, not demonstration — a winning argument is one where the cumulative effect of several different and often inconclusive propositions is enough, relative to a particular context and any other arguments made, to convince someone to pursue one course of action over another. In this way, law and legal reasoning are not usually treated as tools or databanks, but comprise performative activities that are marked more by their style than their substance.

Legal reasoning, therefore, refers as much to an attitude or style of argument as to the techniques of argument themselves. As a particular form of rhetoric, legal reasoning is not about proof but about persuasion. As such, it ought not to be thought of, like links in a chain or chapters in a novel, as part of a linear, one-dimensional process that proceeds from argument to decision. Instead, as the philosopher John Wisdom observes, reasoning more resembles the legs of a chair, where reasoning is related to the ultimate decision as a pragmatic support rather than as a causal *sine qua non.* This quality means that the "soundness" of any particular episode of legal reasoning is to be judged in terms of its capacity to persuade other lawyers (and, in your case, law professors) rather than its analytical approximation to some logical ideal. As in architecture, so in law — form follows function: the formal validity of the argument does not guarantee the substantive correctness of the decision.

"Thinking like a lawyer" or, at least, reasoning like one (and they amount to much the same thing) is not as mystical as law school and some professors seek to make it. It involves learning to become operationally functional in a finite set of argumentative techniques. Whereas their identity is usually left for students to fathom and absorb in the trial and error of the classroom experience, they can easily be listed and mastered. Once you know them and have learned to use them in a whole range of situations, the classroom experience and the exams will be less mysterious. You will have taken a massive step in your efforts to think like a lawyer. Moreover, these argumentative moves will serve you well in a host of non-law circumstances; the ability to argue rigorously and systematically is a skill that cannot be undervalued — although it can get you in a lot of trouble in domestic arguments!

While there is an implicit consensus about the relevance and prevalence of these argumentative moves, there is little agreement about the weight to be attached to any particular manoeuvre. Some of these arguments will not be relevant or usable in every situation. What works will depend on your sense of context, audience, stakes, and so on. At law school, how you deploy these arguments or reasons (in the sense of the weight you give to one or another) will be dictated by the leanings and preferences of professors: they will usually have a preference for some kinds or styles of argument that will ring a sweeter chord on their intellectual register. Like comparing apples and oranges, the choice between the various strategies can be experienced as not internal to law's paraphernalia, but external to it.

A final note is warranted before introducing the basic typology. In many traditional accounts of legal reasoning, much is made of the distinction between reasoning in cases that involve legislation and those that do not. Although there are some important differences (see chapter 3), by and large the differences are not as frequent or as significant as is often claimed. Once it is conceded that statutory interpretation is not an exercise in semantic parsing, the rendering of any rule or principle to be derived from the legislation becomes problematic. This is particularly so where the statute has existed for a considerable length of time and a body of case law has developed around its interpretation. Consequently, not only is formulating a rule rarely straightforward in legislation as well as in common law, but isolating the purpose of a statutory rule is no less difficult and no more obvious than trying to extract a rule from a case or series of cases. In short, there are more similarities in reasoning about legislative rules and common law rules than there are dissimilarities. After all, as I have been at pains to emphasize, the substantive rules are resources to be manipulated within the practical activity of legal reasoning.

A TYPOLOGY OF LEGAL ARGUMENTS

There are a group of argumentative manoeuvres that constantly repeat themselves in legal debate and that can be used to support or undermine one another; they draw heavily on the ideas and inspiration of Duncan Kennedy of Harvard Law School who maintains that "there are no killer arguments outside of a particular context." This typology is obviously stylized and static. In practice, the better exponents of legal reasoning should be able to weave these different argumentative strategies in an organic and elegant web of persuasive advocacy. We have tried to illustrate their operation by reference to actual cases. In order to appreciate fully the play of these argumentative moves, you should read the cases that are referenced. While each pair of arguments might not apply with equal weight and facility to every dispute, almost any legal issue can be worked through using some blend of these techniques. They can be divided into two broad groupings: precedent and policy.

PRECEDENT

The following paired strategies enable you to argue about and reason with statutory rules or past decisions. Contrary to received wisdom, the more expansive or flexible interpretation does not necessarily correlate with the more liberal or progressive outcome, and the more limited or rigid interpretation does not necessarily correlate with the most conservative or reactionary outcome: their effect will depend on the context in which they are used, the particular twist they are given, and the background of entitlements against which they function.

(1) Literal and Purposive Interpretations

- *Literal:* Interpret the meaning of any particular word or phrase by reference to its abstract and general "dictionary" meaning and apply it to the facts of the case without reference to the context in which the rule or the facts arise.
- *Purposive:* Posit the purpose or purposes (for there are likely to be multiple and/or conflicting purposes) that the rule arises from or is intended to achieve and elaborate the meaning of the particular word or phrase in light of that purpose and the factual context.

Either of these interpretations is a simple manoeuvre and is commonly used to great effect. Particularly pertinent to statutory analysis, they can function to warrant entirely contradictory outcomes. For example, the meaning of "to use a weapon" under section 267(1) (a) of the *Criminal Code* can be restricted to the "wielding" and "thrusting" of traditional instruments such as guns, knives, or even hammers, or, by focusing on the purpose of the object rather than its character, can be interpreted to encompass the unleashing of a dog or any other animate entity (see *R. v. McLeod* (1993), 84 C.C.C.(3d) 336 (Y.C.A.)).

(2) Narrow and Broad Interpretations

- *Narrow:* Elaborate the rule or principle in such limited terms that its extension by analogy to any other fact situation will be extremely difficult to pull off and the earlier precedent will have to be distinguished.
- *Broad:* Formulate the rule or principle in such wide terms that its extension by analogy to any other fact situation will be much easier to sustain and the earlier precedent will have to be followed.

Either of these interpretations is a run-of-the-mill move that is explicitly relied upon by judges. For example, the famous "neighbour principle" of Lord Atkin can be pitched at many different levels of generality: it can be (and has been) restated in such a way as to support a range of formulations that run from "(a) Scottish manufacturers in the late 1920s of opaque bottles of ginger beer are expected to check that dead snails are not left in them" through "(m) all persons who make goods or offer services to the public must ensure that they are fit for their intended purpose" to "(z) everyone should act with due care in their interactions with others" (see *Donoghue* v. *Stevenson*, [1932] A.C. 562).

(3) General and Detailed Statement of Facts

- *General:* Describe the facts of the case at such a high level of generality and vagueness that they can be made compatible with a variety of different rule formulations.
- *Specific:* Offer an account of the facts of the case at such a high level of detail and specificity that it is very difficult to make them fit almost any rule formulation.

The idea here is to emphasize the way in which the categorization of the facts and the law are manipulated to create better or worse fits between the two, in conjunction with (1) and (2). Facts and law interrelate; they each determine and refine the other as they are determined and refined by them. Questions of fact are by no means as straightforward or given as they appear in appellate judgments. What is material or relevant will be determined by the law; it is a dialectical relation. For example, in determining issues of foreseeability, it is much easier to support a positive finding when the facts are stated generally (fireworks and negligent employees) than when they are related in fine detail (carrying fireworks, missing train, helping hand, falling passenger, explosion, and unsteady scales; see *Palsgraf*, 162 N.E. 99 (1928)).

(4) Old and Modern Authorities

- *Old:* The rule or principle is so old that it has become a basic axiom of the entire common law and must be followed, or it is so old that it has lost contact entirely with the realities of modern society and must be disregarded.
- *Modern:* The rule or principle is so recent that its worth to the law has not been established and it cannot yet be considered to be a stable feature of the common law, or the rule or principle is so recent that it responds directly to the conditions of modern society and deserves to be taken most seriously on that account.

Either of these manoeuvres is obvious. There are a host of judicial pronouncements by the same judges that pick and choose among these strategies as it suits them. They are popular arguments in property and constitutional law cases.

POLICY

Although public strategies are more openly "political" in nature and sweep than precedential arguments, they are not necessarily more political; they are simply more subtly so. Not only is the choice between the competing pairs of policy arguments not determined by the arguments themselves, but the mounting of each argument involves some preference for one value over another (e.g., positing of a purpose). Also, it is a mistake to assume that one side of each pair will always connect with the same larger political orientation. Apart from the fact that it is not always obvious what is the "left" or "right" thing to do in a particular situation, the shifting details of the context will ensure that different arguments have different political spins and implications at different times. At best, each side of a competing pair tends to tilt generally in one political direction or the other.

(1) Judicial Administration

- *Strict:* A firm or fixed rule is required because it will be easier to administer and enforce; it will enable people to order their affairs with a higher degree of certainty and predictability; and a less firm or fixed rule will lead to outcomes that are inconsistent, confused, or arbitrary.
- *Flexible:* A flexible or variable standard is required because it will be easier to tailor it to an individualized fact situation; it will maintain confidence in the law's status as an institution committed to justice; and a less flexible or variable standard will oblige the courts to reach particular decisions that are mechanical, unfair, or unjust.

This pair of arguments is often used in contract cases. For example, in dealing with the contractual doctrine of "fundamental breach," the courts have swung back and forth between strict rules and broad standards as the most appropriate device to define and monitor the enforcement of unfair agreements. Is it better to employ a mechanical and formal rule to establish if the breach has brought the contract to an end, or to examine the substantive circumstances in which the contract was made? (see *Beaufort Realties*, [1980] 2 S.C.R. 718).

(2) Institutional Competence

- *Competence:* The courts are especially suited and able to deal exclusively with this kind of issue because it involves complicated factual matters that require case-by-case resolution; it invites an impartial and experienced act of judgment; and it demands a capacity to respond effectively to rapidly changing social conditions.
- *Incompetence:* The courts, as opposed to the legislature or an administrative agency, are not well situated to deal with this kind of issue because it involves matters of social justice that need to be settled by an institution with a broader democratic mandate; it demands resort to specialized knowledge about particular social practices and customs; and it implicates matters that have long-term, structural implications for social ordering.

Although the courts usually proceed without any doubts about their legitimate entitlement to develop or to change the law (i.e., the whole of tort law), they occasionally hesitate in certain situations to question whether they should be effecting significant change. For example, the Supreme Court confidently proceeded to rework most of the rules for the assessment of damages in personal injury litigation, but became coy about whether it could move from a once-and-for-all lump-sum payment to a scheme of periodic payments (see *Andrews*, [1978] 2 S.C.R. 229).

(3) Equality

- *Formal:* A rule or principle should be formulated and applied in such a way that it respects the demands of equality by treating everyone the same without fear or favour; to do otherwise would·be to work an injustice on certain groups or individuals.

- *Substantive:* A rule or principle should be formulated and applied in such a way that it respects the demands of equality by treating differently situated groups or individuals differently; to do otherwise would be to compound the inequalities that already exist.

This choice arises throughout the common law, whether it is dealing with the relative capacities of contracting parties (e.g., large bank and poor individual) or the capabilities of differently abled tortfeasors (e.g., young, old, blind, and so on). However, it is most squarely faced in constitutional cases, where courts have to determine what are the categories and conditions of discrimination (see *Bliss*, [1979] 1 S.C.R. 183).

(4) Morality

Arguments about morality are, of course, manifold. All that one can do is to offer some examples of the general kind of twinned arguments that it is possible to make; much will depend on the particular substantive matter (e.g., contract, tort, criminal, and so on) that is being considered. Some typical and common examples of such dichotomous pairings include form and substance, individual and community, single instance and multiple series, individualist and altruist, and content and process. A familiar set of arguments are those based around freedom and security.

- *Freedom:* Persons should only be held responsible for those acts that they have chosen to perform, that are blameworthy, that cause foreseeable and intended harm, and that could not have been avoided by others, or persons should be entitled to engage in activity that does not cause harm to others with a minimum of government interference or regulation.
- *Security:* Persons who are injured or interfered with through no fault of their own are entitled to protection, help,·or compensation from other persons or society at large, or the government has a responsibility to monitor and regulate people's activities in order to preserve the freedom of others.

These argumentative possibilities arise in most cases; property and criminal law are fertile sources. But a particularly stark example of where they come into play is over whether there is a "duty to rescue." Although the courts work from the general proposition that there is no general obligation to come to the rescue of someone else, they have fashioned an expanded set of exceptions that assumes a pre-existing relation between parties that warrants the imposition of such a responsibility (see *Horsley* v. *MacLaren*, [1972] S.C.R. 441).

(5) Deterrence

- *Flexible:* A particular standard or rule will encourage good conduct and deter bad conduct because it will allow persons and corporations to respond better to changing social and market conditions; it will facilitate greater interaction and freer competition among persons and corporations; and, as opposed to a less broad and more strict standard, it will not inhibit persons or corporations from creative or innovative behaviour.
- *Stable:* A particular standard or rule will deter good conduct and encourage bad conduct because it will leave persons and corporations confused as to the limits

placed on their behaviour; it will stymie open interaction and healthy competition among persons and corporations; and, as opposed to a less broad and more strict standard, it will inhibit persons or corporations from taking chances.

This set of arguments is common in contract and criminal law cases. For example, a continuing challenge that the courts face in contracts cases is determining in what circumstances a party is invariably bound to perform certain terms of the contract (see *Hong Kong Fir*, [1962] 2 Q.B. 26 (C.A.)). Another approach to take here is to point up the different capacities of different persons and corporations to know the relevant standards and to adjust their conduct accordingly (see *Lloyds Bank* v. *Bundy*, [1975] Q.B. 326 (C.A.)). This approach involves a shift between formal assumptions and substantive realities.

(6) Cost-Benefit Analysis

- *Incentives:* A rule or principle will increase or decrease the responsibility on certain persons or corporations to incur certain costs, but these individual expenditures or savings are outweighed by the overall benefits to others, and will enhance social utility by encouraging a socially desirable level of activity.
- *Disincentives:* A rule or principle will decrease or increase the responsibility on certain persons or corporations to incur certain costs, but these individual savings or expenditures are not outweighed by the overall benefits to others and will not enhance social utility, because they do not encourage a socially desirable level of activity.

Obvious examples of this form of argumentation occur in tort law. For example, in determining the level of resources that must be invested in safety measures, the court must ensure that potential tortfeasors are encouraged to take appropriate steps to safeguard others, but not so that the cost of those steps or the resulting penalties oblige them to withdraw from a useful endeavour (see *Hedley Byrne*, [1964] A.C. 465). Again, it is possible here to move from an abstract analysis to a more concrete discussion by contrasting the formal assumptions of economic theorizing (e.g., perfect information, or rational actors) with the substantive circumstances of real-world economic activity (e.g., imperfect information or irrational actors). Also, if you juggle the figures sufficiently, the whole equation of costs and benefits can be stood on its head (see chapter 2).

(7) Distributive Considerations

- *Redistribution:* A particular rule or principle that places additional burdens on one group of persons rather than another is justified because that group is better able to afford the costs of that added responsibility, or because greater opportunities or entitlements will redound to the advantage of a less advantaged group.
- *No distribution:* A particular rule or principle that places additional burdens on one group of persons rather than another is not justified because that group will usually be able to spread or pass on that burden to other persons, including those very groups intended to benefit, or because such goals are better achieved through the tax or welfare system.

This set of arguments has particular salience in property law and applies to the whole area of landlord and tenant, especially the vexed issue of rent control. Also, these arguments have obvious application where the court expects more of one party than another (e.g., unconscionability doctrine in contracts) or places one party under a fiduciary obligation to look after the interests of another party (see *LAC Minerals*, [1989] 2 S.C.R. 574).

(8) Choice

- *Paternalism:* A particular standard that imposes duties or responsibilities on persons is favoured because these duties are in the best interests of those persons whether or not the persons themselves believe them to be in their own best interests, or because certain structural conditions prevent those persons from making informed decisions for themselves.

- *Antipaternalism:* A certain standard that imposes duties or responsibilities on persons is not favoured because no one is ever in a better position than the persons involved to assess those persons' best interests without imposing their own interests, or because interfering in one area or instance will only lead to problems and injustices elsewhere.

These manoeuvres are invoked in large questions about the scope of tort law generally or the extent of limits on freedom of contract. A particular focus for these considerations is the issue of "consent." For example, they have salience in criminal cases in which the courts are required to decide whether a person can inflict actual bodily harm in the course of consensual sexual relations (see *Brown*, [1993] 2 All E.R. 75 (H.L.)).

AN EXTENDED ANALYSIS

Most of these argumentative manoeuvres can be brought into play on most legal occasions. In order to demonstrate their relevance and application, we offer a sustained application to one particular situation. Take the following hypothetical case:

> Marie Beaumont throws a large party at her cottage an hour or so out of town. She owns a chain of wineries and supplies most of the alcoholic refreshment herself. Charlie Paylor, a renowned party animal, was invited and drives there with his friend, Jamie Singh. They both drink a considerable amount and Marie is highly amused at their crazy antics. After midnight, Charlie and Jamie leave. On the way home, they are involved in an accident with Tom in which they are all seriously injured. Is Marie liable in damages to Charlie, Jamie and Tom?

The most significant authority is *Menow* v. *Honsberger and Jordan House*, [1974] S.C.R. 239, in which a hotel was held partly responsible for injuries caused to a drunken patron who was thrown out of the hotel and later run over by a negligent driver on a busy highway near the hotel. Assume for the purposes of this demonstration that it is also the only relevant precedent. While some arguments have more rhetorical bite and cogent force than others, it should be obvious that, with a little imagination and ingenuity, it will be possible to run these permutations in almost every case that comes up in class.

On behalf of Charlie, Jamie and Tom and in favour of liability, it can be argued that:

- Although *Menow* was about a hotel, the meaning and reach of any rule imposing responsibility for the care of others is not restricted to "commercial establishments" because its motivating spirit and purpose extends to include private parties.
- The facts of *Menow* were very similar (i.e., a host permitted a severely drunken man to drive home), and the likelihood of harm great enough to warrant the imposition of liability.
- The decision in *Menow* is fairly recent and, because it represents the prevailing desire to curb drunk driving, ought to be respected by enforcing it vigorously and widely.
- A broad and flexible standard of liability is suitable because it will allow the courts to adapt the imposition of liability to the particular circumstances and, by imposing liability in this case, to ensure that justice is served.
- The courts act entirely within traditional understandings of their institutional competence by developing the law to meet new challenges and to reflect contemporary expectations.
- Everyone who acts irresponsibly by supplying drivers with excessive amounts of alcohol should be treated similarly regardless of whether they are in business or not.
- Homeowners who arrange parties, supply alcoholic refreshment, and invite people with a propensity for drunken revelry should assume responsibility for the safety of such guests.
- A well-formulated rule of responsibility will ensure that antisocial conduct is deterred so that the kind of wild partying that led to the present accident will be discouraged.
- Marie could have avoided this accident at a very small cost by offering Charlie and Jamie a room for the night or, at least, by arranging for a sober driver or a cab to take them home; this cost pales in comparison with the potential costs of permanently damaged lives.
- Any burden of imposing liability can be readily carried by the homeowners, who are in a much better position to avoid it by being more selective in issuing invitations or to spread it through insurance than the random group of drunks and their victims.
- Because Marie invited Charlie and Jamie, at least in part, on the basis of their being renowned party animals, she should have assumed responsibility for their welfare when they got into an incapacitated state.

On behalf of Marie and against the imposition of liability, it can be argued that:
- As *Menow* was about a hotel, the meaning and reach of any rule imposing responsibility for the care of others is restricted to "commercial establishments" and does not extend to private parties.
- The facts of *Menow* were such (i.e., leaving a severely drunken man to walk home in the black of night on a very busy highway with no sidewalk) that the likelihood of harm occurring was much greater than in the present situation, where it was late, the local roads were quiet, and Charlie's car was clearly visible.
- The decision in *Menow* is fairly recent and it would be premature to extend its ambit so quickly without a reasonable chance to evaluate its operation and effect.

- A firm and fixed rule of liability better serves the ends of justice because it allows a general degree of predictability that will more than compensate for the harsh and inconsistent imposition of liability in situations like this one.
- The courts exceed their institutional mandate and infringe the legislature's prerogative when they extend the law to such an extent that it will have massive effects on people's private behaviour.
- Rules of liability should be formulated and applied so that commercial operators are treated differently and held to a higher standard from private party givers.
- Because Marie did not invite them under false pretenses, Charlie and Jamie knew what they were getting themselves into and were fully able to take prior steps to look after themselves.
- A sweeping rule of liability will have effects that are absurdly wide and will deter activity like social gatherings that is for the good of almost everyone in society.
- Charlie and Jamie were in a better or, at least, as good a position as Marie to take earlier and relatively cheap steps to arrange for transport or to stay at a nearby hotel; this approach is much more economical than curbing people's willingness to host parties or risking the possibility of drunken accidents.
- The burden of imposing liability will be substantial for social hosts who, unlike commercial enterprises, will find it difficult to spread potential losses in a relatively cheap way; drivers are much better placed to provide for their own insurance.
- Although Marie's conduct cannot be entirely condoned, it is unreasonable to expect her to take greater responsibility for the safety of other grown-ups like Charlie and Jamie than they did for themselves.

A CAUTIONARY NOTE

This modest notion of legal craft as a combination of intuitive judgment and technical proficiency glosses over the more ambitious claims made for it. The effect, if not the intent, of such a limited depiction of lawyers' special and distinctive expertise is that it too easily functions as a ruse for relieving them of their responsibility to justify their power and authority by recourse to the real-world pressure of getting the job done. The value of such skills in the training of lawyers is undeniable, and the knack of using legal materials with adroitness and dexterity is not to be underrated. However, the best legal craftspeople are not those who simply reproduce mechanically and mindlessly old arguments and trite analogies, but those who can rework legal materials in an imaginative and stylish way. Such legal artistry demands more than technical proficiency. To be worthy of their professional prestige, lawyers and judges must nurture a sense of social justice and a feel for political vision, unless they are to become only hired hands for vested interests. In the pithy words of Karl Llewellyn, "technique without ideals is a menace; ideals without technique are a mess." A bare legal craft can too easily acquire the elite habits of a Masonic order and fail to meet the civic specifications of its social calling: a job well done is not always its own reward.

Lawyering is not carpentry. While it is true that legal tables will wobble and precedential doors will jam without crafted care and attention, there is an important difference between the doors and tables of a torture chamber and of a hospital ward; a hospital bed is not a torture rack, although it can become one. Lawyers and, therefore, law students cannot easily evade taking responsibility for the artifacts and outcomes of their crafted performances by taking refuge in matters of technical consistency and internal coherence. This inward and insular stance unnecessarily cuts off law from its sustaining political context and rich historical resources. Lawyers must be carpenters, but they should also be designers and innovators who place their pragmatic craft in the service of society, particularly its disadvantaged and disenfranchised members.

FURTHER READINGS

Boyle, J. "The Anatomy of a Torts Case" (1985) 34 Am. U. L. Rev. 1003.

Burton, S. *An Introduction to Law and Legal Reasoning.* 2nd ed. Boston: Little, Brown, 1998.

Hutchinson, A. *It's All in the Game: A Non-Foundationalist Account of Law and Adjudication.* Durham, N.C.: Duke University Press, 2000.

Kennedy, D. *A Critique of Adjudication fin de siècle.* Cambridge, Mass.: Harvard University Press, 1997.

Levy, E. *An Introduction to Legal Reasoning.* Chicago: University of Chicago Press, 1949.

Llewellyn, K. *The Common Law Tradition.* Boston: Little, Brown, 1960.

Slattery, B. "Are Constitutional Cases Political?" (1989) 11 Sup. Ct. L. Rev. 507 at 515.

Twining, W. & D. Miers, *How to Do Things with Rules*, 4th ed. London: Weidenfeld and Nicolson, 1999.

CHAPTER 6

The Write Stuff:
Putting on the Style

Legal writing is something that many students are apprehensive about. Looked at from the outside in, it does appear to have a certain character and style that is readily recognizable as different from other forms of writing. However, while legal writing is touted as a special style of expression and communication, its precise specialness eludes most efforts to pin it down or teach it. Apart from a lexicon of new words and a slightly different structure, there is nothing that should frighten the intelligent or conscientious student. Legal writing is a craft and, like any craft, it requires practice. Whether you are learning to ride a bike or play a guitar, it cannot be done by merely thinking about being a good bike rider or guitarist; it requires a commitment to constant practice in order, if not to be perfect, at least to be competent. Like legal reasoning, good legal writing is simply the virtues of good general writing applied to law; there are no secret formulae that are sparingly revealed to students in the privacy of the law school classroom.

Students go through a crisis of confidence when they come to law school. They think that they have never been able to write well or even glimpse what that might be. However, students should remember that they must have acquired some basic writing skills and habits to get as far as they have. The challenge is to identify those skills, recognize weaknesses that need to be improved, and start the task of turning those writing skills to good legal effect. If you can develop the ability to write well, you will have taken a large step in becoming a successful and good lawyer. Indeed, in a recent survey of law firms in the United States, it was discovered that almost all firms placed a greater emphasis on the ability to research thoroughly and communicate effectively than on the acquisition of vast slabs of substantive law. Acquiring the habits of good legal writing is at least as important as learning the latest case on contract or tort. It is not an optional skill that some manage to pick up more easily than others. The determination to be a good legal writer is something that all law students must have or must develop. More than anything else, lawyers are wordsmiths; language is their stock-in-trade. As one commentator graphically put it, "language is the lawyers' scalpel. If they cannot use it skillfully, they are apt to butcher their suffering client's case."

In this chapter, I will try to put you on the right path to the write stuff. After outlining some of the problems with traditional legal writing and the flawed foundations that undermine efforts to teach good legal writing, I introduce the basic tenets of good organization that should underlie legal writing. Using examples of bad and good legal writing, I list the basic pointers to be followed if you are to avoid the pitfalls of bad legal writing and to establish the essentials of good legal writing. Finally, the different exercises of legal writing that you will be asked to undertake are explained and dissected to reveal the best and most successful way to approach them.

THE WRONG STUFF

The observation that someone "writes like a lawyer" is rarely made or taken as a compliment. Very few non-lawyers (or lawyers) hold up legal writing as a model or style to be copied. Too often, legal writing consists of very dense and inaccessible prose, larded with the worst forms of circumlocution, prolixity, and obfuscation. Indeed, legal writing seems to be a paradigm of bad writing; it is full of compound constructions, redundant repetition, dangling modifiers, and multiple negatives. It is almost universally condemned as being an unholy combination of vices — convoluted, tortuous, pompous, and boring. The effect of this reputation is to mystify and alienate the public. Remember that a non-lawyer reading law is like a North American reading about cricket; it is an alien and baffling experience. To repeat what the great American judge and jurist Oliver Wendell Holmes Jr said about it, "lawyers spend a great deal of time shoveling smoke."

Many attribute this low opinion of legal writing to the fact that lawyers have been ill-trained in the niceties of grammatical construction or syntactical style. Yet, at least in the last couple of decades, the teaching of legal writing has been taken seriously by most law schools; the standard first-year curriculum contains a course or program in legal writing. However, some maintain that the dissatisfaction with legal writing is more of a smokescreen than anything else. It is suggested that lawyers write badly out of choice rather than ignorance; it serves their economic interest. On this view, the problem with legal writing has less to do with writing by lawyers than with the lawyers themselves; they develop an opaque and occasionally obtuse style of writing because it pays them to do so. It also means they can fence sit, and lets them be non-committal when they choose. They are not clearly committed to anything. John Stark summarizes this general scepticism:

> Poor writing is as much a consequence of the way lawyers look at the world as is their ability to read a contract and find consideration. Lawyers write poorly not because they know too little, but because they know too much. If lawyers stopped writing like lawyers, they might have trouble charging as much for their work. Every time lawyers confound their clients with a case citation, a "heretofore," or an "in the instant case," they are letting everyone know that they possess something the nonlegal world does not. One need not be a Marxist to understand that jargon helps professions to convince the world of their occupational importance, which leads to payment for services.

There are, of course, some occasions when such dubious qualities might be put to useful effect by a good lawyer; the intentional use of language to create confusion or to facilitate avoidance are the occasional tools of the legal craft. But they are not the daily diet or basic stuff of good legal writing. To be a good legal writer does not mean that one has to sacrifice a clear and accessible writing style. The caricature of legal writing is not what you should be striving to achieve. Law students can and should develop a style of writing they can be proud of both as serious professionals and as serious writers.

GOOD WRITING

At the outset, it is important to emphasize that, contrary to common understandings, the good writer is not necessarily someone who is able to use language as a transparent prism through which the light of law's meaning can shine. While the virtues of clear and simple writing can never be overestimated, George Orwell's popular view that "good prose is like a window pane" is of scant assistance in understanding good writing. It rests on an untutored and simplistic notion of language that sets the apprentice writer off on the wrong foot. In this account, thinking is portrayed as a mental process that goes on inside people's heads, while the function of language is to act as the transparent conduit through which ideas shift from one head to another. Used at its best and most efficient, language allows the meaning of thoughts to speak for themselves; confusion is either the fault of sloppy thinking or poor writing. As one commentator puts it, legal writing "is legal thinking made visible"; thinking about law and writing about law are separate, if complementary, activities that can be understood and studied separately.

Without entering into the esoteric world of linguistics and philosophy, there is now considerable agreement that this Orwellian view of language's role and function is naive and mistaken; it tends to misdirect the efforts of those who are trying to understand what it is to be good writers. Language is more than mere words; it both shapes and is shaped by a way of viewing the world. The world of things and ideas does not stand outside the language used to describe or contain them, but is part and parcel of that world or activity. Language is already implicated in thinking, and not merely ancillary to it; the ideas and the medium through which they are expressed are intimately related. This explanation is doubly important in understanding legal writing. Because law is itself a language, the act of thinking and writing about it are one and the same; the meaning of law does not stand outside the words used to express it. Moreover, as we tried to explain in chapter 2, the law is not a "brooding omnipresence in the sky" waiting to be reduced to a transparent prose such that law's basic clarity can be revealed. The whole process of understanding law and legal writing is fraught with uncertainty and confusion. To put it bluntly, in law, writing is thinking and thinking is writing.

None of this should be taken to imply that legal writing can never be clear or that lawyers have a licence to write in clotted prose. Suffice it to say that law students should not drive themselves to distraction or depression by imagining that their inability to write clearly about law is only about writing. It should never be forgotten that writing style and legal analysis are not mutually exclusive; the sophistication of the one has an impact on the sophistication of the other. In the same way that confused and confusing rules of law make for a difficult writing task, so a good and clear legal writing style can help to clarify the muddiness of recalcitrant areas of legal analysis. There are very few good legal analysts who are not also good legal writers, and there are very few bad legal writers who are good legal analysts.

GRAMMAR

In developing a good writing style, it must be remembered that to talk well is not the same as to write well; each skill relies on different conventions and expectations. So, while the dictaphone or voice recognition devices need not be avoided at all costs, it must be recognized that what is acceptable in speech is not always acceptable or as convincing in writing. Because writing lacks the natural inflection and emphasis that speakers give to their words, the craft of writing has developed its own set of conventions and devices to do much the same thing. However, I will not spend much time telling you to be grammatically correct by admonishing you about split infinitives, dangling participles, or misplaced modifiers. While these traditional principles are not bad sources of direction, they ought not to be treated as inviolable or sacrosanct. Punctuation and grammar are often spoken of as if they were universal truths. In fact, they are customary conventions that tend to vary in their details from one English-speaking country to another. Those conventions used at the end of the seventeenth century seem to have become fixed and converted into a set of rules. Nevertheless, little seems to generate as much heat as disputes over the correct placing of commas or the correct differentiation between colons and semicolons. For instance, in the American case of *Ron Pair Enterprises*, 489 U.S. 235 (1989), the whole litigation centred on the significance of a comma in a bankruptcy statute; the U.S. Supreme Court divided 5–4 on its relevance and effect. As well as reinforcing the importance of legal writing and the need for clarity, this episode demonstrates that there is no form of writing that can withstand the determined efforts of lawyers to turn the meaning of words to their clients' best advantage.

Nevertheless, it is extremely useful to know the basic rules of grammar. You should treat them respectfully but not reverentially: they must earn their keep by virtue of their utility. They are some of the important tools of the trade to be put to service by you, but must not be allowed to become ends in themselves. As two of the leading exponents of good legal writing advise, "a grammatically correct sentence is not necessarily a well-written one." You should never sacrifice function to form. While they are not necessarily at odds and will often complement each other, the measure of a well-written sentence is its persuasive effectiveness, not its syntactic harmony. Most word-processing programs now contain a variety of aids, including Spellcheck and Grammatik. An initial reliance on these programs is a good idea. However, remember they are not designed for specialized professional use and can only be considered a partial replacement for rigorous editing of your own or by someone else.

SEX AND LAW

It is important that you develop a writing style that is non-sexist in its structure, orientation, and detail. Unlike French and German, English is an uninflected language in which words do not have a gender. However, English has traditionally solved this problem by being patriarchal and bestowing "masculine" words with a generalized meaning. Although there is still resistance in some quarters, this practice is now beginning to change; English is becoming a more inclusive and less sexist language. Nevertheless, this transformation is not always easy to achieve, particularly in the use of personal pronouns. While plural forms — they, their, them — are non-specific, the singular forms —- he/she, her/his, him/her — are not. Consequently, it is easy to be sexist in English without really trying.

However, it is no longer acceptable (nor should it be) to defend the use of sex-specific terms by reference to customary grammatical rules or by stipulating that the masculine shall always include the feminine; function and substance must not be allowed to fall victim to form and style. Instead, good legal writing demands that positive efforts be made to ensure that all writing is non-sexist. Most times this situation can be avoided by redrafting phrases in the plural or, occasionally, by using the passive voice. But this is not always possible. For example, it is difficult to complete the phrase "no one can enter the building unless ..." in a non-sexist way; it is not possible to use "they" because a singular pronoun is required, and "she" or "he" is sex-specific. In such cases, it is best to use the unwieldy "she or he" or even "s/he" rather than "she" or "he" only; the preferences of stylistic elegance must give way to the demands of substantive content. While precision is vital in referring to quotations, you should develop a personal style of writing and vocabulary that is scrupulously non-sexist. To achieve a non-sexist writing style, there are only a few basic guidelines that need to be followed:

- *Avoid the generic "he."* While "he or she" will do the job, it is cumbersome and grating. Instead, there are several options.

  (1) Make the sentence plural: you can pluralize most sentences with little difficulty and with some economy. For example, change "The stress on the young lawyer can also take its toll on his clients" to "The stress on young lawyers can also take its toll on their clients."

  (2) Substitute "the" for "his": change "A lawyer must respect his client's wishes" to "A lawyer must respect the client's wishes."

  (3) Alternate between "he" and "she." Although a second-best solution, it is better than "he" or "she" throughout a piece. However, you should be careful to avoid using either of them inappropriately; the secretary is not always "he" and the janitor is not always "she."

  (4) Change "he" to "one." This solution is acceptable in a pinch, but it results in a stilted form of writing in the passive voice.

- *Avoid the use of "man" or any of its derivatives.* There are now so many acceptable synonyms for "man" (e.g., human or humankind) that there is no need to use the term except where it actually refers to a male person. This caution also applies to the verb "man."

- *Avoid typecasting.* It is important that you do not describe or judge people in terms of familiar stereotypes, particularly when describing someone's appearance or personal qualities. For instance, there are far too many "spunky and fresh-faced women" and too few "cute and fragile men." Except in very context-specific circumstances, you should use only those words to describe or judge someone that you would be prepared to use for either gender. If you would not comment on a man's appearance, do not comment on a woman's.

- *Avoid referring to a person's gender unless the context demands it.* Many references to gender serve no useful purpose because they emphasize personal characteristics over skills or qualifications. Again, refer to a person's gender only where you would do so for either a woman or a man. For example, you should avoid writing a "woman lawyer" or a "male nurse" unless there is a very specific reason.
- *Avoid patronizing substitutes for "women" and "men."* If you do refer to a person's gender, it is inappropriate to use such terms as "ladies" and "girls" or "boys" and "gentlemen"; these terms tend to emphasize qualities and characteristics that are sexist in nature.
- *Avoid gender-specific titles or salutations.* In most instances, it is better to use someone's name rather than risk a misplaced title. Where you do not know someone's name, you can use "Dear Madam or Sir." Also, unless the woman has expressed a preference to the contrary, you should use "Ms." instead of "Miss" or "Mrs."
- *Avoid using non-inclusive words.* Although many words originated in a gender-specific form (e.g., chairman and seamstress), there is almost always an acceptable gender-neutral word that can be used (e.g., chair and dressmaker). This restriction is especially applicable when you are using negative expressions (e.g., henpecked or sissy) or common turns of phrase (e.g., not "every man for himself" but "all for themselves"; not "old wives tale" but "superstition" or "popular misconception). However, there is no need to use such tortured expressions as aviatrix or authoress; aviator or author is better.

GETTING IT TOGETHER

Like all good writing, good legal writing is a judicious blend of "unity, sequence and coherence in the right proportions for any given document." It should carry the reader along so that the flow and force of the argument seem natural and inevitable; they will not be helped by a structure that is disjointed and jagged, or by a style that is uneven and rough-edged. Moreover, what is considered to be a good piece of legal writing in one context may be a bad piece of legal writing in another context. Lawyers engage in a variety of forms of writing — pleadings, affidavits, contracts, wills, letters, office memoranda, factums, examinations — and the good legal writer will develop a style that is appropriate to the particular context. As you begin to get an idea of what are considered to be good examples of legal writing (and what fits your own style of writing), you should develop a small collection as a convenient reference pool. Indeed, as an initial exercise, it is useful to find a piece of writing that you like and to analyse why you like it. Also, find a piece of writing that you do not like and analyse why you do not like it. In this way, you will begin to develop a style of legal writing that is both impressive to others and is comfortable for you.

In developing a good legal writing style that will serve as a basic resource in all your work, remember that, while law students are ill advised to use a flippant levity in their writing, there is no need to cultivate a lugubrious solemnity; a style that is balanced but firm, polite but direct, is always a useful asset. Also, the twin evils of unnecessary dogmatism and excessive equivocation should be studiously avoided. Although there are times when an unequivocal statement of the law is required, there are other times when a more cautious and conditional assessment of the law is advisable. The best advice on good legal writing is as trite as it is true: *be brief yet brilliant, clear yet concise, and professional yet persuasive.*

The ability to be a good legal writer is a subspecies of being a good writer. You need a particular skill to write clearly and simply about confusing and complicated matters like law. But the imperative to cultivate a clear and simple writing style does not mean that the writing has to be unsophisticated or inelegant: the lean Ernest Hemingway was no less a literary stylist than the dense Victor Hugo; both succeeded in fashioning very different but exemplary writing styles. However, there should be no doubt that the ability to write well is a basic requisite to being a good legal writer. Without a basic understanding of the essentials of good writing, it will be difficult to become a good legal writer and even a good lawyer. This means that for those who have not yet acquired or honed the dos-and-don'ts of good writing, learning the skills of legal writing will be a considerable challenge. But do not forget — the difficulty is more about writing in general rather than about legal writing in particular. So, while we cannot offer a complete primer on writing, we can do a quick survey of some of the techniques that almost all good writers have or will need to adopt. Again, as with legal reasoning, there is no enduring set of canonical rules to be followed that will guarantee good legal writing; they are more a shifting series of instructive principles that writers should deploy with judgment and insight. They should be treated as baselines from which any deviation must be justified — the more the deviation, the stronger the argument needs to be.

GOOD ORGANIZATION

One of the keys to success in developing a particular craft is to be organized. You should be organized not only within your writing but also in your general approach to writing. Although the best writers leave the reader with the distinct impression that their words fall effortlessly from pen to paper or keyboard to screen, this enviable effect is almost always the end result of an arduous but organized process of writing; Shakespeare may have had the genius of perfect, one-draft writing, but most people have to learn to rely less on creative instinct and more on practised organization. Consequently, as with any good writer, the legal writer would be well advised to follow a three-step procedure that consists of preparation, writing, and editing. Adapted to the particular needs of the individual and the exigencies of the situation, this simple process will provide you with the necessary organization within which to hone the more refined techniques of good legal writing. As you become more confident, you will probably become less structured in your approach and shift between these step as you progress.

PREPARATION

Being sufficiently prepared before beginning to write is an obvious and indispensable first step to good legal writing. Although much of this preparation will consist of legal research (see chapter 7), it is essential that you answer certain important questions before you run off and lose yourself in the library. The first is to ascertain the context of your research and writing: What are the limits placed on your legal writing? Are you to restrict yourself to certain sources? How exhaustive does your research have to be? How much time do you have? An important organizational ability that you must learn as a law student and later as a lawyer is time management: the ability to divide your time between competing demands and to use the available time to optimal effect. There is little to be gained from giving "made-to-measure" treatment to an "off-the-rack" problem, or vice versa. Cut your cloth according to the garment to be tailored.

Second, before beginning your research, you must establish the anticipated audience for your writing: Is there one audience or are there many different ones? What are their knowledge and expectations? What are their objectives? What questions or concerns will they likely have? What level of formality do they expect? These and other questions will need to be answered before you begin to prepare in earnest. Without a sense of the audience to be addressed, you will not be able to pitch your arguments at the level of comprehension and sophistication that will be most effective.

Third, after you have done your research and feel confident that you are on top of the substantive material, it is advisable to sit down before you begin to write and ask: What am I trying to say and achieve in this particular piece of writing? By focusing your attention, you will realize that good preparation includes bringing together not only the material you intend to use but also the order in which you want to present it, the detail you plan to use, and the material you wish to leave out — a "kitchen sink" approach to legal research and writing is not desirable. Finally, before you begin writing, it might be a good idea to write a short outline or even sketch a tree diagram to give you a sense of what you want to achieve. Unlike writing a novel or some other piece of fiction, it is not a good idea to start writing unless you have a pretty good idea where you are going.

WRITING

There is no one good way to write; it will depend on the audience, the objective, and the context. At times a more casual and less formal style might be tolerated; at other times a more official and less conversational tone is required. However, there are certain pieces of advice that you should only ignore at your peril:

- *Ensure that there is a well-marked sequence and coherence to your arguments.* It is preferable to provide a "road map" at the beginning of your work so that people will have a better chance of not getting lost in reading through the body of your writing.
- *Ensure that your argument progresses and moves along.* It is much easier to win over a reader if you construct an argument that advances smoothly and directly to its conclusion rather than meandering and digressing along the way.
- *Ensure that your argument is dynamic rather than passive.* You will be much more effective and persuasive when you engage the reader and take a positive attitude to the argument to be made. In trying to nurture a style that is active and vigorous rather than static and dull, it is a good idea to rely on verbs rather than on nouns to convey action and affect. Avoid the tendency to overuse nouns that are derived from verbs (for example, authorization from authorize, application from apply).
- *Ensure that you tie everything together in a solid conclusion.* All your good work can be lost if you fail to bring your arguments to a tidy and decisive ending.

EDITING

Many students seem to think that when they have finished writing, they have completed the assignment. But, in many ways, the hard work has only just begun: thorough editing of what has been written is the difference between acceptable and excellent legal writing. The ability to write well necessarily encompasses the ability to edit well. However, editing is a skill that many people lack, and, indeed, the most gifted of writers are not always the best editors of their own work. Too often, a potentially excellent piece of legal writing remains just that: potentially excellent, but actually mediocre. Very few writers are fortunate enough to be able to produce a first draft that is good enough to be the final draft. As the famous American judge Louis Brandeis said, "There is no such thing as good writing: there is only good rewriting." If you want to become a good legal writer, it is essential that you leave yourself plenty of time to give your work the serious editing that it should deserve and probably requires.

The mind-set of the editor is very different from that of the writer. Good editors are good readers, and it is essential that the legal writer be able to become a good legal reader as well. Editing is not simply about checking for grammar and idiom; it is about trying to elicit the underlying organization and structure of a piece so that it can be enhanced. Of course, it is easier to be an editorial critic of someone else's writing than one's own. Good editors do not impose their own style on the work to be edited, but begin from the inside and seek to make the other writer's style the best that it can be without fundamentally altering that style. However, as a student, you may not have the luxury of someone else editing your work. Indeed, in some circumstances, it might be perceived as a breach of the academic regulations about submitting only your own work.

In editing your own work, certain maxims are worth bearing in mind:

- *Treat the manuscript as if it were written by someone else.* Try to come to the work afresh, though, if time is short, this perspective is difficult to achieve.
- *Assume that the work is in need of improvement.* It is the final product that you want to be proud of, not the first draft.
- *Rethink the organization of the piece.* In addition to ensuring that the writing is stylistically sound and appropriate, good editing means going back to basics to check the structure of the overall work.
- *Divide the edit into several steps.* Do not try to achieve everything that a good edit requires in one pass; begin with the big issues (overall structure and tone), and move down to the smaller matters (sentences and proofreading).
- *Do not be afraid to omit material.* The most difficult task for writers is to condense or delete the material they have worked so hard to produce; try not to be too enamoured or possessive of your own writing.

SOME BASIC POINTERS

What follows are some pointers and exercises about the kind of writing style you should strive to acquire and the basic temptations that you will need to resist if you are to become a good legal writer. There are, of course, many other techniques you will have to learn, but these are the ones that most commentators on good legal writing seem to place most weight on. All these examples are drawn from or inspired by ideas and examples in Robert Eagleson's work.

- *Avoid legalese*

Legalese is the scourge of all good legal writing. Lawyers never seem to have heard of the old saw that "enough is as good as a feast." Although legalese has been a staple of legal writing for centuries and was once considered good legal writing, it is no longer acceptable. A typical sentence of legalese might read as follows:

> In the event of the tenant wishing to take a renewal of the lease for a further term, he shall prior to the expiration of the term hereby granted give to the landlord or his agent not more than six (6) months' and not less than three (3) months' previous notice in writing of his intention so to do and provided he has duly and punctually paid the rent reserved by this lease at the times therein appointed for payment thereof and shall have duly performed and observed all the covenants and agreements contained in this lease up to the expiration of the term hereby granted on his part to be performed and observed, then the landlord will at the cost to the tenant grant to him a further term at a rent payable by him which would at such time be current market rental of the premises.

The problems with this paragraph are manifold: it is too long, too unwieldy, repetitious, archaic, and jumbled; it is almost all the things that good legal writing should not and need not be. To remedy these faults, you must first try to capture the main ideas to be expressed — lease renewal, period of notice, and so on. Having done this, you can reduce the sentence to manageable chunks so that a more focused reworking can be carried out. The first part of the sentence seems to run from "In the event of ..." to " ... intention so to do." This chunk itself can be broken down into two separable ideas and parts. The first part consists of eighteen words and, without too much effort, it can be tightened and cleaned up so that repetitions, redundancies, and circumlocutions are omitted. Compare:

> In the event of the tenant wishing to take a renewal of the lease for a further term,

> If the tenant wants to renew the lease,

Much the same can be done with the second, thirty-nine-word part of the first chunk. It can be reordered and shortened so that its meaning is actually clarified. Compare:

> he shall prior to the expiration of the term hereby granted give to the landlord or his agent not more than six (6) months' and not less than three (3) months' previous notice in writing of his intention so to do[.]
> the tenant must give the landlord or the agent not less than 3 months' and not more than 6 months' notice in writing before the lease ends.

- *Keep the essential components of a sentence as close together as possible*

The flow and meaning of a sentence are much harder to read and follow when the sentence's essential components — subject, verb, and object — are separated by qualifying clauses. For example:

> An employer, who is not a company, or a working subcontractor, who is not a company, to whom a certified assessment under section 30 applies may within 14 days from the date of service of notice of that certified assessment appeal to the appropriate provincial or federal court or tribunal which may hear and, if it wishes, determine the matter.

In this sentence not only are the subjects of the sentence — employers and subcontractors — separated from the verb — may appeal — by subordinate phrases, but the two parts of the verb itself are interrupted by several intervening clauses. A more straightforward arrangement of the sentence might read:

> Provided that they are not companies, employers or working subcontractors may appeal to the appropriate provincial or federal court or tribunal within 14 days from the date of service of notice of a certified assessment under section 30.

- *Write in a positive and direct style*

A common fault among lawyers is to write in a negative and indirect way rather than a positive and direct style; they say that "it is not impossible that ..." or "you will not succeed unless ..." rather than "it is possible that ..." or "you will succeed if ..." In particular, law students too easily slip into using double or multiple negatives to express themselves. While this turn of phrase might not always be avoidable, it should be used only as a last resort and not simply as a matter of course. The negative mood of the following instruction is much easier to understand when reframed more positively. Compare:

> In the case of a person who has more than one nationality, the term "the country of his nationality" means each of the countries of which he is a national, and a person shall not be deemed to be lacking the protection of the country of his nationality if, without any valid reason based on well-founded fear, he has not availed himself of the protection of one of the countries of which he is a national.

Persons are considered to have the protection of each country of which they are a national unless they have a valid reason for not seeking that protection. This reason should be based on a well-founded fear.

- *Avoid archaic (or trendy) words*

The inclination to use archaic (or trendy) words is something that law students should work particularly hard to resist. Good legal writing is not the art of learning and including as many long or technical words as possible, preferably in some foreign language, in order to baffle the uninitiated reader and to display one's newfound erudition. While it is important to ensure that correct and appropriate technical terms are used in legal documents, there is no reason to treat that as an excuse to lard a sentence with unnecessary jargon or redundant words and phrases;

the use of such expressions is a sign of shallow pretension, not great learning. In particular, look out for and avoid unnecessary lawyerisms — hereinafter, aforesaid, hithertofore, hereinbefore, wheresoever, heretofore, whereof, thenceforth, hereunto, and so on. The following example can be easily and effectively translated into a sentence of modern prose that better captures its essential meaning:

> This indenture is made between the Mortgagor described in the Schedule hereto (hereinafter called "the Mortgagor") of the one part and the Mortgagee described in the Schedule hereto (hereinafter called the "Mortgagee") of the other part whereas the Mortgagor is the beneficial owner in possession free from all encumbrances of the Chattels described in the Schedule hereto (hereinafter called "the Chattels") . . .

> As described in the Schedule, the mortgagor and the mortgagee confirm that the mortgagor is the owner of the property and that the mortgagor has a clear title to that property . . .

There are definite circumstances in which the test of good legal writing is not its easy accessibility to the general reader. Many documents, like wills and mortgages, must be legal-proof in the sense that they must be able to withstand, as best as possible, the attempts by other lawyers to subvert their plain meaning or to complicate their simple phrasing. As always, it is essential to pitch one's legal writing at a level and length that is appropriate to the particular audience and the intended function. Nothing is to be gained by crafting a document that is understood fully by the client, if it can be thoroughly ripped apart by the other party's lawyer. While it is important to avoid verbosity for its own sake, clarity should not be sacrificed for brevity; the economy of writing is related to the substance of that to be communicated.

- *Do not be afraid to use diagrams or charts*
Lawyers and, therefore, law students seem reluctant to use diagrams and charts in their documents and writings. This fear is unwarranted. Do not be afraid to reduce statistical data or technical information to a graphic series of tables or diagrams. As old mathematics teachers are fond of saying, a picture is worth a thousand words. In the following example, no matter how good a legal writer you are, it would be difficult to convey the necessary information in a clear and uncluttered way without relying upon a simple chart:

> With the exception of alternate Thursdays, the first Monday of the month, and any weeks in which a national or state holiday is celebrated on a weekday, students are only permitted to use the Law Library ("use" being defined as being present in the Law Library and reading law books — the only use of the facility that is permitted, loitering being specifically forbidden and not permitted for any reason whatsoever) on Mondays and Tuesdays between the hours of 9 o'clock a.m. and 12 noon, 6 o'clock p.m. and 9 o'clock p.m., Wednesdays, between the hours of 2 o'clock p.m. and 5.30 o'clock p.m., Thursdays, after second roll call clears (unless it clears after 12 noon, in which case Tuesday's schedule applies), and 5 o'clock p.m., Fridays, after 4 o'clock p.m. and 9 o'clock p.m. and Saturdays, between 7 o'clock and 9 o'clock p.m.

A much better alternative to this convoluted and inaccessible set of instructions is the construction of a simple chart. After all, the purpose of the paragraph is supposedly to convey important and straightforward information to some section of the public:

Law Library: Hours
Students may use the Law Library at the following times:

Monday	9 - 12 midday
	6 p.m. - 9 p.m.
Tuesday	9 a.m. - 12 midday
	6 p.m. - 9 p.m.
Wednesday	2 p.m. - 5.30 p.m.
Thursday	After the second roll call clears:
	until 5 p.m.
	(If the second roll call clears after midday:
	9 a.m. - 12 midday
	6 p.m. - 9 p.m.)
Friday	4 p.m. - 9 p.m.
Saturday	7 p.m. - 9 p.m.

The library will be closed on the following days:
1. alternate Thursdays
2. the first Monday of each month
3. national or state holidays falling on a weekday

Note: Students may use the library only to read books.
It is not meant to be a meeting place.

- *Avoid strings of synonyms*

Lawyers have a penchant for using a string of synonyms. They believe it is better to kill a bird with two or three stones than one: Why use one word when two will do? Better to avoid couplets and trinities unless their use can be individually justified or is mandated by their legal usage (e.g., joint and several liability). While such indulgence lends a document or a piece of writing a certain legalistic patina, it does so at the expense of prolixity. Some of the more common and unnecessary alliances include:

all and every	have and hold
by and with	sole and exclusive
final and conclusive	type and kind
for and during	costs, charges and expenses
full and complete	rest, residue and remainder
over and above	bear, sustain or suffer
any and all	legal, valid and binding
by and between	rules, requirements and regulations
do, execute and perform	

THE LEGAL STUFF

There are many different forms of legal writing. Although they all share certain characteristics and allow for a basic reliance on a common writing style, they all vary slightly in the organization, audience, or emphasis required. Form shapes substance as substance is itself shaped by the form; the form of the writing can affect its substantive meaning, and the substance of that to be communicated can affect the form of its expression. The major types of legal writing that law students confront and will be asked to present include the case brief, the case comment, the legal memorandum, the term paper, and the legal factum.

CASE BRIEFS

There is much debate around the value of case briefs. While students need some record of what a particular case stands for or holds, the compilation of case briefs tends to reduce the law to a series of individualized and discrete decisions rather than a developing sequence of rules and principles. Consequently, it is important to brief cases in such a way that they interrelate and cross-reference each other. Too many students manage to accumulate a vast knowledge of particular cases; they can recite the dates, citations, facts, and holdings in impressive detail. However, they have little idea of how to relate those cases to one another in a revealing or illuminating way — the very core of what it is to be a good law student or lawyer. It is no use being able to describe lavishly the bark and leaves of every tree in the forest if you cannot also gain a sense of the overall nature of the forest so that you can find your way around it.

The detail and particular components of any particular case brief will depend on the significance of the case. The most common structure of a case brief will include the following components: name and status of the parties (plaintiff, defendant, appellant, respondent, etc.); a citation; facts of the case; the contending parties' main argument; the central issue or question to be decided; the final disposition of the case, including who won and who lost; the reasons for the decision, including how the court relied on other cases; interesting asides or *obiter*, and critical comments on the decision or judgments.

LEGAL MEMORANDUMS

The purpose of a legal memorandum is usually to research a point of law. As an "in-house document," it tends to be less adversarial and positional and more even-handed and balanced. It must, therefore, be a reliable and comprehensive account of the law; a memo is not the time to fudge difficult issues or overstate the argument. There is no detailed or fixed blueprint for writing a legal memo; its precise structure will be determined by the nature of the issues, facts, and law to be addressed. However, the basic structure is most likely to be:

- *Statement of the material facts of the problem.* Detail can be added later and put in the context of the applicable law. You must remember that a statement of facts can be the best part of your argument. It enables you to emphasize the key points and to begin to direct the reader's thought along a certain path. Although his writing style is not something that students should emulate, Lord Denning's presentation of the facts in an arresting and partial way is a fine example of how a recitation of the facts can become a major part of the argument: "Broadchalke is one of the most pleasing villages in England. Old Herbert Bundy was a farmer there. His home was Yew Tree Farm. It went back for 300 years. His family had been there for generations. It was his only asset." Guess who won in a dispute between Bundy and a bank for repossession of his farm? And, "In summertime, village cricket is the delight of everyone." Guess who won in a dispute between a cricket club and some complaining neighbours?

- *Succinct statement of the major issues.* It is best to set out the central questions that you intend to answer and, where appropriate, a summary of the answers. This short section should be thought of as an analytical road map. Again, how the issues are framed can influence the type of answers and responses to be elicited.
- *An analysis of the basic law.* This section is obviously the main body of your memorandum. It should be organized in a fluent manner, with the important links in the argumentative chain laid out sensibly and reasonably; avoid a too emphatic statement of the arguments. As well as covering all the major arguments supporting your analysis, you must also deal with likely rebuttals or counterarguments. By taking opposing arguments seriously, you strengthen your own position.
- *Conclusion.* This section gives you an opportunity to tie together all your arguments and to show that they point in a certain direction. At times, it will not be possible to suggest a clear and unequivocal answer. However, one should be clear and unequivocal in informing the reader that your answer is not clear and unequivocal, and why that is the case. It might also be appropriate to include a set of recommendations as to what actions might be taken or what strategies might be pursued.

In order to give you a better understanding of a legal memorandum, appendices A and B contain a couple of examples.

CASE COMMENTS

Whereas the case brief is usually more of a note for your own reference and future use, a case comment is an essay that is to be submitted for evaluation or grading. It fulfils much the same function as the book review: it is an occasion to introduce, explain, and give an opinion on an important event. Students are required to do case comments in order to develop their legal reasoning skills as much as their writing abilities. Indeed, such comments are a primary example of the intimate connection between "thinking about law" and "writing about law." As such, the instructor will be looking for a finished product that not only is well written and well organized but also derives from serious and thorough research and demonstrates a sophisticated grasp of law and legal thinking. In an important sense, therefore, the ability to research, plan, and write a case comment is one of the basic skills of the aspiring law student. As a result, and because it will likely be one of the first serious assignments that students are required to undertake, the handing in of a case comment can be a very anxious and unsettling experience. However, provided that you understand what is expected of you, such a comment can be completed reasonably painlessly and successfully. Indeed, you might actually enjoy preparing it!

The general pattern of the case comment is not very different from the case brief; it demands a similar structure of presentation. However, it is obviously intended to be more expansive and critical. The case chosen will usually be an important and topical decision of an appellate court, often the Supreme Court of Canada. The first thing to do is ... THINK. Don't dive into the library or the web and read every possibly related case and text on the subject to be discussed. Read the case thoroughly and take stock of its main analytical and argumentative thrust. Write out a couple of the most salient and general responses that come to mind before you begin your research; these notes will help to structure your initial efforts, although most likely you will revise or abandon your original observations as your research and thinking progress. As you research further, you should begin to get a better sense of the strengths and weaknesses of the decision and its judgments. At each stage of your research, keep going back to your original thoughts and adjust them accordingly. Try not to lose sight of the forest through all the detail you are amassing about particular trees. The hardest thing for a law student and/or lawyer to do is not to do more research or read more cases, but to think about that research and those cases in a general and reflective manner. After a little practice, anyone can read a case or track down a precedent; the hard part is knowing how to use effectively and optimally the ideas and insights you have gained.

The best case comments are those that are able to provide a different or unusual perspective on a case: to highlight a particular way of approaching the issue at hand, to expose the limitations of earlier understandings of the matter, and to suggest a more compelling way to grasp or resolve the problem. Of course, it may be that you come to the opinion that the decision or judgments are spot on, in which case you must demonstrate how and why they are superior to other approaches. However, although there is little point in being critical for its own sake, there is no need to refrain from criticizing a decision or its supporting reasons. Provided that the criticism is measured and balanced, students should resist the implicit pressure that is often present to celebrate or apologize for the judgments of courts. While it is important to avoid *ad hominem* arguments, the honing of the critical faculty is an important exercise and ought not to be neglected. Nevertheless, whether you praise or pillory the case to be commented on, you must ensure that you cover all the bases and place the case in its broader doctrinal and policy context. Before you apply the icing, ensure that you have baked a first-class cake from the best ingredients and by the tried-and-trusted methods.

The basic organization of a case comment is fairly straightforward. Again, it is a matter of working from a general structure and adapting it to the circumstances of the case and the preferences of the writer. There are four main components:

- *The introduction.* This part should set a general tone for the comment, highlight the issues to be addressed, explain the methodology to be employed, and indicate the paths to be trod.
- *A contextual account of the case.* This part should provide the facts, litigation history, the reasons for judgment, and its overall cogency.
- *A critical evaluation of the case.* This part should evaluate the case's internal consistency, institutional desirability, legal and social consequences, and contribution to broader discussions of justice and fairness.
- *The conclusion.* This part should tie all the strands together in a plausible and persuasive manner.

The best case comments and any other form of student writing, particularly exams and term papers, are those that are able to blend together a statement of what was said or done with a critical evaluation of those statements and acts. This combination is a sophisticated skill that few intuitively possess, but it is one that everyone should seek to acquire and one that will ensure success as a student or a lawyer. Scout around the library and read a few published case comments in the *Canadian Bar Review* or a similar journal and get a flavour of things.

FACTUMS

Factums are the written arguments that are put before a court on an appeal hearing and that form the basis for the oral argument. Most law schools require students to prepare and write such documents as part of the mooting exercise. Chapter 8 is devoted to an explanation and guide to this whole process. Appendix C contains good student examples of an appellant's and respondent's factum.

CONCLUSION

As the legal profession comes under closer public scrutiny and criticism, lawyers will be required to account more for themselves and their writing. The old habits of convolution and the customary instincts to obfuscation will have to be checked. And for good reason. By developing a writing style that is clear and open, law students can not only enhance their own standing with professional ranks but also contribute to the democratic mission of law as a friend, not foe, to the general public. If you begin early and do not fall victim to the legal tendency to gobbledegook, you will be able to spend less time shoveling smoke and more time clearing the air. Your legal writing should be a source of pride, not embarrassment.

A final note is warranted on the effect of the computer on legal writing. Unlike some Luddites, I believe that it is the boon, not the bane, of good legal writing. It allows for better note-keeping, easier editing, and crisper presentation of work. Because word-processing allows for better organization and because organization is the key to good writing, the word-processor can be an invaluable tool. Also, most software packages come with available legal templates for all kinds of documents and forms. While these "precedents" have been around for years, they are now readily accessible to the novice legal writer. However, although their use is commonplace and indispensable in legal practice, law students should be very cautious in resorting to them. Such aids are helpful, but they are no substitute for the skills of legal drafting and writing; they should be used as a basic reference rather than as a convenient crutch. Once you have got the hang of what you are doing, you should, with the skilled use of macros, have sufficient confidence in your own style and structure of writing to create your own model formats.

FURTHER READINGS

Armstrong, S. & T. Terrell. *Thinking Like a Writer: A Lawyer's Guide to Effective Writing and Editing*. New York: Clark Badman Callaghan, 1992.

Dick, R. *Legal Drafting*, 2nd ed. Toronto: Carswell, 1985.

Eagleson, R. *Writing in Plain English*. Canberra: Australian Government Publishing Service, 1990.

McFarlane, J. & W. Clements. *The Globe and Mail Style Book: A Guide to Language and Usage*. Toronto: Penguin Books, 1995.

Mellinkoff, D. *The Language of the Law*. Boston: Little, Brown, 1963,

Stark, J. "Why Lawyers Write Badly" (1984) 97 Harvard L. Rev. 1989.

Williams, J. *Style: Ten Lessons in Clarity and Grace*, 3rd ed. New York: Harper Collins, 1989.

Wydick, R. *Plain English for Lawyers*, 3rd ed. Durham: Carolina Academic Press, 1994.

CHAPTER 7
Making Friends:
The Basics of Legal Research

All law students need to do legal research at various times and for various reasons. In an important sense, the key to being a good lawyer is not knowing tons of law, but knowing where and how to find the law quickly and efficiently when required. It is futile to think that you can learn everything you need to know and keep up to date as well. Indeed, it would be a negligent lawyer who tried to work from memory. In your first year at law school, the likely reasons for doing legal research will be to complete a memorandum of law, write a case comment, prepare an essay, or look up and review the work of certain professors. Later on, in articling and throughout your legal career, you will use your research skills to an even greater extent than in law school. Whether you are writing memoranda of law, factums, or client letters, you will always benefit from a well-honed set of research skills. In important ways, legal research is no different from any other kind of research for writing: the only differences are the places where you look and the tools that you use. All that you are attempting to do, regardless of the purpose, is to find information. Like legal writing, legal research is simply a specialized form of research. The law library, whether in physical or electronic form, is first and foremost a place of reference; students do not so much read materials from cover to cover as consult a variety of materials to glean certain information and insights about the law. Finding your way around these legal resources and turning this formidable maze into a helpful friend rather than an inscrutable enemy is the first step to success as a smart lawyer.

A generational change has taken place in the way lawyers do research. It is no longer viable or even possible to utilize the old methods that assumed that what is law is what is written on paper. Today, any law student must be proficient in the use of a computer and its gateway to the world of online research. If you have a dose of techno-phobia, now is the time to overcome it — good and even not-so-good lawyers must have a working grasp of how to do research online. You must think of the law library as being truly huge; it stretches from your law school library across cyberspace to include a galaxy of ever-expanding information. Unfortunately, most guides to legal research view the technological tools as an add-on to the traditional methods of research. This is a pity and typical of law's general tentativeness about electronic technology and the Web. When it manages to overcome treating them as a threat rather than an opportunity, it still refuses to embrace its possibilities entirely.

There is no need for you to make the same mistake. To be an effective legal researcher, you must be able to integrate old and new to your best advantage: a mix-and-match approach is advisable. But you simply cannot afford to treat research's technological possibilities as anything other than a boon, not a barrier. If you don't appreciate it already, the computer and its awesome access to the world can be the best friend that you ever had.

' Many books and articles have been written about legal research. This chapter attempts to give you an overview of the way to do basic legal research. If legal research becomes one of your passions, you should (after seeking psychiatric help) refer to the other sources listed in the bibliography at the end of the chapter. Accordingly, this chapter will outline the basic tools and techniques of legal research that you will need to perform a tolerable job in the early parts of your law school career and to provide a good grounding for the rest of your career. As such, this chapter is not about teaching you how to do the actual research. But it is about giving you a general overview of what is out there, familiarizing you with some general approaches, and suggesting how you might develop a realistic framework for the acquisition of important and useful research skills. Like everything else, it is only when you know the rules that you can bend them and play with them to your own advantage and style. Accordingly, to be competent at legal research, it is necessary to have a sense of the various tools that are available, how they interact and complement each other, and how the overall toolbox functions as a set.

WHERE TO LOOK

Legal research is merely finding answers to legal questions. In essence, it is about finding the law. However, the law is neither static nor easily determined. Again, like life, law has a distinct tendency to be what you make it. There is no one source of the law on any particular subject. What passes for the law on a particular question at a particular time will depend on the nature of the question, the type of answer required, and the amount of time and money that is available to be spent on finding the answer. It is not so much that the law changes for each question, though this may be true, but that the question and its surrounding factors affect what law is required. For some questions, the answer will lie in a statute (e.g., the notice period required to be given by a tenant to a landlord). If the client is the landlord, however, and she wants to argue that insufficient notice was given even though the statute was followed, then other sources of law must be consulted and found. This need will lead to case law or precedent, which may give examples of situations where landlords have argued successfully or not the point you are trying to make. In all cases, it is important to ensure that your research has been thorough and comprehensive. It is not only a matter of unearthing regulations or cases that are supportive of your client or position; it is about scouring the whole legal landscape for a sense of how such provisions have been or are likely to be interpreted.

Research is about being confident that you have got a full and complete grasp of the available law; massaging it into a more partial and persuasive shape in the interests of your client or position is for later. In approaching legal research, you need to have the right attitude. And there are two very important things to remember. First, currency is vital in law; being *almost* up-to-date is simply not good enough. You must be as current as today; yesterday's law can be not only less useful, but might actually be positively harmful. And, in this regard, the various online databases are excellent; what they lack in synthesis, they gain in currency and comprehensiveness. Secondly, as the old adage goes, "one search is not research" — it is re-search and re-search again. A casual job will produce casual results. While that might be acceptable in some rare instances, it will usually not be and might do more harm than good.

THE BASIC SOURCES

There are four main classes of legal literature — the Constitution, legislation, law reports, and academic literature. Although these are covered at greater length in chapter 3, a recap is worthwhile.

- *The Constitution:* The Constitution of Canada is the paramount law throughout Canada. All statutes, federal and provincial, must be consistent with the Constitution. The Constitution outlines the division of power between the provinces and the federal government, and defines in the *Charter of Rights and Freedoms* those rights that people have in their dealings with the state. Remember that the Constitution comprises the relevant case law as well as the formal documents. There are also more informal conventions that are part of the Constitution.
- *Legislation:* The statutes and regulations that have been made by the legislature are called legislation. There are federal statutes as well as provincial statutes. Each statute generally covers one area of law. They can be lengthy and involved, as is the case with the *Income Tax Act* or the *Criminal Code*, or they may be a single page. Statutes are also changed by judicial or administrative interpretation, by subsequent Acts that negate or alter existing Acts, and constitutional challenges resulting in a finding that certain Acts or portions of Acts are unconstitutional and therefore invalid. Regulations are attached to specific statutes. They direct how the relevant statute should be implemented in more specific and concrete situations. Regulations are subordinate to statutes and must always be interpreted with a view to the overriding purpose of the statute.
- *Law reports:* These reports are extensive in number and bewildering in content. Whether interpreting a statute or working with earlier cases, judges make law. However, the binding force of such decisions is dependent on the level of court, the balance of judgments, and, occasionally, the particular judge; a dissent in the Supreme Court of Canada can be the harbinger of future change. While it is the *ratio* alone that is considered to be formally binding, the only certain thing that can be said about *ratios* is that they are uncertain in both presence and value. Judges talk about *ratios*, and some law professors insist that they exist, but they are ghost-like in their elusiveness: the *ratio* should be thought of as what a particular judge said in a particular case based on particular facts at a particular time. If the *ratio* is the principle or rule of a case, the *obiter* is the rest of the comments made by the judge; it is not formally binding, but it can be of persuasive authority. All this really means is that you can use any part of a judgment that helps your case and try to call it the *ratio*, while you discount all the other comments as *obiter*.

I have listed some of the leading modern Canadian, English, and American reports you will encounter in your study of the common law, along with the conventional forms of citation.

Canadian
Dominion Law Reports [Old Series] (D.L.R.), 1912–22
Dominion Law Reports [New Series] (D.L.R.), 1923–55
Dominion Law Reports [Second Series] (D.L.R. (2d)), 1956–68
Dominion Law Reports [Third Series] (D.L.R. (3d)), 1969–84
Dominion Law Reports [Fourth Series] (D.L.R. (4th)), 1984 onwards

Ontario Reports (O.R.), 1822 onwards
British Columbia Law Reports (B.C.L.R.), 1976 onwards
Saskatchewan Reports (Sask. R.), 1979 onwards
Manitoba Reports: Second Series (Man. R. (2d)), 1986 onwards
Recueils de Jurisprudence du Québec (R.J.Q.), 1986 onwards
Alberta Reports (A.R.), 1976 onwards
Alberta Law Reports: Second Series (Alta. L.R. (2d)), 1976 onwards
New Brunswick Reports: Second Series (N.B.R. (2d)), 1968 onwards
Nova Scotia Reports: Second Series (N.S.R. (2d)), 1970 onwards
Newfoundland & Prince Edward Island Reports (Nfld. & P.E.I.R.), 1970 onwards
Northwest Territories Reports (N.W.T.R.), 1983 onwards

Canadian Criminal Cases (C.C.C.), 1898 onwards
Reports of Family Law (R.F.L.), 1970 onwards
Canadian Cases on the Law of Torts (C.C.L.T.), 1976 onwards
Carswell's Practice Cases (C.P.C.), 1976 onwards

English
Appeal Cases (A.C.), 1891 onwards
Chancery Division (Ch.), 1891 onwards
Queen's or King's Bench (Q.B. or K.B.), 1891 onwards
Family Division (Fam.), 1971 onwards

All England Law Reports (All E.R.), 1936 onwards
Weekly Law Reports (W.L.R.), 1953 onwards
Criminal Appeal Reports (Cr. App. R.), 1908 onwards

American
United States Reports (U.S.), 1790 onwards
Supreme Court Reporter (S. Ct.), 1882 onwards
Federal Reporter (F. 2d), 1880 onwards
Federal Supplement (F. Supp.), 1932 onwards

- *Academic literature:* Although this material is never strictly binding on courts, judges tend to refer increasingly to the academic literature as the law becomes more complex and sprawling. If used appropriately, it can be an excellent and up-to-date source of ideas and arguments in your research; it can provide a general and sophisticated overview of the area of law to be researched. Also, it can add weight to more imaginative or speculative claims about the law. As long as you remember that some books and periodical articles can take a very partial slant on legal doctrine, you should take advantage of this rich source of information and ideas.

THE BASIC RESOURCES

The challenge of legal research is to know how to find your way efficiently and effectively around these voluminous sources. The amount of legal information that is available is truly amazing; there are more law reports, statutes, and academic books and articles than most people could read in two lifetimes. Moreover, it is growing exponentially. And the advent of technology — CD-ROMs, online databases and the Internet — has accelerated that tendency. Any lawyer who attempts to learn and keep on top of this massive plethora of legal material is on mission impossible and destined for a nervous breakdown. The only sane course is to give up any hope of mastering the full range of primary resources of law in all their mind-numbing detail. Instead, it is much more profitable and realistic to concentrate on perfecting your use of the secondary sources or tools of law — encyclopedias, digests, abridgments, gazettes, textbooks, citators, and so on.

All of law's many bibliographical aids are still available in the traditional print format, although this is unlikely to continue indefinitely. Your law school library will almost certainly possess these materials and you must familiarize yourself with their whereabouts and accessibility. However, before introducing some of those basic bibliographical aids, it is useful to sketch briefly the different technological resources that are now available. They can be grouped into three main groups:

- *Online databases.* The three main online database collections are QUICKLAW, LEXIS-NEXIS, and WESTLAW. Each of these has its strengths, although you might not be able to get access to all of them as a law student. QUICKLAW is the most Canadian with a rapidly growing collection of US and other common law jurisdiction databases and it gives access to QuickCite, which is a noting-up service that allows for the retrieval of a case's history and provides alternative citations; LEXIS-NEXIS has a broad coverage and includes sources from the United States and the Commonwealth generally; and WESTLAW is an American-based service that has access to most American legal periodicals with a recent Canadian section. Each of these resources produces its own online and print handbooks on how to access and use them. Also, the *Canadian Abridgment* is available online from e-carswell and on CD-ROM.
- *CD-ROMs.* A vast range of material is now available on CD-ROM. In addition to being convenient and updatable, they have good search capabilities and can be used off-line. Importantly, the Canadian Abridgment is available on CD-ROM. Some other leading resources that are available on CD-ROM are included in the listing at the end of the chapter.
- *Internet.* There is a massive amount of material available on the Internet; most of this can be accessed through common search engines, like YAHOO, GOOGLE,

and LYCOS. As with any Internet material, you must rely on it with caution. Although it is getting better, the system is anarchic, changeable, and basically free to anyone able to get access to a properly equipped computer and modem. There are many official sites and they are excellent resources for accessing and downloading material. However, these official sources are limited in their search and organization capacities. There are many Web pages that you can access to provide tips and suggestions on all manner of topics. All the law schools have Websites (see chapter 1) and they contain lots of information that all students can use. Also, many professors (and some students) have their own Web pages where they provide materials, notes, and the like. For my money, one of the best general sites to begin is the Jurist website — http://jurist.law.pitt.edu. This is an American site, but has links to sister sites in the United Kingdom, Canada, and Australia; it is superbly organized, very up-to-date, and extremely informative. Some of the most useful sites for Canadian legal information are included in the listing at the end of this chapter.

Although a full discussion of computer-based research is beyond the scope of this book, the "virtual library" is not far away. Students who are unable or unwilling to join the technological wave are likely to find themselves left high and dry in the coming years — the writing is on the screen. The advantages of computer research are many and include the speed of retrieval, guaranteed accuracy, astonishingly up-to-date and vast databases, and the fact that they are downloadable. Also, most students are eligible for free membership to many commercial sources, such as QUICKLAW. For first-year students, however, although the availability of computerized research makes it an enticing prospect for exclusive reliance, they are still well advised to cut their teeth on more traditional sources and outlets: the high expense of computer-based research means that it will not always be available or viable. These traditional skills will not only lay a solid base of legal research skills in case your future employment does not facilitate access to technological resources, but they will also make your computer-based research more efficient and, therefore, less expensive in later years. Computers are information-rich but analysis-poor. It must be remembered that computer research, even more than other research tools, is dependent on the researcher asking the proper question. The computer will only answer the questions you ask — nothing more and, as important, nothing less. It is often a case of feast or famine. You must input the proper keywords or phrases if you are to receive anything at all or not be overwhelmed with the amount of material you receive. Indeed, in computer-based legal research you need a more, not less, refined grasp of the organization and dynamics of legal research.

In all matters, but particularly for computer research, you should seek out assistance from the law library's staff. Do not be afraid to ask the reference librarians for assistance; these talented people are an underutilized resource and they will tell you (in no uncertain manner) when you are asking them to do more than they are supposed to. Research is no occasion for bluff and bravado; it is no weakness to concede that you are out to sea (or even lunch) when it comes to research. Indeed, as again with most matters, it is a sign of strength to recognize and admit your weaknesses; it makes it so much easier to remedy them and turn them into strengths so that you gain the edge over prouder, but less savvy students.

THE BASIC TOOLS

More than almost any other subject, law has a highly developed and fully integrated set of bibliographical aids. Here are the most helpful of these research tools:

- *Textbooks* are an excellent place to start. They are published on almost every area of law. They will provide more detailed and in-depth coverage of a particular subject area. You will get a good grounding in the topic or subject area from someone who has relatively sound credentials and credibility. Remember, though, that the textbook is current only to the date it was published, and you must update cases found in a text.

- The *Canadian Encyclopedic Digest*, or *C.E.D.*, is a legal encyclopedia. It consists of multiple looseleaf volumes arranged by subject area. Each subject area consists of numbered paragraphs that outline broad statements of the law in that area. Relevant cases are footnoted within the paragraphs. The *C.E.D. Ont.* covers Ontario and federal law, and the *Western C.E.D.* covers the Western provinces, the territories, and federal law. Both publications also refer to case law of other common law provinces, the United Kingdom, and other Commonwealth jurisdictions. Remember, though, that the *C.E.D.* will provide only a general overview and, therefore, will not cite all the relevant case law on any topic. The *C.E.D.* is updated about once a year in the "Yellow Pages" that are found at the front of each volume. After checking the main section of the volume, you should update by looking for the corresponding paragraph number in the Yellow Pages. If the paragraph number does not appear, there have been no additions since the last entry in the main body. The main part of the *C.E.D.* is current to the date found in the bottom right-hand corner of each page. Always note-up (keep up to date) cases found in the *C.E.D.* by checking with the *Canadian Case Citations* of the *Canadian Abridgment*, or *QuickCite*.

- The *Canadian Abridgment* is the basic tool needed by any researcher to gather relevant case law. Conquering the *Abridgment* is a necessary task for any law student determined to do complete legal research. It is made up of a number of main volumes, arranged alphabetically by subject. In addition to these main volumes, the *Abridgment* has other parts that are used to complete various research tasks:

  - finding aids to case law relevant to specific areas of law from numerous Canadian courts and tribunals: main volumes, supplement volumes, *Canadian Current Law: Case Law Digests*;
  - the history and judicial treatment of cases (the noting-up function): *Canadian Case Citations, 1867–1990*, and update volumes;
  - the history and judicial treatment of statutes and rules of practice: *Canadian Citations: Statutes Judicially Considered/Rules Judicially Considered* and update volumes;
  - judicial interpretation of words and phrases, including case law citations: *Words & Phrases Revised* and updated in the *General Index* and *Canadian Current Law: Case Law Digests*;

- alternative citations: *Consolidated Table of Cases*; and
- legal literature, including books, articles, case comments, notes, government publications, legal education material, and law reform reports: *Index to Canadian Legal Literature*, updated in *Canadian Current Law: Canadian Legal Literature*.

Using the *Abridgment* may seem daunting at first because there are so many volumes and parts. However, once you understand the basics of using it, you can soon turn it into a solid and reliable friend. The chart reproduced in figure 3 is usually posted in every law library right next to the *Abridgment* and can be a handy reference guide. Most first-year law programs include instruction in legal research in the legal writing component. The best way to learn how to use the *Abridgment* effectively is to use it: practice makes perfect. If you get lost, refer back to the guide in the text above, check the chart, ask the librarian (after you have tried yourself), and, if you are still confused, contact the publisher of the *Abridgment,* who is available online or offers a toll-free help line. In using the *Abridgment* online, remember the provisos about computer research — you can access information only by keyword or phrase. Therefore, you must not assume that you have found all the information there is to find unless you are sure that you have asked for every possible keyword or phrase. The computer cannot read your mind: you will get out only what you put in — "garbage in; garbage out."

- *Periodicals* contain articles, case comments, and notes written on a specific area of law. They can be a valuable resource, as they offer comprehensive interpretations on a myriad of topics. In addition, because periodicals are published frequently (often more than four times a year), they can contain much more current information than textbooks. As well, many of the articles will be written about evolving areas of law. In truly new subject areas, such as reproductive technology, periodical literature will be the main source of information. There are also reports of the various provincial law reform commissions, as well as materials from conferences or seminars, that can be helpful.

- *Looseleaf services* include legal encyclopedias, like the *C.E.D.*, consolidated statutes or regulations, annotated statutes, and court forms or precedents. Commerce Clearing House (C.C.H.) publishes more than fifty looseleaf publications on various subject areas, such as *Canadian Labour Law Reports*, *Canadian Employment Benefits and Pension Guide*, and *Canadian Commercial Law Guide*. To determine if there is a C.C.H. volume on your subject, consult the *Rapid Finder Index*, which is published yearly. Many are now published on CD-ROM.

- *Topical law reports* are reporters containing case law on a particular topic. Some examples include *Canadian Cases on the Law of Torts*, *The Canadian Environmental Law Reports*, and *Carswell's Practice Cases*. If you know your subject area, often a topical reporter can be a great shortcut. Go to the topical reporter for your subject area and scan the index for your particular subtopic. Again, many are now published on CD-ROM.

- *Other research tools* deal specifically with words and phrases. A good legal dictionary is an invaluable tool, not only when you are a first-year law student attempting to make sense of unintelligible words or Latin phrases but also for use throughout your legal career. These dictionaries define legal words and phrases and give definitions of ordinary words and phrases that have been used and defined by courts. You may be amazed to learn that words you had thought of as obvious in their meaning (e.g., keep, or find) can mean something completely different in court. There are several leading research tools:

- *The Encyclopaedia of Words and Phrases, Legal Maxims* is a looseleaf publication that covers definitions from Canadian courts from 1825 to 1985. It is updated by cumulative supplements.
- *Words and Phrases Legally Defined* is a British publication that provides interpretation of words and phrases from the House of Lords, the Privy Council, and the superior courts of England, Canada, Australia, and New Zealand. It references cases where the words or phrase were used, and refers to *Halsbury's Laws of England* if applicable. It is updated with a cumulative supplement.
- *Stroud's Judicial Dictionary of Words and Phrases* includes references to English and Commonwealth cases and English statutes. It is updated by a cumulative supplement.
- *The Dictionary of Canadian Law*, by D.A. Dukelow and B. Nuse (1991)
- *Canadian Law Dictionary*, by J. Yogis (2nd ed. 1990)
- *The Canadian Law Dictionary*, by R.S. Vasan (1980)
- *Black's Law Dictionary*, by J.R. Nolan and J.M. Nolan-Haley (6th ed. 1990)
- *Jowitt's Dictionary of English Law*, by J. Burke (2nd ed. 1977)
- *Second Supplement to Jowitt's Dictionary of English Law*, by E. Williams (1985)
- *Osborn's Concise Law Dictionary*, by L. Rutherford and S. Bone (8th ed. 1993)
- *Mozley & Whitely's Law Dictionary*, by H.N. Mozley (11th ed. 1993)

Finally, your research project will more often than not require you to access English legal materials — a full topic in its own right. Many sources are now available on-line or in CD-ROM format. Here is a brief overview of the available sources:

- *Halsbury's Laws of England* is roughly the British equivalent to the *C.E.D.* The most recent fourth edition has fifty-two main volumes, as well as other volumes of tables and indexes. It is arranged by subject matter in numbered paragraphs, with each paragraph discussing a particular topic and providing footnoted references to statutes and case law. Relevant Canadian cases are included. As with the *C.E.D.*, each subject area begins with a detailed index of the particular areas covered.
- *Halsbury's* is updated by referring to the *Cumulative Supplement* that updates the main volumes. Cases found in the supplement and decided after 1973 are digested in the *Annual Abridgment*, which provides information on the development in the law and reference to recent periodical articles. A monthly looseleaf publication called the *Current Service* further updates the supplement. Unlike the *C.E.D.*, *Halsbury's* is a recognized authority and can and should be cited in your research.
- *The Digest* (formerly known as *The English and Empire Digest*) provides summaries of all English case law as well as that of Scotland, Ireland, Canada, Australia, New Zealand, and other Commonwealth countries. It performs a similar function to the *Abridgment*. It is updated with continuation volumes and an annual supplement.
- *All England Law Reports* cover cases reported since 1936. The *Consolidated Tables and Index* will lead you to relevant case law by subject heading or by case name. It

Figure 3 *The Canadian Abridgment*

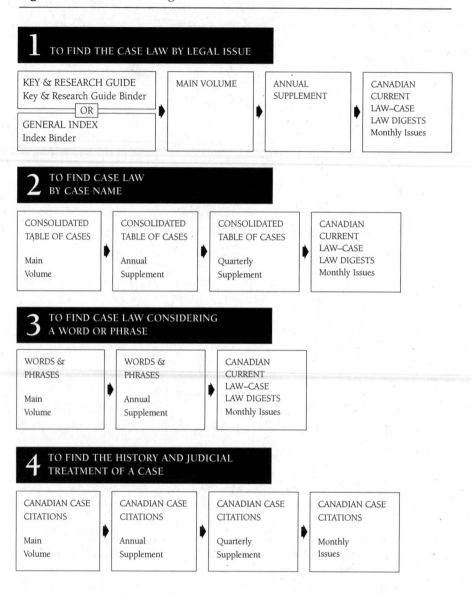

1 TO FIND THE CASE LAW BY LEGAL ISSUE

| KEY & RESEARCH GUIDE
Key & Research Guide Binder
OR
GENERAL INDEX
Index Binder | MAIN VOLUME | ANNUAL
SUPPLEMENT | CANADIAN
CURRENT
LAW–CASE
LAW DIGESTS
Monthly Issues |

2 TO FIND CASE LAW BY CASE NAME

| CONSOLIDATED
TABLE OF CASES

Main
Volume | CONSOLIDATED
TABLE OF CASES

Annual
Supplement | CONSOLIDATED
TABLE OF CASES

Quarterly
Supplement | CANADIAN
CURRENT
LAW–CASE
LAW DIGESTS
Monthly Issues |

3 TO FIND CASE LAW CONSIDERING A WORD OR PHRASE

| WORDS &
PHRASES

Main
Volume | WORDS &
PHRASES

Annual
Supplement | CANADIAN
CURRENT
LAW–CASE
LAW DIGESTS
Monthly Issues |

4 TO FIND THE HISTORY AND JUDICIAL TREATMENT OF A CASE

| CANADIAN CASE
CITATIONS

Main
Volume | CANADIAN CASE
CITATIONS

Annual
Supplement | CANADIAN CASE
CITATIONS

Quarterly
Supplement | CANADIAN CASE
CITATIONS

Monthly
Issues |

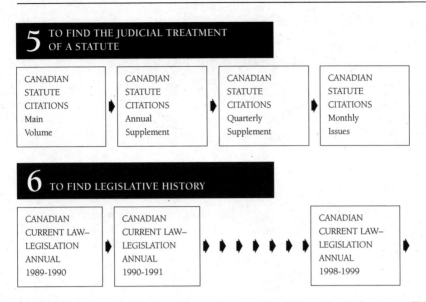

5 **TO FIND THE JUDICIAL TREATMENT OF A STATUTE**

| CANADIAN STATUTE CITATIONS Main Volume | CANADIAN STATUTE CITATIONS Annual Supplement | CANADIAN STATUTE CITATIONS Quarterly Supplement | CANADIAN STATUTE CITATIONS Monthly Issues |

6 **TO FIND LEGISLATIVE HISTORY**

| CANADIAN CURRENT LAW– LEGISLATION ANNUAL 1989-1990 | CANADIAN CURRENT LAW– LEGISLATION ANNUAL 1990-1991 | CANADIAN CURRENT LAW– LEGISLATION ANNUAL 1998-1999 |

Traces the developments in the legislative history of statutes and regulations and tracks the progress of bills from first reading to royal assent and proclamation.

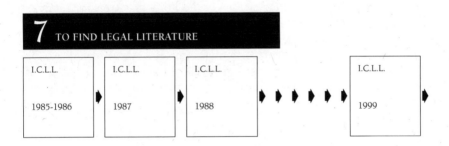

7 **TO FIND LEGAL LITERATURE**

| I.C.L.L. 1985-1986 | I.C.L.L. 1987 | I.C.L.L. 1988 | I.C.L.L. 1999 |

is updated by the annual *Cumulative Tables and Index* and the more frequent *Current Cumulative Tables and Index*. A *Canadian Supplement* lists cases which have been reported in the *All England Law Reports* and which were cited in Canadian cases.

TRACKING DOWN STATUTES

Law students soon develop a familiarity with the law reports; they can quickly locate and understand the judgments of various courts and offer a reasonably sophisticated analysis of their contents. However, they find it much more difficult to familiarize themselves with legislative sources. This distinction derives in part from the emphasis that the first-year courses place on case law, including those courses that are ostensibly organized around legislative material. Nevertheless, it does not take students long to realize that familiarity with the law reports is only part of the story; a solid grasp of the where and what of statutes is vital to their legal education. I have compiled an introduction to the arcane world of statutory literature: where to locate it; how to update it; how to track its judicial interpretation; and how to be up to date.

LOCATING STATUTES

Statutes are laid out alphabetically within the *Revised Statutes* sets. However, often the name of the statute is not readily apparent; for example, the relevant Act in Ontario for doctors, nurses, and other health professionals is called *The Regulated Health Professions Act*. If you were looking under "health," or "doctors" or "nurses," you would not find it. Therefore, it is a good idea to scan the *Table of Public Statutes* for the relevant province or Canada. If this tack fails, seek assistance from the librarian or, alternatively, search for statutes through the QUICKLAW database. The *C.E.D.* will also refer you to a relevant statute within the particular subject area. In addition, looseleaf versions, office consolidations, and annotated statutes exist for many statutes; look for these tools as well.

UPDATING STATUTES

How you update a statute will depend on whether it is a federal or a provincial statute. To update a federal statute, you should:
- Find the statute in the *Canada Statute Citator*.
- Check the green pages of the *Citator* — the *Monthly Bulletin*.
- Check the individual parts of the *Canada Gazette, Part III*; these parts are dated after the latest *Bulletin* in the *Citator*. Also, you can check the current issues of *Canadian Current Law: Legislation* dated after the latest *Bulletin* under the name of the statute in the "Progress of Bills" section.

Updating provincial statutes is somewhat different, depending on the particular province. In Ontario, for example, you should:
- Find the statute in the *Ontario Statute Citator*; amendments after the *Revised Statutes Ontario, 1990* are included.
- Check the pink pages in the *Citator* — the *Monthly Bulletin*. You can also update by looking at the latest annual volume of the *Table of Public Statutes*. This last sug-

gestion is very time-consuming, though, because you will find only a list of the amendments since the statute was introduced and you must then check each amendment individually.

- Check the "Progress of Bills" section of *Canadian Current Law: Legislation* for the period after the date in the *Citator*.

NOTING-UP STATUTES

Statute citators are available for federal statutes and for many provincial statutes. These are looseleaf services that outline the current status of a statute since the last revised versions were released. In order to note-up its interpretation in the courts, you should either use that part of the *Canadian Abridgment*, entitled *Canadian Case Citations: Statutes Judicially Considered*, or refer to the *Statute Citator* that will have the judicial treatment of statutes. However, it is current only since the last revision of the statute: 1985 for federal statutes, and 1990 for Ontario statutes.

KEEPING CURRENT

Again, checking for new Acts, recent amendments, or repeals differs for federal and for provincial statutes. For federal legislation, go to the *Canada Gazette* for third readings of Bills and search in the index. For provincial legislation, go to the *Statute Citator Weekly Bulletins*.

When working with statutes, keep in mind that many jurisdictions have an *Interpretation Act* that defines and outlines the guidelines for interpreting statutes. Remember to check the "application" section to determine whether using the *Interpretation Act* is proper. For example, the federal *Interpretation Act* specifically exempts the Crown from liability in certain areas.

A PLAN OF ACTION

Before introducing the basic steps in any research effort, it is important to tailor your research to the particular assignment you have been asked to complete. As far as first-year students are concerned, the occasions for doing research are broadly divided between essays for courses and memo or opinion writing. While the general method of research should not change, the purpose of the research will affect what you do. If you are writing an essay worth 100 percent of your mark, you should be sure to be as comprehensive and thorough as possible. However, if the essay is worth 10 to 20 percent, you will be more selective in your use of time. This does not mean that you will be less complete, but that you will budget your time to focus on the most relevant and valuable resources. You would not, for instance, look at all Commonwealth cases on the subject or read twenty-five articles. If you are given an option in a course to do a paper worth 100 percent or less than 100 percent, it is usually better to pick the 100 percent option. This same reasoning applies to course credits. The more credits you can get for a paper, the better. Once you start doing research, it is hard to do only a little to do it well: no matter what the purpose of the research is, you need to look at all the sources — to read the cases, read at least some articles, and note-up everything.

Figure 4 Legal Research Flowchart

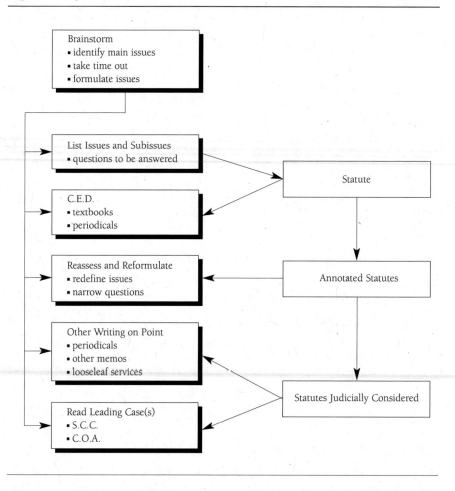

Some people brag about getting through law school without ever writing an essay; they were good at writing exams and were able to maintain an excellent academic record without doing any serious legal research. However, these same people will be adrift when they do articling or are asked to prepare law office memoranda. In the highly competitive world of law school, students will use whatever method they can to maximize their grades. But do not imagine that your avoidance of legal research will hold you in good stead in the future. Surveys show that law firms are most happy with those junior lawyers who can write well and perform effective legal research. Law school can be a place where you have some time to develop good research habits, and this skill will be valuable in the struggle to gain a competitive advantage in the rough and tumble of legal practice. Figure 4 gives a quick reference guide of the basic steps that should be followed in doing research.

The methods of doing research are as varied as the people doing it, and the results are only as good as the method used. There are four approaches that you would do well to avoid:

SUBJECT AREA DEFINED

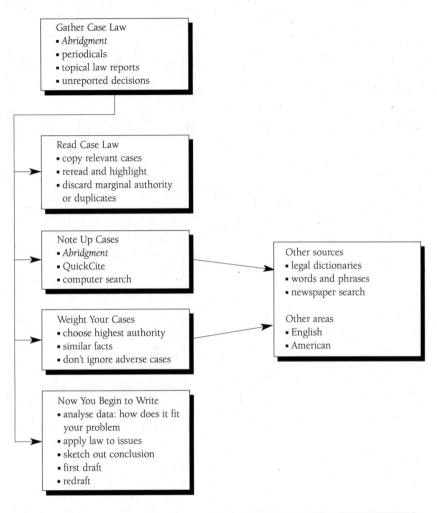

- *Search and destroy:* In this method, you find all the cases and law on the topic, read through them all, get rid of everything you think is irrelevant, and write the memo. This method may work on a one-off basis, but, as a long-term strategy, it is fraught with problems. First, there is never or rarely one topic. Even though you start out your research thinking that you have the question nailed down, invariably the question will change as you go through your research. You will find that there is a pertinent statute, even though you thought at first there was not. Under any of these scenarios, you are in the unfortunate position of having to start over because you have not kept any of the cases or other materials that you first thought were irrelevant, but that now turn out to be exactly what you need.

- *Hunt and peck:* This method is similar to "search and destroy," but is more tentative and, therefore, even less comprehensive. You find one or two cases on point, think they say what you need, and base your answer on them. However, you later realize that you have missed many other cases that are important, as your professor will tell you when you try to pass this work off as comprehensive research. You start again.

- *Blanket:* This approach is exactly what it sounds like: research with no focus and no subtlety. You find every case, every article, and every authority that ever mentioned your topic or topics, you photocopy them all, read them all, get completely confused, read them all again, and stay confused. But you know that you have to write something, so you grind out a fifty-page memorandum that includes every case or authority that you found. Your professor will not be impressed. You start over.

- *Luck of the draw:* This method is similar to "hunt and peck," but can occasionally be successful. You happen upon the most recent authority (or a recent article that canvasses the area) and use it as a basis for your memorandum (mostly plagiarizing the article you found). While your professors might initially be impressed, you run the considerable risk that they will recognize the source. You are in deep trouble. You start again, if you get the chance.

You should decide not to use any of these methods. Of course, in their place, you need not use the approach that this chapter recommends or that anyone else suggests. But whatever method you come up with, there are some fundamentals that should be included:

- *Think first and think again:* Do not put pen to paper or finger to keyboard until you have thought out the issues. Then, take a break from thinking about them and think about them again. As you think about the issues, you can make short lists of what you think the issues are. Time spent early in determining your routes will save you from unnecessary and time-wasting detours later. Even if you are convinced that you know what your issue is from the outset, think about the many and different ways it can be treated. As much time is wasted by focusing in too early on a preferred line of argument as there is in doing research that is off topic. If you have time, talk about the problem with someone else; brainstorming can produce some interesting (as well as unhelpful) directions for future research.

- *Determine the level of research:* Now that you have determined the issues, you need to decide on the level of research that you have the time or the inclination to do. There are certain things that must be done for every research project, but the scope and depth of research can be expanded or limited depending on the factors of time, knowledge, importance, and grade value. The determination of the issues should not vary regardless of any other factor. In fact, the proper determination of the issues is even more important if you have less time. You can think about the levels of research in terms of air travel: economy class is when you are pushed for time or there are few marks at stake; business class is when you have more time and more grades to shoot for; and first class is when the stakes are very high and the best is required. As you do more research, you will begin to develop your own comfort level and learn that, whereas it is something of a waste to travel first class on a short hop, it is much more reassuring on those long flights.

FURTHER READINGS

Castel, J.R. & I. Latchman. *The Practical Guide to Canadian Legal Research*. 2nd ed. Toronto: Carswell, 1996.

Cotton, B. "Advanced Legal Research and Writing: How to Build a Cadillac" (1991) 13 Advocates Quarterly 232.

Cotton, B. "Basic Research: How to Gather Raw Research Material" (1993) 15 Advocates Quarterly 332.

MacEllven, D. *Legal Research Handbook*. 4th ed. Toronto: Butterworths, 1998.

Yogis, J.A., I.M. Christie, M.J. Iosipescu & M. Deturbide. *Legal Writing and Research Manual*. 5th ed. Toronto: Butterworths, 1999.

SELECTED WEBSITES

1. General Sites
ACJNET: Access to Canada Justice — http://www.acjnet.org/
Jurist Canada — http://jurist.law.utoronto.ca
Virtual Law Library — http://www.droit.umontreal.ca/doc/biblio/en/index.html

2. Legislative Materials
ACJNET — http://www.acjnet.org/cgi-bin/legal/legal.pl?lkey=al&ckey=
Consolidated Statutes — http://canada.justice.gc.ca/loireg/index_en.html
Parliamentary Internet — http://www.parl.gc.ca/
Canada Gazette — http://canada.gc.ca/gazette/gazette_e.html
Ontario — http://209.195.107.57/en/index.html

3. Courts
S.C.C. — http://www.lexum.umontreal.ca/csc-scc/en/index.html
Federal Court — http://www.fja.gc.ca/en/cf/index.html
C. H. R. Tribunal — http://www.chrt-tcdp.gc.ca
C. H. R. Reporter — http://www.cdn-hr-reporter.ca
Alberta — http://www.albertacourts.ab.ca/
British Columbia — http://www.courts.gov.bc.ca/
Ontario — http://www.ontariocourts.on.ca/english.htm

4. Law Schools and Libraries
Canadian Law Libraries — http://www.ucalgary.ca/library/law/lawlibs.htm
Canadian Law Schools — http://www.canadalawschools.org

5. Law Firm Directories
ACJNet — http://www.acjnet.org/cgi-bin/legal/legal.pl?lkey=al&ckey=lawfirm&tkey
Canadian Law List — http://www.canadianlawlist.com

6. Law Publishers
Butterworths Canada — http://www.butterworths.ca
Canada Law Book — http://www.canadalawbook.ca/

Carswell — http://www.carswell.com
CCH — http://www.ca.cch.com
Irwin Law — http://www.irwinlaw.com
Lexis-Nexis — http://www.lexis-nexis-canada.com
Maritime Law Book — http://www.mlb.nb.ca
Quicklaw — http://www.quicklaw.com
West Publishing — http://www.westgroup.com/

7. Legal Writing Guides
Bluebook (1997-98 ed.) — http://www.law.cornell.edu/citation/citation.table.html
Legal Research and Writing — http://www.ll.georgetown.edu/lr/rs/leglwrite.html
Webster Dictionary — http://www.m-w.com/netdict.htm

Selected CD-ROM Collection
Aboriginal Land Claims British Columbia
Aboriginal Land Claims North
Bankruptcy Partner
Bibliography of Early American Law on Cd-rom
Canada Statute Service
Canadian Case Digests
Canadian Encyclopedic Digest Ontario
Canadian Statute Citations
Civil Practice Partner: Federal and Ontario
Corporate Law Partner (Federal & Ontario)
Criminal Law Partner
Employment Law Partner
Environmental Assessment: the Canadian Experience
Environmental Law Partner
Family Law Partner
For Seven Generations
Immigration Law Partner
Index to Law School Theses and Dissertations
Legaltrac
Ontario Citator Service
Securities Partner plus
Taxfind
Taxpartner
Treaties with Canada

CHAPTER 8
Stand and Deliver:
Doing a Moot

While each law student's experience of law school and legal education will differ, one of the shared experiences will nearly always be mooting. In almost all law schools, every law student is required at some point to prepare for and argue in a moot. For some students, this occurs in the first year; for others, it will be in the upper years. There will, of course, be a small number of students who relish such an opportunity and who will become part of their law school's mooting team in the many interschool, competitive moots that are scheduled each year; they enjoy the challenge of debating or public speaking and hope for a career in litigation. For many students, however, the moot looms as one of the least appetizing and most fearful requirements of their legal education; it is up there with the exams on the scale of educational torments.

This chapter is for both groups — the enthusiasts and the enlisted. For those who are thrown into a state of paralysis at the very thought of mooting, there is a thorough and simple prescription for turning "mootophobia" into a bearable and even rewarding occasion. For those eager to participate in mooting, I present a clear and concise method for developing and enhancing your mooting skills. This chapter covers the preparation, the writing of a factum, and the presentation of the oral argument. Also, a short overview of the many competitive moots that are available to eager mooters is included.

SO NICE TO MOOT YOU

Mooting consists of preparing written submissions in the form of a factum and making those arguments in an oral presentation before a mock bench of judges. Moots usually involve an appellate review of a recent and controversial case: you will be given the judgment of a lower court and expected to work up an appeal from it. It can be in any area of law. For compulsory in-school moots, the most common areas are constitutional and criminal cases. Competitive moots run the gamut of possibilities, from *Charter* cases through corporate law to Aboriginal claims. Mooters are required to do research (often extensive in competitive moots), write the factum, and make oral submissions. In most law schools, students will moot in pairs. Even if you have no intention of entering legal practice and/or becoming a litigator, this preparation gives you invaluable experience. As well as providing an opportunity to hone and test your research skills (see chapter 7), mooting gives you valuable experience in furthering your writing abilities in a specialized context (see chapter 6) and, most distinctly, it obliges students to develop the habits of oral argument and presentation — a talent you will be asked to perform in some situation or another whether you become a lawyer or enter a different profession. The experience of mooting will hold you in good stead by refining your argumentative techniques, by emphasizing the importance of stating your position succinctly, and by giving you the confidence to speak publicly.

Approached with the right attitude, mooting can be and should be a positive and, dare it be said, fun experience. It is a time when you get to present your view of how a particular case should be resolved under two unique conditions. First, there is no client to be concerned about: no one's freedom or property or money is on the line. This circumstance allows you a chance to make original and daring arguments that you would likely not try in a real case. Also, you have the luxury that your reputation or job are not at serious risk. Second, mooters often get to argue their case in front of senior judges or lawyers — an opportunity that will not come their way for many years, if ever. In the in- school compulsory moots, the most likely judges are experienced litigators; young law students, eager to make an impression on a senior associate or partner from a local firm, have a chance to shine and develop future valuable contacts. In the interschool competitive moots, students may find themselves presenting their arguments to a bench that consists of experienced judges of the various provincial courts, courts of appeal, and the Supreme Court of Canada; these judges often participated as students or young lawyers, and they feel strongly about continuing the mooting tradition and its perceived strengths. Though this prospect may seem daunting and may add to the anticipated tension of the whole mooting experience, you should not forget that the worst that can happen is that you do not win the moot. Of course, you could faint or make a fool of yourself, but this is highly improbable; if mooters have reached the final argument stages of a competitive moot, it is unlikely they will crack. As should be obvious, schmoozing is an important and effective technique in the small world of the lawyering ranks.

Many compulsory moots are based on a pass/fail basis or are worth a minimal mark of 5–10 percent of one course. The factum is usually marked separately from the oral submissions and, in some law schools, will count for a more substantial portion of the grade than the oral presentation. Whatever stories you hear about the moot itself, you can be reassured that, unless you fail to show up or to speak, you will pass. However, it is best to begin with the belief that you will not merely survive but thrive. As with all assignments and evaluation, you can do well only if you set yourself the strong ambition of succeeding rather than the weaker goal of not failing. If students begin by setting their sights on writing C papers or making C arguments, they should not be surprised when they receive C grades. To achieve an A grade, you have to set yourself an A task — usually a question of imagination and self-confidence as much as talent and insight.

One of the most helpful things to remember about a compulsory moot is that it is an ordeal that everyone must endure: all the participants will be nervous (even if they claim not to be) and, as important, they will survive. A strong sense of anxiety will be present for even the most seasoned litigators, let alone the accomplished mooter. Being nervous before such a public event is not only normal but probably necessary. Obviously, terror is not conducive to productive or competent work. If you think that your natural anxiety is beginning to run over into raw fear, you should reduce the expectations on yourself and recognize that the moot is not the make-or-break experience of your law school career. For most students, a manageable level of anxiety is more likely to precipitate action than paralysis: it will make you read and reread the cases, articles, and texts on point; it will make you write and rewrite your argument; and it will make you practise your oral argument repeatedly, but not to the obsessional extent of driving yourself and your family and friends crazy. The anxiety will be overcome by doing all the things that anxiety makes you do.

The best result will be when you put your anxiety to such good effect in your preparation that you accumulate a warranted confidence in the thoroughness of your research and the cogency of your arguments. Confidence is as important to successful mooting as the research and preparation itself. Unlike real appellate advocacy, which is for the most part won on the law (or at least the interpretation of the law by the judges), moots are more often won on style, confidence, and presentation. That does not mean that you do not need to know the law in a detailed and rigorous way. Quite the contrary — the best mooters are those who instil a genuine confidence in the judges which is based on a comprehensive grasp of the relevant law and literature. Good mooters come to believe in the soundness of their position. Not that they assume that there is no merit to the other side, but they realize that, if you cannot persuade yourself that you have a good and strong argument, it is unlikely that you will be able to persuade a neutral or sceptical judge of the validity of your arguments and position. However, in the same way that false bravado is of little use to the student mooter, so smug presumption will blind students to the inevitable weaknesses and gaps in their work. Never forget that there is little point in winning on the law, if you proceed to lose the moot. After all is said and done, mooting is a simulated exercise in persuasion and argument: victory more often goes to the rhetorically articulate than the always legally correct.

In almost all moots, you will be working with a partner. Where possible, it is important to choose your partner (or be chosen) wisely. Mooting is a team effort and it is vital that you have confidence and trust in your partner. With the right partner, student mooters can bring the best out of themselves, achieve a level of performance that is unexpected, and participate in the pleasure of a shared endeavour. From the outset, you and your partner will need to set the ground rules, coordinate your working styles, and set up realistic as well as firm deadlines. If you are assigned a partner, these ground rules are even more vital. Because both parts of the argument must be cohesive and consistent, both of you must be familiar with the argument of the other. You must work together on your approach to the problems and the theory of the case. Also, you must be able to answer a question that deals with your partner's part of the argument in at least a general way, and then advise the bench that your co-counsel will deal with that issue in more depth later. The ability to work with another lawyer and to appreciate the dynamics of professional cooperation is something that will bear size-able dividends in your future career.

BEFORE YOU SPEAK

The first step is to separate the assignment into issues and divide the issues between you and your partner. In most compulsory moots, this division is already done for you and, in some competitive moots, it may also be outlined in the materials you are given. You should approach your mooting problem cautiously: don't put pen to paper until you have spent a good deal of time brainstorming the issues. One of the advantages in mooting is that you have a partner with whom you can discuss the intricacies of the issues and the possible lines of argument. Give yourself time to let the problem percolate in your mind, and you will find that your research will end up being more focused. Also, you should set deadlines for all phases of the work; plan to meet at a specific time each week or every couple of days to discuss the progress that each of you are making. Stick to these deadlines and meetings, and you will find that the work will proceed much more effectively.

In competitive mooting, each team is usually assigned a coach and/or researcher. At some schools, these roles are taken by other students who are experienced moot-ers and are coaching for credit. In other situations, especially the more prestigious competitive moots, professors (and, occasionally, local practitioners) act as coaches or mentors. With luck, your coach will be keenly interested in mooting and will also have a background in the area of law in which you are mooting. It will be extreme-ly helpful if your coach is committed to being available on a consistent basis for advice and discussion. You should not shrink from trying to get the professor to a weekly or a regular meeting at which to discuss the progress of the project and any problems encountered. Not only will such an arrangement offer the possibility of invaluable guidance and assistance but it will compel you and your partner(s) to be prepared in a timely and effective manner.

Once responsibility for the issues has been allocated and you have brainstormed sufficiently, it is time to do some serious research. The plan of action outlined in chapter 7 will form the basis of your research. However, some provisos are worth bearing in mind.

- *Do not go off on tangents*. Unlike a research essay or a memo in which you have time and opportunity to discuss many aspects of the issues, mooting is time limited and the issues are largely predefined. Usually, you are given a maximum of twenty minutes to present your argument and, during this time, you will almost certainly be interrupted with questions from the bench. You must be able to out-line clearly and concisely what your position is and its supporting authority. You do not have time to discuss every case that ever dealt with your problem. One of the difficulties that law students frequently confront is knowing when they have done enough research and have generated sufficient information. You must be ruthless about this understandable tendency to overresearch when doing research for mooting. Of course, your work should not be slipshod or cursory. But reading too many articles or cases will serve only to confuse you. You must stop yourself when you begin to realize that you are not reading anything new or different. Make a deal with your partner at the outset that you will serve as each other's monitor. Be thorough, but do not be obsessive: reading another case is always so much easier than thinking hard about your precise arguments and presentation.

- *Go to the secondary sources first.* Start your research with secondary sources of materials rather than going directly to case law. For instance, because mooting usually involves arguing a decided case, often there will be considerable academic commentary on topic. If you are very lucky, you may even find case comments on the original appeal. Since many mooting problems are derived from split Supreme Court of Canada decisions, you can often find a hefty body of writing on the topic. Also, the rules of mooting usually limit the numbers of cases you are allowed to cite. This restriction quells the competitive nature of law students in general and mooters in particular. In this way, everybody is limited to a maximum number of cases that can be used in the factum, as well as a lesser maximum number of cases that can be cited in the oral argument. Typically, this works out to something like twenty cases being allowed for citation in the factum, and a maximum of five being for use in your oral argument.

- *Know your court.* It is important that you understand the status and standing of the moot court before which you are mooting. It will make a difference to the kind and strength of the arguments you make if you are arguing before a provincial court of appeal (in which case, you will have to defer to most decisions of the Supreme Court of Canada) or before a fictional court that stands hierarchically above the Supreme Court of Canada (in which case, you can give less binding weight to lower court decisions and do more on policy).

- *Begin writing sooner.* You might want to consider putting pen to paper or fingers to the keys sooner in preparing your moot than you might in other kinds of legal research. Because you will have limited time, starting to write will force you to give shape and focus to your arguments. Also, since the factum is made up of distinct parts, you can deal with some of the easier sections early on and get them out of the way. This is particularly true of the facts and the requested disposition of the appeal. The way in which you frame the facts will have a direct bearing on how and what you research. Remember that a moot is primarily about law, not facts; you must accept the factual findings of the trial court and work with them as best you can.

- *Consult with the other side.* One of the advantages of mooting (as opposed to actual appellate litigation) is that you have access to the arguments of the other side. You will all get better by discussing your arguments together. In competitive moots, your scores are determined by each participant's performance, and, since you do not argue against each other, you have no reason not to help each other. In a compulsory moot, however, since you know who the other side will be, you may be tempted not to help them in an effort to improve your own mark. However, since those moots are usually judged on a pass/fail basis or represent only a small percentage of your overall mark, there is no compelling reason why you should not be willing to work together. In the highly charged competitive atmosphere of law school, it is another excellent opportunity to collaborate and cooperate.

WRITING THE FACTUM

The research that you do will be put to two different but complementary uses: your oral presentation and your factum. The factum is the foremost document that is placed before the court on an appeal. Other than the cases or the other legal materials, factums are the only written documents to which the court will make reference. This important fact is not to be taken lightly. Any oral arguments that you make before the bench will have to be contained within the factum, or the bench will not entertain them; no spur-of-the-moment arguments are allowable. In many ways, writing factums is a strange assignment in law school because it is something you will only have to do "for real," if ever, many years after you leave law school. Nevertheless, the discipline and organization involved in writing factums can be of considerable value in developing the more general skills of researching, writing, and reasoning.

Because the factum is of such importance and is the cornerstone of the mooting exercise, it is usually evaluated separately in both the compulsory and the competitive moots. In compulsory moots, it is often a component of your legal writing course, which also may include writing a case brief, case comment, and legal memorandum. In competitive moots, there is usually a separate competition and prizes for the team that has written the best factum. Not surprisingly, because of the different skills involved, the best factum writers are not always the best oral advocates. It is quite common in competitive moots for different teams to win the factum and the argument sections of the competition. However, it remains the case that, if you can write an organized, concise, and comprehensive factum, you are likely to understand the issues better and be well placed to do an excellent job in the oral segment of the moot.

With this in mind, here are ten top tips for factum writing:

10. Start out by stating the facts: be accurate and concise.
 9. The facts lead to the law: know where you want to end up.
 8. Do not overdo it on the law: less is more.
 7. List your issues in order of importance: start with a winner.
 6. K.I.S.S. [Keep It Simple, Stupid]: no one will read it all.
 5. Write your issue headings in the form of questions.
 4. Each submission should be a statement of law.
 3. Think "water": clear and cool is best.
 2. Do not argue: save it for the oral.
 1. The factum should speak for itself.

Appendix C includes two factums. They are based on factums in the Wilson Moot in 2000. Although it has been partly edited down, there remains the essential features and flow of what is required. As will be obvious, it is divided into four parts and organized into consecutively numbered paragraphs:

- *Part I: Nature of the Appeal.* This section is usually found only in the appellant's factum, on the page following the cover page. Here you must state the decision from which you are appealing and restate its main findings; the text should be short and to the point.
- *Part II: Statement of Facts.* In this section, you outline the facts. Although you must take pains to be precise, you should recite the facts in a way that will enhance your case while making it difficult for the other side: highlight the neg-

atives of the other side and the positives of your own. Appellants should outline the facts, and the respondents should indicate those facts with which they agree, emphasize different slants they wish to put on the facts, and add any other facts they think are pertinent that were not mentioned. Avoid rhetorical language, but tell a compelling story that leads a court to your desired outcome.

- *Part III: Statement of the Issues and the Law.* This section forms the guts of the factum where you will lay out your arguments. At the outset, list the issues to be addressed, then proceed to deal with each issue separately and thoroughly. After having stated your answer to the issue question, provide authority for your statement. Each numbered paragraph will support your initial submission on that issue. Ideally, each paragraph will be a separate statement of authority for your position, with an appropriate citation.

- *Part IV: Order Requested.* Moot courts are not likely to pronounce a ruling on the case or indicate the relief granted: it is a mooting exercise intended to identify the better mooters. However, you must include, as a formal part of your factum, a paragraph at the end outlining the relief sought. Whereas the respondent usually asks for a general dismissal of the appeal, the appellant seeks a specific mode of relief. Generally, in competitive moots, factums are submitted anonymously. Usually, you will sign merely as counsel for the appellant or respondent. In fact, many competitions forbid any identifying marks on the factum at all, so that judging the factum can be unbiased for or against any particular school. Be sure to check the rules of your particular moot before submitting the final product. In compulsory moots, the factum is graded and is probably identified only by your examination number.

As outlined in chapter 6, good writing is clear, direct, and simple to understand. Nothing is gained and much may be lost by confronting your reader with overly long sentences, convoluted phrases, or legalistic jargon. Many factum writers fall into a bad habit of starting too many paragraphs (and too many sentences in oral argument) with "It is respectfully submitted that . . ." This cliché should be avoided, except in the concluding paragraph of each issue. In this way, the preceding paragraphs will set up the concluding paragraph. As with oral argument, the pace of your written argument is important. Some commentators suggest that you follow a three-paragraph rhythm of law-fact-argument: state the proposition of law found in the authorities that you cite; apply the proposition to the facts; and make a submission on the ruling that should be made. Throughout, you should strive to be straightforward and uncluttered. By doing so, your factum will provide a solid foundation for your oral presentation and stand a better chance of being part of a compelling and persuasive argument — which is, after all, the purpose of the exercise.

Although each side shares a similar goal and should heed the same general advice in writing its factum, it is important to remember that the appellant and the respondent have a slightly different role to play. Consequently, each side should bear the following considerations in mind:

- *Appellants:* Your factum must establish that there was an error in the judgment below and that the law compels this court to overturn the lower court finding. You must demonstrate justifiable reasons why the court should reverse the earlier finding. As the appellant, you have the advantage of framing both the facts and the issues to your advantage. The respondent does just what the name suggests: it responds to the appellant's argument. The appellant is in the driver's seat; do not waste this advantage.

- *Respondents:* The role of the respondent is to answer the argument of the appellant and outline for the court why the lower court decision should be upheld. Although the respondent's factum should follow the appellant's organization of the issues, this procedure does not mean that you answer the appellant only by denying its position. Even though the appellant has the advantage of being the underdog, you have the advantage of having a decision before the court that is in your favour. If you are able both to refute the position of the appellant and to highlight the rightness of the decision reached below, you will be in a winning position.

Even though mooting is not really about overturning or upholding anything, the judges who are listening will usually enjoy the power of pretending that they are deciding a real case. In addition, since mooting problems are frequently based on real and often controversial decisions, the judges will be keen to act out their role and imagine how they would have decided the case if they had been in on the decision. Even though the bench in a moot court will rarely give a decision on the outcome of the case, the judges will ask questions based on how they see the case.

Finally, there are a number of dos and don'ts that you should heed in planning and organizing the writing of your factum:

- Do try to control the urge to fill the factum with "the Law."
- Do not include twenty cases when five will do.
- Do include pithy and relevant short quotations.
- Do not quote lengthy passages.
- Do pick the best quotes of the best judges from the best cases.
- Do not forget that there are other courts besides the Supreme Court of Canada.
- Do cite periodical articles written by accepted experts.
- Do not be afraid to cite non-case authorities.
- Do remember that there is valuable authority in non-legal writing.

In compiling and writing your factum, do not be afraid to integrate policy arguments. The reliance by superior courts on policy and social science research is becoming increasingly common. Indeed, mooting judges will not be satisfied by exclusive reference to legal cases and doctrine. Because the moot is often imagined to be taking place in the Supreme Court of Canada or some other lofty institution, the court will want to be supplied with and have explained to it the more pertinent policy arguments that relate to this issue in hand. Most mooting cases are on novel or controversial points of law, and the judges will welcome your efforts to frame the problem in both legal and policy terms.

ORAL ARGUMENT

Now that you have completed and submitted your factum, you must prepare for the oral argument itself. While some students will approach this performance with excitement, others will be much less enthralled at the prospect. Although the oral argument is the last stage in the moot, it is the part for which you have been researching and preparing. If you have been following the advice in this chapter, you will have been thinking about your oral presentation from the outset; the oral argument should have been foremost in your mind as you researched and re-researched and as you wrote and rewrote your factum. The factum will stand on its own as the formal presentation of your position. But, while the factum will be your guide, it is the oral argument that must make it come alive for the judges. Of course, to succeed in the oral argument, you must know your factum inside and out. But you must not fall into the trap of simply regurgitating its contents by way of a stilted and flat reading. The oral argument is much more than a rehash of the factum. It presents the mooter with the opportunity to connect in a personal and immediate way with the judges. You need to bring them into the story and ensure that they see your position on the case as the one that should prevail. Above all else, your oral presentation is an exercise in persuasion; it is not a recitation of legal facts or a soliloquy of dramatic force. In its bare essentials, it is an attempt by you to tell a group of (usually) three people that they can and should rely on you to dispose of the case properly — "Listen to me and I will tell you all you need to know to decide this case in a legally compelling and policy-justified way."

All mooters must find their own technique to allow their personality to come through, while maintaining an appropriate level of formality and respect for the process. The best way to settle on a technique that works for you is to watch other experienced mooters or advocates: you can incorporate some of the approaches you like and add them to your own style. Each time you watch someone else, look at what they do that works with the judges. As you gain more experience, you will learn what works for you. While you may be impressed with someone else's mooting style, you will follow it only if you feel you can carry it off. Along with being well prepared, good mooters will work to be comfortable with both the subject matter and the manner in which they will present it. In striving to be a mooter who is composed and competent, a number of techniques are helpful for someone preparing for a first moot as well as someone with more experience. But remember that not all these tips will be useful for everyone; practice and experience will be your best guide.

- *Construct a theory of the case.* You should be able to come up with an explanation of your position that would be accessible and meaningful to another law student who has absolutely no idea of what the case or the relevant law is about. If you can describe your "theory" in two or three sentences so that anyone can understand it, you will be able to do the same with the judges. Do not assume that the judges in your moot will have expert knowledge or understanding of the case; they most likely will not. Besides, even for a well-known case or where the judge is an authority on the topic in issue, you should describe it to the bench with the specific spin that you want to put on the cases and the arguments. The theory forms the basis for your factum and ultimately for your oral argument. The clearer and simpler you can make it the better.

- *Develop an appropriate style.* Like sweaters, good mooters come in many styles. Some adopt a formal approach to the judges and the process; others choose a more relaxed approach. Mooters must decide for themselves what suits them best. The only caveat is that you should avoid extremes of either style. Try not to be so formal that you appear rigid. After all, you are not arguing a real case; there is room for some deviation from the straight-backed, stone-faced look that some older counsel affect. On the other hand, do not approach the moot as if it was a casual and informal chat. Whether a competitive or a compulsory situation, you are being judged or evaluated on your presentation. Remember that mooting is more about form than substance — moots are won as much on style as on substance. However, do not make the mistake of thinking that your dazzling wit will get you through: humour can make for welcome light relief from the heavy matters in hand, but it must be used sparingly and appropriately. You must know the case and the law, or your style will quickly be revealed as all light and little heat. So be confident, but not cocky; be assertive, but not aggressive; be persuasive, but not repetitive.

- *Talking the talk.* When you stand to deliver your argument, remember that you have about twenty minutes to convince the panel of judges that you know the case inside out, that the law is on your side, and that they must reach a judgment in your favour. You will not do that by reading your factum. One of the most common mistakes of first-time mooters is to prepare a written speech and then stand up and read it. Even if you have prepared the most compelling speech imaginable, you will lose the interest of the judges (and the moot) very quickly with this approach. In addition, they will no doubt interrupt you in an attempt to force you away from your speech, and this break will surely incite panic in the mooter unprepared for such exchanges. Better to avoid preparing a word-for-word text of your intended presentation; outline your argument in point form and have verbatim statements of essential rules or crucial quotations only. Some mooters adopt the practice of writing out a script, rehearsing it as a speech, and then reducing it to point form for the actual presentation. Do this only if you do not take the full text into the moot with you and you are able to present your argument in such a way that you don't sound as if you are delivering a speech. Finally, always follow the argument as it is presented in the factum. Provide the judges with reference points throughout as to where you are in the factum, but avoid repeating what you have provided in the factum. Remember to use quotations sparingly: only the best, and the shorter and pithier the better. It might be obvious, but:
  - Speak slowly and clearly.
  - Stop speaking if the judge interrupts.
  - Do not interrupt the judge.
  - Maintain eye contact with the judges as much as possible.
  - Smile, but do not grin/laugh/scowl.
  - Do not apologize for your position.
  - Do not misrepresent your position, your opponent's, or the law.
  - Control personal habits: pen waving, swaying, hand movements, etc.
  - If the judges are writing, slow down to let them catch up.
  - Be personable, but not personal: "I submit" or "It is our position," not "I believe" or "I think."
  - Be direct and decisive: "Our position is that" is better than "It seems to me" or "It appears that."

- *Start with a zinger.* When you first stand up to present your argument, you must get the attention of the court. They may be bored, tired, distracted, or uninterested. It is up to you to change that. You will not do it by reading your factum or launching into a disorganized but well-memorized recitation of your position. You must start out with a line that will make the court sit up and pay attention. How you do this will vary with the case, your personal style, and where you are in the speaking order. If you are first, a good way to begin is to start out with:

"My Lords, my Ladies, this case is about X."

If you are a respondent, it is especially effective to start out with a line that reiterates what the appellants have said, but turns the position to your favour:

"My Ladies, my Lords, my friend has suggested that this case is about choices. I agree, and the choices made by the appellant were the wrong ones."

In a criminal case, you can often use stronger language:

"My Lords, my Ladies, the test of a fair and just system is how it treats the least advantaged of its members. This case is an example of how that system has failed."

A mooter should be aware that overwrought rhetoric or emotion is to be avoided. But, in very serious criminal or constitutional cases, there is room for some attempt to humanize the issues. Even if the court disagrees with how you characterize the case, you will have its attention.

- *Draw a road map.* Always use a three-stage set of directions: tell the court where you are going, go there, and then tell the court where you went. This approach is the basis of any successful oral presentation because, to be able to do it, you must have organized your argument in a reasonably logical fashion; to do that, you will have had to understand it; and, if you understand it, you are halfway to making someone else understand it. Also, the judges will appreciate your efforts to draw a road map: they will be able to follow you and will know when you are almost finished. This is how you do it:

"My Ladies, my Lords, I will be making submissions on two issues; the first issue is . . . and the second issue is . . ."
"On the first issue, I have three submissions to make; they are . . ."
"My first submission is that . . ."
"Those are my submissions on first point. My second submission with respect to issue 1 is . . ."

When you complete your submissions on that issue, indicate that those are your submissions on issue 1:

"Those are my submissions on issue 1. I will now move to issue 2."

Restate issue 2 and indicate the submissions you will make under issue 2. Follow the same pattern throughout, telling the court as you go along what you are doing, when you are concluding, and when you are moving to a new point. Following this pattern also makes it easier for you to remember your own argument and, therefore, lessens the need to read from a prepared text. In addition, it allows the judges to make notes as you speak.

ANSWERING BACK

Experienced mooters view the question-and-answer exchange as the best part of the mooting experience. Although new and inexperienced mooters might feel relief that they have managed to finish their argument without any questions, this silence is not a good sign. Questions indicate that the bench is awake, aware, and interested: lack of questions probably means that you did not engage their interest or challenge their views. You most certainly should not assume that you were so persuasive and compelling that they were dumbfounded and had no answer to your arguments. The ability to answer questions clearly, concisely, and confidently is what separates the gifted mooter from the competent mooter.

So how do you develop that confidence? There is no magic formula or secret rite of passage: you acquire it in much the same way that you develop any other skill — with lots of preparation and lots of practice. There are no shortcuts. With serious and rigorous preparation, you will gain an understanding of the problem that will allow you to know the answer when the question is asked. More importantly, preparation will give you the insight into the problem in a way that will indicate what the most obvious difficulties are likely to be. As you prepare, you should be able to see where the weak points in your case are and you should assume that the judges will as well; simply hoping that they will have overlooked such matters is more wishful thinking than sound preparation. Practice will give you confidence, help settle your nerves, and allow you to develop a technique to use during tough questioning. But there are some tips to follow when faced with questions from the bench.

- *Listen to the question.* If the court interrupts you, stop talking and listen to the question. Do not interrupt the question, even if you think you know the answer. Pause after the question is completed and appear to be considering the answer, even if you know it. If you do not know the answer, this pause will give you more time to come up with something and in a less hurried fashion. One trick is to have a glass of water with you at the podium. When the bench interrupts to ask a question, stop immediately, listen, and pause when the question is completed, take a drink of water, and then respond in a clear and specific manner to the question asked. It is especially effective if you preface your response with an introduction:

"I have two points to make in response to your question, my Lady: first . . ."

This technique is truly impressive to the bench. Not only do you have an answer, but you have a structured and reasoned response.

- *Avoid asking the judges to repeat questions.* You should ask a judge to repeat a question only as a last resort if you have truly not heard or understood it. Judges do not always remember what they asked and, therefore, will be unable to repeat it. Or, worse, the judge might think that you do not know the answer and are stalling for time. If you are unsure of the meaning of the question, rephrase it as part of your answer:

  "If I understand correctly, my Lady is asking what evidence there is to show that members of the legislature put their minds to this issue ..."

  Pause here to allow the judge to correct you. If no correction is forthcoming, proceed with your prepared answer.

- *Hold your ground.* Occasionally, you will answer a question from the bench and the judges will pursue you on the point, trying to get you to change your position and come to their way of seeing the issue. Beware of this situation. You must stick to your position. The bench is not necessarily pressuring you because you are wrong, but more likely because they want to see how strong your commitment to that position really is and how well you withstand pressure. Take a "never-say-die" approach. If the bench continues to press you and you have given all the answers you have on that point, you might say:

  "I take your comment, my Lord, but I cannot help you any further on that issue."

  The only time you should ever give in on a point is if you are shown to be blatantly incorrect. For example, this might be the case if you have mischaracterized the facts of a case you are referring to or have quoted an authority incorrectly. In these instances, you should own up immediately to your mistake, apologize, and move on.

- *Avoid deflecting questions.* Often a judge will ask a question that is part of your submission later in your presentation. Beware of putting off the bench by telling them that you will be getting to that point later. If they are asking the question, it is bothering them then, and the best thing to do is answer the question when it is asked. In these circumstances, the extent of your preparation and your mooting skills will be put to the test. If you are entirely comfortable with dealing with the question immediately, run with it: answer the question fully and indicate to the court where those submissions are found in the factum. Tie in your answer to the submission you were discussing when the question was asked, and end by steering your argument back to where you were interrupted. If you choose to delay your answer in full, it must be because you truly believe the question is off topic, too distracting from the point you are making, or is dealt with in your partner's submissions. Never tell the court bluntly that you will deal with the question later. In the event that the question is off topic, give a short but relevant response and try to move on. If you do say that you will deal with the question later in your argument, give a brief but instructive response and then tell the court exactly when and where you will be dealing with it. Remember that this tactic will only work if you do return to that issue; don't get caught trying to fool the bench with a promise to return to an issue and then fail to do so. Also, it is best to remind the bench when you do get round to answering more fully their earlier question.

- *Do not steal your partner's thunder.* Where the question refers to a matter that is to be dealt with by your partner, do not put the bench off simply by telling them that your partner will deal with it later. Answer the question as best you can and tell the court that your colleague will be able to provide them with a more comprehensive discussion later. However, avoid the temptation to display the full extent of your knowledge, leaving your partner with nothing or little to say; you would not appreciate your partner doing such a thing to you, so do not do it to your partner. This scenario shows why it is so important that mooters know their partner's argument as well as their own; it also indicates that you are working together effectively as a team.

- *Do not patronize.* While you may think that the question asked is off point or that it reveals a woeful ignorance of the basic law on the topic, resist the urge to put the judges in their place: it will only be you who ends up being chastised. It is a bad move to begin your answer to any question with the words:

"That is an interesting (or difficult) point . . ."

Whether you agree or not, the judges are likely to think that their questions are interesting and they hope that they are difficult. Even if they are not, they will not want you informing them of that fact.

- *Asking questions.* Some people maintain that mooters should ask the bench at the end of their submissions if there are any questions. They usually ask:

"Those are my submissions, my Ladies. If the bench has no further questions, my colleague will now present submissions on issues 3 and 4."

This request for questions is unnecessary and somewhat patronizing. If the bench does have any questions, they will ask them; there is no need to remind them. It is preferable to conclude your remarks simply by saying:

"Those are my submissions. Thank you."

Wait a couple of seconds in case they suddenly think of a question. If there is none, sit down. Your colleague will introduce herself or himself, there is no need for you to do so.

THE COMPETITIVE MOOTS

Many moots are run competitively and on an interschool basis. The most popular and important moots are:

- The Canadian Corporate/Securities Moot is sponsored by the Toronto law firm of Davies, Ward & Beck. It is an annual competition focusing on the fields of corporate and securities law.
- The Gale Cup Moot, named after the former Chief Justice of Ontario and sponsored by the Canadian Bar Association, is held in Toronto in early March and is open to all Canadian law schools. The moot problem is usually in the area of constitutional or *Charter* issues, and is frequently criminal in nature. Also, Osgoode Hall Law School and the University of Toronto have an annual moot, involving teams of first-year law students, based on the Gale Cup problem.
- The Philip C. Jessup International Law Moot is sponsored by the International Law Students Association based in Washington, D.C.. Law schools in more than thirty countries hold national competitions. The top school or schools — Canada's top two — go to the world championships, which take place during the annual meeting of the American Society of International Law, usually held in Washington, D.C., in early April. Also, first-year law school students from Osgoode Hall, Queen's University, the University of Toronto, and the universities of Buffalo, Cornell, and Syracuse participate in an annual competition based on the problem being mooted in the Jessup Moot.
- The Laskin Moot is an annual and national bilingual competition focusing on the areas of administrative and constitutional law. It is named in honour of the former Chief Justice of Canada, Bora Laskin. Each team in the Laskin Moot must include a mooter fluent in each of Canada's official languages. The University of Toronto and McGill University compete against each other in a competition modelled after the Laskin.
- The National Aboriginal Law Moot was first held in 1993–94 and was organized by the Native Law Students Association and the Faculty of Law of the University of Toronto.
- The Niagara International Moot Court Tournament is sponsored by the Canada–United States Law Institute and focuses on international law issues. Twelve teams from Canada and the northeast United States meet annually at a different school.
- The Wilson Moot is named in honour of former Supreme Court Justice Bertha Wilson. It is sponsored by her former law firm of Osler, Hoskin & Harcourt in Toronto. The moot focuses on equality issues.

CONCLUSION

Like much else in life and law school, mooting is what you make it. Even if you are pretty clear that advocacy is not going to be your chosen vocation, you can learn a tremendous amount about research, presentation, and argumentation that will hold you in good stead in almost all legal settings. Indeed, you will particularly learn something about yourself and your response to such situations and challenges — this, of course, could be good or bad, but, either way, it should help you to make a better lawyer. Remember that a strong lawyer is not someone who has no weaknesses, but one who knows and guards against them. Also, some of the leading advocates are not the silver-tongued smoothies that television leads you to believe must be the case. The two leading advocates of their generations that I have met both had a marked stammer. It is about being effective and that depends on good research, sound organization, and situation-sense; the good mooter is the good lawyer on stage. Also, unlike in law school, you often have to go before the same judges on numerous occasions, so you are well advised to develop a court persona that is reliable and trustworthy. While the one smart trick will win you a case, it might well lose you five or six down the road.

FURTHER READINGS

Walton, K.A. *Strategies and Tactics for First-Year Law*. Larchmont, N.Y.: Emanuel Law Outlines, 1990.

William, S. & J. Walker. *A Practical Guide to Mooting*. Toronto: Emond Montgomery, 1994.

CHAPTER 9

In the Belly of the Beast: Writing Exams

There is nothing quite like law school examinations: they seem to afflict students in ways that only an imminent visit to the dentist can come close to repeating. They are both a special form of examination and a special form of legal writing. Unlike most exams to which you will be accustomed, law school examinations are not simply about memorizing large amounts of material and regurgitating them in a stylish fashion to obtain a good grade. The ability to memorize, recall, and state the information is a definite and useful talent, but the main focus of most law exams is on the practical application of that information. Having a photographic memory certainly helps, but it will get you only part of the way. Law school examinations test whether you understand the material by requiring you to use that material in an effective and cogent manner. Accordingly, knowing the course and cases backwards and forwards is a necessary but not sufficient preparation for examination success. It has to be understood that law school examinations are not a trivia quiz; they rarely test students' knowledge of the minutiae or detail of legal judgments and statutes for their own sake. As such, law school examinations are not about memory, but about issue-spotting and argument: the examination is an occasion when students are given a platform to display their ability to argue persuasively. In this way, law school examinations test the combination of skills that derive from an effective grasp of legal sources, legal reasoning, and legal writing.

No two law professors agree on much, least of all the perfect examination question or answer. Indeed, it is a mistake to imagine that there are perfect answers at all. At best, there are better and worse models of how to approach and answer examination questions. However, there are certain fundamental skills and insights that you would do well to learn if you want to succeed at law school examinations. What follows is an attempt to provide you with an appropriate context of information about examinations so that you will be able to study and write them with less anxiety and more success. First, I will introduce the broader context in which evaluation and examinations take place, and then provide a series of suggestions and tips on how to study for and write examinations. Although incorporating these techniques into your array of other studying skills will not assure you of an A standing, it will assure that you fulfil your potential and be in the top half of your class. Remember that few people fail exams; it is simply a question of how well you do.

THE BROADER CONTEXT

Before addressing the nitty-gritty of preparing for and writing exams, it is instructive to consider the general and institutional background against which law school evaluations take place. Although there are many pedagogic and educational reasons to move beyond the three-hour, 100 percent examination at the end of the course, most Canadian law schools rely on this form of evaluation as a major device for grading students. There is considerable debate around the whole question of whether there is a need for any grading at all within law schools. After all, you had to do exceptionally well to make it this far. Whereas some argue that grading systems merely pander to the legal profession in that they provide a convenient way to sort through and sift applications from prospective articling students, others maintain that some form of grading is necessary if an appropriate level of effort and learning is to be achieved by students. Nevertheless, this debate is not something that need concern students, at least not at exam time. Most law schools have a grading system and will continue to do so for the considerable future. Your challenge is to know the system and to turn that knowledge to your advantage so that you excel within it.

Although the details on any grading system will vary from law school to law school, most law schools tend to impose some kind of grade profile; that is, professors are required to grade examinations so that there is a spread of grades that generally conforms to a bell-curve in which there are a few high and low marks, but the great majority cluster around the middle. In larger law schools, where there is more than one section in each subject, some kind of profile seems particularly important to allow equity among different groups and different professors. However, it is not the existence of the profile that is usually challenged, but the particular profile that is in operation. Some law schools operate on a fixed spread of grades in which a certain number of students must be graded within each letter grade, while other law schools simply require that the overall grading of the class maintain a certain grade point average, allowing for a more flexible distribution of grades. In light of this diversity, students should inform themselves about the basic grading procedures that are in play at their own law school. Nevertheless, whatever that profile is, students should not drive themselves to distraction by complaining or arguing against the profile while they are preparing for exams. Changing the grading profile or evaluation procedures is something for another day.

Because grading by its nature is relative, all professors have to decide on the best way they can to assess the relative merits of each student's examination paper. Obviously, whatever system is adopted, there will be a considerable degree of subjectivity and personal opinion. Again, however, students will not be helping themselves by railing against this lack of objectivity. Since it is unlikely that law schools have any serious plans in the next few years of moving into an evaluation process that relies largely on multiple choice questions, students should study for exams in such a way that they are in the best position to benefit from the inescapably subjective nature of the evaluation procedure. The professor who taught you will be marking the examination, but this does not mean that you have to pander to his or her prejudices. What it does mean is that you have to be constantly aware that the style and the agenda of questions that are raised in class are likely to be the ones that interest the professor most and dominate the examination. Accordingly, students must always remember that they are never simply studying or writing an examination in torts or contracts, but are studying or writing an examination in torts by Professor Hexx and in contracts by Professor Whyy. Although there are many general proposals and guidelines for studying and writing examinations, the identity of the professor should never be far from students' minds.

There are several types of examinations that are common in law schools, and students should tailor their studying to the particular format that is to be used in a particular course. At the beginning of the course, ask the professors to make clear the particular type of examinations they will be setting. Examinations can take several different forms:

- *Closed-book examination.* This type of examination will be familiar to most students. In its purest form, students are not entitled to take any material at all into the examination room; failure to observe this rule will lead to severe punishment. However, there are some examinations where students will be provided with a case list or a table of contents for the course book once they are in the examination room. In this type of exam, greater emphasis is placed on the student's ability to memorize and recall vital information. Obviously, this slant should have an important influence on the way you prepare for an examination. A greater balance of your time will be spent memorizing large amounts of information, and greater credit will be given by the professor for the recitation of such material in the examination. While this "ambush" form of examination is less common in law schools than it used to be, it is still a fact of life for some law students, and they must develop various methods for coping with the anxiety and stress that accompanies such ordeals.

- *Open-book examination.* This type of examination is probably the most common form in modern law schools. Students are entitled to take into the examination any material they think will help them in answering the questions, although library materials are often not allowed. This system will be new to most students, though experience suggests that students generally overestimate the advantage of open-book examinations and often turn a potential advantage into an actual disadvantage. It is best to think of this privilege more as a kind of a safety valve than as a main feature of the examination process. There will be no time in the examination to do the kind of reading or preparation that should have been done before the examination. Apart from taking in your outline and course book, it is highly unlikely that you will have time to read anything else. Moreover, the student who has to engage in such further reading during the examination is already in deep trouble. Although you might wish to carry more materials into the room in case you have a panic attack or are completely bamboozled by the examination, you should be extremely selective in the material you take into an open-book examination. The student who is surrounded by a stack of books and papers is not one who is likely to fare well in the examination.

- *Term papers.* Most students will have had some experience with writing term papers. They are a staple feature of much undergraduate education, and the talent to write a sophisticated term paper is one that will hold law students in good stead in the upper years of law school. However, few first-year law courses give students the option of writing term papers. While this process is beginning to change, students should not expect that they will be able to get through law school by avoiding most open- or closed-book examinations: the option of a term paper is more of an exception than the rule. Nevertheless, some courses do allow the option of completing several small papers or one large term paper as part of the course evaluation. In deciding to pursue such an option, students should ensure that they begin such an undertaking only if they are certain that they will be able to complete it. There is nothing worse than putting in considerable work on researching a paper and deciding later on in the term that you cannot complete it. You have spent considerable time and energy in generating material that you will not be able to use effectively in an examination, and you may well have paid less attention to the course and the preparation for examinations than you needed to.

- *Take-home examination.* This type of examination is becoming an increasingly popular option in some law schools. Students are given an assignment or examination that they are required to complete within a specified amount of time, usually anywhere from twenty-four hours to a week. During that time, students are expected to complete the examination in their own time and in a place of their own choosing. Again, like the open-book exam, this option can sound more attractive than it actually is. While much of the stress of a three-hour, 100 percent examination is avoided, it can be replaced by the extended anxiety of having to worry about the examination for a period that is much longer than three hours. It is essential in writing take-home examinations that students still prepare thoroughly for the examination and organize their time effectively during the take-home period. Also, because students are given considerable time to reflect on the examination and, in some circumstances, to research the questions, professors will likely expect a much higher standard of performance. At a minimum, they will expect that the answers will be presented in a much more sophisticated and organized fashion.

A comment needs to be made about how professors grade papers. Apart from the vaunted (and mythical) "staircase method," they tend to adopt one of two approaches. Some professors use a marking sheet and preassign a certain number of marks to the spotting and handling of particular issues: at the end of the grading, they simply add up the marks that each paper has earned, place them in ascending order, and impose the profile on those numerical marks. Other professors take a more general and impressionistic approach: they read answers or whole examinations generally and sort the papers according to their relative merit. In both cases, it is likely that professors will begin by reading several examination answers to get a sense of the overall response, and they will likely return to several examination answers at the end to ensure that they have been consistent.

Finally, it is fair to assume that most professors take no satisfaction in failing people or handing out poor grades; they are usually prepared to give students the benefit of the doubt in most matters of judgment or interpretation. The days of Kingsfield and *The Paper Chase*, if they ever really existed in Canada, are long gone. Indeed, most professors go out of their way to find and assign marks; they take their responsibility very seriously. In some ways, the profile works in your favour because it means that you can safely assume that everyone begins at the mid-point (usually some sort of B) and a few are moved up or down to meet the profile. Accordingly, you should forget about getting above the fail-line and concentrate more on how to get out of the Bs — it is hard to do well if you are constantly looking back over your shoulder at dreaded Ds rather than looking ahead to the allure of the As.

STUDYING FOR EXAMINATIONS

There are a host of different suggestions on how best to prepare yourself for a law examination; much will depend on your own particular disposition and habits. Nevertheless, we can list some sensible guidelines.

- *Know your professor.* Although there are some basic guidelines that you can develop in studying for exams, remember that you are not studying generally but for a particular examination in a particular subject by a particular professor. Each professor has her or his own method of teaching, understanding the law, and setting examinations, and the same professor who is teaching the course will also be setting and grading the examination. The agenda of issues and questions that are raised and aired in the course are likely to feature predominately in the examination. As well as attending class regularly, you are well advised to track down any of the professor's publications on the subject being studied. There is no need to pore over these publications; it is enough to get the general drift and direction of the professor's ideas and thinking. Also, having got a fix on the professor's particular slant, there is no need to pander brazenly to those views; most professors are suspicious of students who convert to the professor's way of thinking for the duration of the course. The reason for informing yourself about these matters is that you will be better able to sense what is likely to appear on the examination and what kind of discussion the professor will find impressive. Your professor will be looking for proof that you listened, thought about the issues, formulated a position, and are able to explain why you have come to that position. Regardless of whether your position mimics that of the professor, you must be able to identify issues, recognize the law that applies, apply the particular law to the facts in question, and come up with a cogent and well-reasoned conclusion. However, be careful: some professors talk a policy line or ramble on in class, but like to see a traditional form of examination answer. Again, you must read their previous exams to guard against surprise — forewarned is forearmed.
- *Obtain copies of the professor's previous examinations.* Reviewing past exam papers is the first step to take in studying for any examination. Such review is of course difficult in the case of young professors or professors who are new to a particular course. Students are fully within their rights, however, to approach such professors to obtain some indication of the format and style of the coming examination. Most professors are predictable in both the form and the substance of their examination. While they will not recycle exactly the same set of questions from

year to year, they will pursue new variations on old and established themes. As well as studying their previous examinations, students should approach professors for copies of any model answers they may have or for students' past examination answers that the professor thought impressive. Accordingly, students should always be studying for examinations with a copy of old examinations in front of them. And, if in doubt, simply ask your professor — How many questions will there be on the exam? How many questions will we have to answer? What are the time restraints for each question? What exactly can we bring in to the exam? How do you want cases cited? Do you have any formatting preferences, such as single or double spacing? and How do you distinguish between an excellent exam and a good exam?

- *Study all and only the relevant material.* Students should study not only in the right way but also the right material. Before beginning serious preparation for the examination, you must ensure that you understand precisely the material to be covered so that you do not waste your time studying the material that will not be on the examination. After ascertaining the material to be studied, you must set yourself an appropriate task. Remember, the learning of large amounts of legal information is not an achievement in itself, but simply a necessary means to achieving the more important end of knowing how to apply that material in particular fact situations. You should never lose sight of the fact that you are only part of the way to success when you learn and understand the cases and the materials; the final and most important part of your journey is to develop the ability to apply the information you have learned in an effective and persuasive manner.

- *Obtain a good summary.* A major focus of your studying will be a summary. There are many different views on how to assemble a good summary (see chapter 4). The most important thing to remember is that a list of cases does not amount to a summary. The best summaries are those that not only contain all the relevant cases and issues but are able to synthesize and integrate these cases and issues in relation to each other. As should be obvious by now, be careful about obtaining a summary on criminal law if it is not a summary that derives from a course taught by the professor who is teaching you. Also, the most important and helpful part of a summary is in the act of assembling it, rather than in the finished product; it is in this process that you will do your most important learning. It is worth paying great attention to producing a good summary because it will be extremely difficult to obtain an A grade from a C summary.

- *Decide whether to be in a study group or not.* This issue causes fledgling law students particular concern: is it best to study independently or to become part of a study group? Any decision will depend on students' own judgment about their personality and peculiarities; some students thrive in a gregarious environment, while others do their best work alone. However, there is no reason why students cannot effect a judicious and personalized blend of the two. In the same way that there is little to be gained from joining a study group on the basis that someone else will do all the work for you, there is also no logic in believing that other students have nothing to contribute to your own knowledge or understanding. Accordingly, students should effect a balance between working on their own and meeting in a group. A study group is particularly good for going over problems and ironing out particular difficulties; one student's strength is likely to be another student's weakness. By working in a team, you will find reassurance that you are on the right track. Also, most students find that their study group doubles as a social focus for relaxation and fun.

Most students' success or failure will depend as much on what they do before the examination as on what they do during the examination itself. Because you will be asked to apply your legal knowledge, you can devise and plan certain strategies in light of expected questions. For instance, you can write a short draft of a couple of sentences on particularly difficult or conflicted areas of law so that, should these topics arise in the examination, you have already done some of the initial spade work; you will not only save time, but ensure that your examination answer is more polished and professional. You can even draft an answer to possible essay or policy questions. Of course, you should ensure that you use such preparation selectively; there is little point in deciding to include certain ideas or information before you have even seen the actual examination. However, many students realize after the examination that they could have done much more by way of detailed and direct preparation before the examination.

In some ideal world, students would be best advised to have completed their studying a couple of days before the examination; they can then take this period of time to relax, refresh themselves, and put themselves into a positive frame of mind to sit the examination. Needless to say, most law students (and law professors) do not live in anything approaching an ideal world: there is always too much to be done in too little time with too little energy. Nevertheless, there is little point in having spent many days and hours studying for an examination, only to arrive at the actual examination in a fraught and fatigued state. In seeking to amass as much information as possible, students ignore the psychological side of exam preparation. Getting yourself into the right frame of mind to perform well is something that deserves your attention, and you should think ahead about how you might realistically spend the evening and hours before the examination. From past experience, students should begin to realize that they may need to develop certain coping techniques to deal with their anxiety: talking or not talking with other students, eating or not eating, dressing or not dressing in a particular way. It would be a pity to waste all your hard work by failing to take a few moments to psyche yourself up (or down) appropriately for the examination.

So what's my best advice? Try to approach the exam as you would any other performance event — try to get a good night's sleep and get yourself in the right zone. You want to sleep well a couple of days before the exam because you probably won't sleep too well the night before with all the adrenaline and anxiety. Set two alarms and get up early enough to eat a healthy breakfast — your mum or dad was right about the need for something nutritious to get you through the day. But don't eat too much or drink too much coffee before the exam; you will be wired enough and don't need to be rushing out to the bathroom constantly. After the exam, it is probably best not to discuss how you did on the exam or ask others how they did. Try to forget about the exam you just took and study for the next one. And take a time-out; you deserve to spoil yourself and the break will benefit you. But don't get completely wasted until after your last exam!

WRITING THE EXAMINATION

Few students enter an examination without some level of anxiety or nervousness. Indeed, most people need a certain level of anxiety to produce their best performance. Although it will be difficult, you should resist the temptation to hit the exam with your pen in motion; some examinations prohibit writing in the first half-hour or so. While some people may need to write a little something to settle their nerves, it is a mistake to begin writing without a fairly definite sense of where you are heading. Some professors suggest that you spend up to half the allotted time for each question preparing your answer before you begin writing. For many students, this proportion will seem excessive and will only induce even greater anxiety. Nevertheless, it does seem good advice to take about one-third of the time available to plot and plan your answer. For those students who are tempted to spend longer, you should not forget that it is your answer for which you will be evaluated, and not the preparatory notes and planning; outlines are not answers.

As with any piece of good legal writing (see chapter 6), you must be clear in your mind about the audience to be addressed in completing your answer. When it comes to writing examinations, this is a very tricky issue. While you are obviously writing for the particular professor, you should not assume that the professor knows the answer to the problem and, therefore, engage in a discussion that touches only the basic material and concentrates on the more fascinating or peripheral issues. You should engage in the somewhat artificial posture of thinking of the professor as a sophisticated lawyer, but one who does not know about the particular doctrine or rules in question. Although it may seem odd, you are best advised to imagine your professor with a temporary case of amnesia; assume that she has forgotten large areas of the law and is in need of your prompting and direction. To do otherwise is to risk missing some of the more basic points and, therefore, failing to capture the lion's share of the marks on offer.

THE HYPOTHETICAL

The stock question in a first-year law examination is the hypothetical fact situation. The student is presented with a rambling and often bizarre set of facts and controversies to analyze in terms of the relevant law and policy. It is essential that you do not "fight the hypothetical." No matter how unlikely or ludicrous the facts may be, you must simply go about your work and take them seriously. Whether the facts can be proven by appropriate evidence is not your concern, unless you are involved in an examination on Evidence. You are to answer what you are asked, and not answer what you are not asked; you should not pose different sets of facts to answer, and you should not address matters that the facts do not raise. Furthermore, there is no need to cover ground that is to be assumed. For instance, if a person is described as acting carelessly, there is little reason in a Tort examination to proceed to discuss the standard of care, although there might well be a reason to discuss the state of mind required in a Criminal Law examination. Furthermore, if legally important facts are omitted from a hypothetical, you will be required to canvass the likely possibilities and to show their effect on your legal analysis. However, most questions will include more than enough information; it is the red herrings for which you should be on the lookout.

In grappling with these hypotheticals, you should not work from the assumption that there is only one correct and uniform answer to the problem. In most circumstances, the hypothetical will have been constructed in such a way that it addresses an area of law that is still open or conflicted. However, some answers and some issues are less open to differing analysis than others, particularly in the eyes of particular professors. You should remember that the point of the exercise is to write a good examination answer; it is not to treat the hypothetical as though it were a real instance in real life. The professor is not concerned with an answer to the hypothetical for its own sake. The hypothetical is a vehicle through which the professor wants you to address certain important legal issues. A good strategy is to work back from the hypothetical to the legal issues that the professor wanted addressed and around which she or he decided to construct the hypothetical. In this way, you will be more likely to concentrate on the more pressing and central issues. And remember that you are being asked these questions as a lawyer, not a historian, social scientist, or political philosopher. Only approach an exam question from a non-law perspective if you are directly asked to do that, which will be very rare.

It is alarming how many students fail to read the examination properly. While this reaction may be a matter of nerves, there is no excuse for not having read the questions and the instructions thoroughly. After reading the general instructions at the beginning of the examination so that you know how many questions to answer and in what way, you should try to read through the whole of the examination. Once you have the general picture of the overall examination, you can begin to focus on particular questions or parts of a question. As you reread the questions, you should highlight the main issues and write notes on how to address them. Before beginning to provide an organized outline of your answer, you must check that you are answering the question asked. You may be asked to discuss a problem generally or to advise a particular party. In either case, ensure that you do what is requested, and not address a question of your own making. If you are asked to advise one particular party, it does not mean that you are to canvass only those arguments that favour that party: the best answer is the one that deals with all the viable arguments and counterarguments to the most rigorous and searching extent. While you should raise all arguments, you should not spend time on those that are simply losers or entirely marginal — go for the main course, not the crumbs. Always weigh relative strength or weakness of the arguments you raise. In other words, you should evaluate the arguments you raise and allot your time accordingly.

FORMAT

Most students enter the examination with a similar knowledge base. Although it will be cold comfort to many, what separates students often is their ability to present what they know in an organized manner. Indeed, the ability to write an organized answer is the key to doing not only well but exceptionally well: it is an ability that is most often respected in its breach. Too often, students happen to begin on one page and happen to come to an equally unexpected halt a few pages later, and in between there is a jumble of issues and answers. This kind of kitchen-sink approach is the best way to obtain a poor mark. Also, while the questions in one examination may raise issues that are relevant to other courses, you should restrict your answer to materials in the course for which the examination is set. There is no need to treat each issue equally; a good examination answer will weight the discussion of particular issues according to their importance and difficulty. In organizing your answer, you would do well to follow the following format:

- *Issues:* Introduce the main issues to be covered so that the examiner, should he start to get lost, will at least have some rudimentary road map to guide him.
- *Law:* Provide a tidy and focused analysis and counteranalysis of the relevant rules, principles, and policy.
- *Application:* Relate the law to the particular facts of the hypothetical in such a way that it touches the most important issues in the problem.
- *Conclusion:* Tie together your legal analysis and your factual application in a decisive but not dogmatic fashion in response to the particular question you have been asked.

Not everyone is a fan of the ILAC method. Indeed, two co-authors insist that they can "never recall seeing an exam answer organized around this so-called method that merited a grade higher than a C-plus." Their opposition is cautionary, but it is not fatal to the ILAC approach. The method is only offered as a basic schema that is often more honoured in the breach than in the observance. Certainly, do not structure your presentation around a mechanical ILAC format by using subheadings in which you repeatedly label portions of your discussion issue, rule, application, and conclusion. Like most rudimentary tools, it becomes less useful and more limiting as its user develops more subtle and sophisticated skills. At the root of its limited value is the point that all but the most formalist professors concede; namely, that it operates on the unstated (and indefensible) assumption that there is one "rule" and one way to "apply" it once an "issue" is spotted. On the contrary, there is not only often more than one rule, application and issue, but also there is more than one way to state those rules, applications, and issues. That is why I prefer to call it ILAC rather than IRAC as many do — talk of Law generally is better than Rule specifically. The mistake is to believe that it is possible to squeeze any question, no matter what size or shape, into the ILAC's four-step rhythm. The two most serious defects of ILAC are based on two competing observations about good exam-writing — that different kinds of questions call for different kinds of answers and that a simple formula is no substitute for a careful analysis. Accordingly, treat ILAC as a beginning tool. Much like trainer wheels on your first bike, it gets you started. When you get the hang of things, you will have little use for it.

As many of your high school math teachers probably told you, it is not the bottom-line that is the most important part of your answer, but the way you arrived at and reasoned your way to the answer. This axiom is particularly true of law school examinations. The professor is not simply interested in a set of legal conclusions; it is the argument and the law that support those conclusions that will be of most interest and that will gain most marks. Although a few professors take a different tack, most expect students to support their arguments by reference to legal cases, rules, and principles. There is no need to provide a full or cited reference to a case, but it is best to mention any cases on which you are relying. Further, in organizing your answer, remember that professors will be awarding grades on three general bases: coverage (a list of issues and matters that you should spot and answer); knowledge (a sophisticated and detailed knowledge of the law as required by the particular issues); and application (applying the law to the facts in a persuasive manner).

TIMING

It is vital that you organize your time effectively. If there is one error that students make that is entirely avoidable and that has the most unforgiving consequences, it is the failure to stick with the recommended time allocation for each question. The professor will expect an answer whose sophistication and detail will vary in accordance with the time allotted for each particular question. There is little point in spending more time than is necessary on one question because this will only disadvantage you on later questions. It is a miscalculation to believe that the extra minutes spent on perfecting one answer are better spent than using that same amount of time on beginning a new answer: it is always easier to get the first few marks for an answer than the last few. There is no point in adding a few more swirls to the icing on one cake if you have no time to mix the batter for the next cake. An examination is a test of your ability against the clock; the sooner you understand and accept that fact, the better.

Although there is never enough time to plan or write as much or as well as you want, it is important that you cover a healthy extent of empty paper. The quality of the answer is what counts, but it would be wrong to assume that quantity does not also have some importance. If your answer is too brief, it is unlikely that you will have discussed all the important points as thoroughly as required. Consequently, mindful that legibility is always a great asset, students are well advised to develop a speed of writing that enables them to produce a reasonable number of pages in a short time: few marks are awarded for what might have been if the student had a little more time or could have written a little faster. The difference between good and not-so-good grades is smaller than most students (and professors) realize or care to believe. No marks are given for simply filling the page with gibberish, but you cannot receive any marks unless you write something. So, even in those situations where you are not sure what you are being asked (or you are sure that you do not know what it is you are being asked), it is better to write something rather than nothing. Also, you should write as clearly as possible — professors are not well disposed to students whose writing is barely decipherable.

Finally, most examinations are graded on an anonymous basis. Anonymity ensures that you receive fair treatment, and it protects professors from allegations of favouritism. Most law schools and professors take a dim view of students who try to communicate their identity to the examining professor by some characteristic remark or familiar anecdote. Moreover, students work from the dubious assumption that by identifying themselves they will somehow do better: the opposite might well be true! Also, it is best to avoid the "Merry Xmas" or "I really loved your course" ending.

ON THE CAT WALK

In the same way that law is a craft, studying and writing law school examinations are skills that improve only with practice. Once you have located some previous examinations by your professors, set aside some time and do a few practice runs. It is, of course, most beneficial to practice under near examination conditions; to do otherwise is to defeat the purpose of the whole exercise. Some professors can be prevailed upon to look over your answers and give you an idea of the quality of your answers. You can ask your friends or members of your study group to "grade" them. Indeed, getting some practice at "grading" examinations is one way to put yourself in the position of the examiner and thereby to learn further insights about what goes into a good examination answer.

To get you going and to give you something to work with, Appendix D includes two examples or "model answers" around which you can begin to formulate your own approach and to develop your own style of writing examination answers. The questions come from first-year examinations in Torts and Civil Procedure in 1999. These examples are not put forward as perfect answers, but they are good answers to questions set on the material that was covered in class: they are done by students who were awarded an A on the exam. You could do much worse than follow the framework and flow of those answers.

Here are some valuable do's and don'ts that you might consider —

You should
Prewrite some standard accounts on key topics and hot cases.
Eat and sleep well.
Read the Instructions carefully — and then read them again.
Leave space at the beginning to write your introduction after you've finished your answer.
Cover all issues.
Answer the actual question asked, not something like it.
State any assumptions that you make.
Leave your prejudices and hobby-horses at home.
Write legibly.
Be analytical, not conclusory.

You should not
Restate facts — few marks are awarded for transcription.
Repeat yourself — time and space are too tight.
Waste time on the perfect outline — you rarely get credit for an outline.
Answer the question that you would like to have seen on the exam.
Identify yourself or ingratiate yourself — it hurts, not helps.
Bullshit, except as an absolute last resort.

CONCLUSION

The end of examinations is, of course, a time of celebrations. All work and no play will make law students an even duller lot than they might already be. However, once you have duly celebrated and recovered from the shock of examinations, you must begin to steel yourself for the ensuing results. Although it would be silly and insulting to suggest that examination results are not significant, it is also important to remind students that their results in the first term of first year of law school are not the deciding factor of their legal career. Many students take time to find their feet, and this delay will often be reflected in what they consider to be a disappointing set of first-term examination results. Many extremely successful lawyers and even prize-winning law students have begun their legal careers in less than stellar fashion. The most important thing is not to be dispirited by less than excellent results.

The real sin is not in making mistakes, but in failing to learn from your mistakes. Most professors provide an opportunity for feedback on the examination. Apart from providing a general session in which they go over the examination, professors are often obliged by school rules to see those students who request an individual opportunity to go over their examination. The students are well advised to take advantage of this chance whether they have done well or poorly. It is just as important to discover why you did well as to discover why you did badly. You will soon realize that the difficulties of exam writing are not all they are cracked up to be. They are not the brick wall that they are often portrayed to be, but a series of obstacles that get lower and lower as your ability to jump them gets better and better. Like everything else, it is the fact of working in the dark that is the killer, not the exam itself. Hopefully, this chapter has shed a little light.

FURTHER READINGS

Emanuel, S. *Some Thoughts about the First-Year of Law School*. Larchmont, N.Y.: Emanuel Law Outlines, 1991.

Neumann, R. *Legal Reasoning and Legal Writing*, 2nd ed. Boston: Little, Brown, 1994.

Roth, G. *Slaying the Law School Dragon: How to Survive and Thrive in First-Year Law School*, 2nd ed. New York: John Wiley & Sons, 1991.

Paul, J. & M. Fischl, *Getting to Maybe: How to Excel on Law School Exams*. Durham, N.C.: Carolina Academic Press, 1999.

Walton, K. *First-Year Law: Learn the Secrets of Top Exam Performance*. Larchmont, N.Y.: Emanuel Law Outlines, 1990.

CHAPTER 10

Is There Life After Law School?
Articling, Lawyering, and
Other Possibilities

You have negotiated the travails of law school and come through better and wiser: What next? How can you or should you deploy the skills and qualifications you have acquired? There are, of course, many answers and responses. An LL.B. comes with no guarantees of fame or fortune, happiness or security, wisdom or judgment. There are so many ways in which you can put your law degree to work. The most obvious and frequent is to enter into the private practice of law. But there are also other paths to travel — government, politics, business, social advocacy, to name a few. Most students usually take the step of qualifying for the Bar, so that they at least have the option to become a practising lawyer. Nevertheless, you must resist the temptation to remain on the conveyor belt that tends to run from law schools to large urban firms. It is the easy thing to do, but it is not the right or the best thing for everyone. Rather than decide by default, you owe it to yourself to make a positive and informed resolution about your future career.

In this final chapter, I explore some of the possibilities and challenges that will present themselves to you after law school. After surveying the basic structure of the legal profession, there is an account of what articling is like and how to get an articling position. Next, I provide a brief glimpse at the prospects and possibilities for employment in private practice and elsewhere. Finally, there is an introduction to the ethical dimension of lawyering. Calling into question the traditional approaches, I suggest a different and more suitable style of lawyering. If you know some of these matters at the beginning of your law school career, you will have a broader context both for your studies and for law school in general.

GOING TO THE BAR

Lawyers in Canada are part of a joint profession. Students are called to the bar as solicitors and as barristers. This distinction between those who do and those who do not litigate as advocates in court is traceable to the English profession, which remains split, with very different entry requirements and training for barristers and for solicitors. Although there is a de facto split in the Canadian profession, with a small group of lawyers dominating the litigation process, there is still a much greater and healthier shifting between roles; many general practitioners do a small amount of court work. Moreover, there is no such entity as *the lawyer*, a fungible professional model that can stand in for and represent the rest of the profession. There are many different kinds of lawyers and ways of lawyering — small firms, large firms, sole practitioners, urban practices, rural practices, generalist firms, specialist firms, female firms, ethnic firms, and so on.

All provinces have a governing body that is controlled by lawyers and that has a monopoly over the certification and discipline of lawyers. Although the requirements for call to the bar vary slightly from province to province, the basic pattern is that all students must possess a law degree from an accredited law school. In the case of foreign-trained or overseas lawyers, they must have their credentials validated by the Joint Committee on Accreditation in Ottawa; such accreditation will often entail foreign lawyers being required to do some studies at a Canadian law school before they can proceed to the more professional phase of qualification. After successfully completing a law degree, students must fulfil a period of articling or apprenticeship with a lawyer and some combination of course work and examinations in subjects such as business, corporate, family, tax, and criminal law. The post-LL.B. bar admission requirements across Canada are set out in table 2., although changes are afoot in some provinces.

Table 2 Bar Admission Requirements

Jurisdiction	Articles	Course work	Examinations
Newfoundland	12 months	6 weeks (3 in November and 3 in February)	Exams after each 3-week course
Nova Scotia	10 months	2 months	Exams at end of course
New Brunswick	44 weeks	8 weeks broken up into four 2-week sessions	Exams after each course session
Prince Edward Island	12 months	8 weeks (1 week in PEI and 7 in NS)	Exam after PEI session
Ontario	52 weeks	1 month prior to articles and $3\frac{1}{2}$ months after articling	9 exams during the $3\frac{1}{2}$-month course
Manitoba	50 weeks	Courses attended each Friday from mid-August to mid-April	Exams following each Friday course
Alberta	12 months	1 month in July/August 1 weekend in November 4 weeks in May	Exams after May courses
Saskatchewan	12 months	2 weeks in July & August 6 weeks in January, February, & March	Exams in March
British Columbia	9 months	10 weeks	2 exams
Yukon	12 months	British Columbia course	2 exams
Northwest Territories	12 months	Alberta course	Exams in March

ARTICLING

All provinces require a period of articles; it is only the length that varies. Of course, articling has a long and illustrious pedigree that harks back to the aristocratic aspirations and affectations of the English legal profession. For barristers, a formalized version of the traditional apprenticeship still applies today; solicitors follow less archaic rites of initiation into the secrets of the law. In Canada, while the aristocratic air is gone, the practice of training for hierarchy remains.

AN ENDANGERED EXPERIENCE

Articling is a largely unstructured affair in which students are supposed to learn more by osmosis than education, and to prove their mettle under the pressure of deadlines rather than to acquire professional values and skills. Not surprisingly, the rap on articling is mixed. On some days, it is about being a lackey for the boss — getting the coffee, picking up dry cleaning, endless photocopying, and a whole series of "joe jobs." On other days, it is about being in over one's head — drafting contracts, fighting motions, interviewing witnesses, and doing other complicated tasks on your own. Today, there is nothing to do; tomorrow, you are pulling an all-nighter. Articling is an emotional roller-coaster of a year in which you are struggling to get by, get on, and get used to working for a living. Your colleagues are your best friends and your fiercest competitors. It is excitement, insecurity, fear, loathing, and relief — the best and the worst of times. As one student put it, "it beats indentured servitude: but only just."

While there is a vast variety of experience, articling remains too much a rite of passage and not enough a period of instruction. For the lucky few, articling may be gruelling, but the remuneration is high and the training can often be exacting. In large urban firms, an articling salary is over $50,000 plus generous benefits, with the allure of considerably more to follow. However, for many others, articling is something to be endured rather than relished. And, for a growing number on the outside looking in, there is no opportunity to form any opinion at all. In Ontario, at the mid-point in any year, there can be up to as high as 20 percent of those who registered for the bar exams still without an articling position. And, of those who find articles and proceed to being called, as many as 30 percent still might not have a job as a lawyer. At the same time, the national unemployment figure stood at 11 percent.

One response of Ontario's Law Society was to encourage law firms to take an extra articling student for free. This intervention received mixed reviews and was soon nixed by the Law Society. For some, this kind of initiative speaks not only to the failure of the articling process but more generally to the parlous elitism of the legal profession; it is a twentieth-century job with nineteenth-century trappings. Among Ontario's so-called equity students (visible minorities, Aboriginals, and people with disabilities), almost a third have sometimes been unable to secure an articling position. Moreover, these figures do not take into account discrimination against parents, particularly women and single mothers, and openly gay and lesbian students. Although the economic climate is bright, articling remains a process in crisis. After many years of education and accumulated debts, students have a qualification recognized only by a profession they cannot enter. And, even when they do obtain articles, the quality of that experience is decidedly mixed.

Many provincial law societies are in the almost perpetual throes of re-evaluating and reorganizing their post-LL.B. entrance requirements. Most changes tend to be modest and limited rather than radical and structural: possible alternatives being considered include the introduction of some kind of provisional or restrictive licence that might limit work that is not done under supervision. However, many contend that, following opening gambits in Australia, South Africa, and England, more radical changes in the organization and training of the legal profession need to be countenanced. Instead of exploring partial responses, such as shared articles or restricting the number of students admitted to law school, the abolition of articles altogether deserves to be taken more seriously. Overcoming its natural reluctance for major upheavals, the profession needs to ask whose interests articles serve, and whether established interests are being put ahead of those of young lawyers and unrepresented clients?

If articles were to be abolished, entry to the legal profession would be open to those law school graduates who had attended a short and compulsory Law Society course. The focus of this course would not be a return trip to a core selection of substantive subjects: most students have done them, and many have no intention of practising in those fields. Instead, emphasis would be put on the acquisition of practical skills, professional values, and business basics. It is not more law that students need, but a greater grasp of working techniques and ethical responsibilities. This reform would bring Canada more in line with the experience and practice of the United States. Although once a requirement for admission to the bar, only two states — Delaware and Vermont — still require law graduates to serve a six-month apprenticeship. The bulk of states abolished articles because the experience was not only difficult to monitor but its quality varied enormously and, in some instances, amounted to "a form of near-peonage." Bar exams are taken directly after law school and require no attendance at the equivalent of Law Society courses. Once completed, the freshly minted lawyers are free to hang out their shingles and take on clients. Ironically, in 1992, an American Bar Association Task Force on legal education and professional development (the MacCrate Report) recommended that some changes had to be made. Although largely unheeded, it proposed that professional training reflect the fact that the acquisition of lawyering skills and values was a continuing process throughout lawyers' careers.

This shift away from a once-and-for-all initiation into the legal profession to a continuing responsibility to maintain and re-learn the lawyering craft seems to be a substantial step in the right direction. Law societies are beginning to recognize that new law school graduates are no more of a threat to the public than old practitioners who have not bothered to inform themselves about changes in the substantive law or in lawyering techniques: it is not inexperience that is the only or major source of lawyer malpractice. As a *quid pro quo* for abolishing articles, lawyers would be required to attend annual professional courses devoted to substantive updates and fresh skills training. In some areas of practice, it might be thought appropriate to place some limited restrictions on what can be done; these curbs can be removed after a period of years spent practising and taking appropriate professional courses. However, the main aim would be to ensure that lawyers understood that a call to the Bar was a privilege that had to be constantly re-earned in order to maintain good professional standing.

Not everyone believes that the abolition of articling is the best way to go. Some lawyers maintain that such a reform does not address the main issue. If lack of jobs is the problem and discrimination is the disease, abolishing articles is not the solution. Insofar as there is discrimination in the legal profession (and the statistics on unplaced students strongly support this conclusion), some believe that it will not be resolved by discreet alterations in the articling process: the problem is much deeper, with a root-and-branch transformation in lawyers' attitudes and practices being required. Although there may be an increasing number of lawyers in a crowded market, there are still insufficient accessible lawyers for those impoverished and disaffected people who are most in need of help and support. As long as present arrangements disadvantage those students who want to serve such people, the legal profession must be prepared to countenance radical change, not merely cosmetic surgery. Moreover, the increase in law school fees and the greater debt load of students can only exacerbate that trend.

GETTING ARTICLES

The difficulty of finding articles varies from region to region. Most law schools (and some law societies) have student-run articling offices that collate and distribute information about vacancies and placements. In Toronto, Vancouver, Calgary, and Edmonton, there is a matching program that provides a structure and a set of rules that students and firms must abide by in the recruitment of articling students. After interviews, students and firms list their preferences, and offers cannot be made until a specified date, nor accepted unless there is a match between student and firm. To register for this program, you need to sign up with the National Matching Services. In addition, the National Articling Database compiles information about articling opportunities. Developed by QL Systems and the Ontario Association of Law Schools Articling Committees, it lists articling positions throughout Canada, although the focus is primarily on Ontario. In order to access this database, you must have a Quicklaw password, which is free to all law students.

The fact is that, across Canada, good articling positions have become something of a scarce commodity. However, after much badgering by disaffected students, law societies and law schools in Canada's largest provinces are altering their training formats to accommodate graduates who have difficulty landing articling positions. As well, some law societies have launched special initiatives to link graduates with law firms.

- British Columbia graduates can article with one or more firms and can take up to two years to complete their articles. In addition, the CBA – British Columbia Branch is developing a directory for firms interested in sharing an articling student.
- Nova Scotia and several law societies, including Alberta, allow students to article at different law firms — rather than at one firm as has traditionally been the case — in order to encourage more firms to create positions.
- New Brunswick now permits law firms to share students, a process designed to cut firms' costs and to open up more articling positions. If necessary, students can article over a three-year period.
- In Ontario, the Law Society of Upper Canada has put the most aggressive program in place to help students find articling positions. Society rules stipulate that fifty-two weeks of articling can be completed at one or more Ontario firms, or divided between six months in Ontario and six in any other province, or eight

months in Ontario and four in another country. Students can also article part-time over three years. Unlike most jurisdictions, the Ontario society allows law school graduates to take the final phase of the Bar Admission Course, including the examinations, without having an articling position. The Law Society has also launched a number of initiatives to encourage law firms to create more articling positions, including a notice to the legal profession in the *Ontario Reports* to encourage firms to hire more graduates; a letter to sole practitioners to promote joint and part-time articling; a reminder in the *Benchers' Bulletin*; coordination of a résumé writing, interview skills, and job search workshop for unplaced students; and matching joint articling programs to create full articling terms.

- Prince Edward Island recently agreed to allow law school graduates to article part-time over two years so as to encourage less busy firms to hire graduates. The part-time scheme is also designed to give students with other commitments, such as children at home, a better opportunity to receive the necessary experience.

Those who have done particularly well at law school have the chance to obtain a clerkship at the Supreme Court of Canada or in the appeal and trial divisions of the federal and provincial courts. These positions last for a year and count as all or part of the law societies' articling requirements. Although they offer exciting and valuable experience, clerkships do not necessarily prepare you well for the rigours of legal practice. However, they will open many doors of opportunity for you, including the possibility of teaching.

Also, "summering" is becoming a feature of the job market. Students apply to spend the summer at a law firm at the end, usually, of their second year, although there is a shift towards the summer after first-year in some places. Apart from the valuable practice in putting together your résumé and negotiating interviews, the summering experience has several benefits — it pays reasonably well; it allows you to get a glimpse of what being a lawyer will be like; and it gets your feet in the door of a prospective full-time employer. Indeed, many law firms use their summer employment program as a dry run for the articling selection process; those who make a good impression in the summer will usually get an offer of articles at the end of law school. The downside of summering is that you can get stuck with the same law firm for the rest of your career, without having tried out other firms or other possibilities generally. Also, your summer after second year is likely to be your last full summer to yourself: you can practise law for the rest of your life, but you are a student only for a few short years.

Putting together a professional résumé is a vital task and deserves considerable effort on your part. It is your calling card and, for better or worse, it is the only thing that prospective employers will have in front of them when they give your application its first (and perhaps last) thirty-second perusal. There are many guides to résumé writing, to achieving a professional-looking and well-organized document that fully documents your academic record.

- *Be bold.* Résumé writing is not a time for modesty or understatement. In the inflated rhetoric of résumé-speak, you will be doing yourself no favours if you choose to hide your light under a bushel. Your ability to speak another language, play music, or be involved in politics is of interest to future employers.

- *Be honest.* Putting a very favourable spin on your achievements is acceptable, but there is a thin line that divides puffery from hyperbole and worse. Walter Scott had some good advice worth following: "what a tangled web we weave, when first we practise to deceive." You are simply setting yourself up for a fall if you cannot in person measure up to or back up the promise of your résumé.
- *Be expansive.* Although you should avoid padding your résumé, do not be afraid to present a well-rounded picture of yourself. Recruiters might not be impressed by the fact that you were a patrol leader in Cubs or Brownies, but they do want to know about your extracurricular activities; the fact that you can be a talented student and still have time to devote to worthy or community projects, including sports, is an important dimension of yourself and your professional potential.
- *Select referees wisely.* It is important that you choose referees with a high profile and a strong reputation, and you should be as confident as possible that your referees will be saying what you expect (that you are a spectacular candidate and that any employer would be foolish to ignore your application). If you are in any doubt, it is perfectly acceptable to ask politely whether your referee will be able to support you. It is better to take a certain glowing reference from a lesser-known professor than a middling one from a well-known professor. Also, avoid the temptation to choose referees who are related to you in some way.

MAKING A CAREER OF IT

Traditionally, more law students find their way into the private practice of law in Canada than in either the United States or England. However, as the economy tightens and the demand for lawyers flattens off, more law students have begun to explore avenues of employment in which their law degree is a valuable asset, but they do not function strictly as lawyers. Also, there is a growing disenchantment among some young lawyers, especially in large, urban firms, with the way that law is practised; they complain that the quality of life is so poor that the relatively high rewards do not compensate for their lack of time and energy to pursue non-legal pursuits. Accordingly, the path to the private bar is not as accessible or pleasant as it used to be. Whereas in the past, law students were on a direct and fast track to a safe existence as private lawyers, they now must be prepared to weigh other options and to take some risks in their choice of career.

Law school does not do a great job in preparing you for legal practice. This ought not to be surprising as many law professors, rightly or wrongly, do not believe that this is the main purpose of their teaching and instruction. However, although debate continues to rage over whether law schools give you the appropriate range of legal skills to make a go of legal practice, it seems indisputable that law schools do little to prepare students to be business professionals. Although most new graduates will have succeeded in developing some rudimentary basics in time management, the world of practice will demand a set of management and administrative techniques that few students have. Professional practice is first and foremost a business that happens to deal in legal products. If you want to be successful, you will have to acquire a passable bundle of office skills — billing, office management, filing, client development, supervision, etc. — so that you will be able to keep your head above water and actually do some lawyering. Although the extent and range of skills that you require will vary depending on the size of the law firm for which you work, you need to be on top of these challenges. Some of the best successful lawyers are not necessarily the smartest or gifted lawyers, but the most organized lawyers.

As with law school, you need to realize that all work and no play not only makes for a dull life, but can also make for a poor lawyer. Although the economics of lawyering still place great emphasis on hours worked rather than work quality, if you are to retain your enthusiasm for the lawyering life, you need to develop or maintain some life outside the law firm. For some, this will be a responsibility as much as a choice — families deserve and demand a lot of time and attention. You owe it to yourself to craft a life that is rewarding both socially as well as financially. Because you will likely spend much of your waking hours at the law firm and dealing with your colleagues, it is worthwhile taking steps to find out something about the culture of those law firms that you might join. Ask questions of the firm and its junior people and try to get a handle on the kind of lifestyle that your associates lead. Also, you should try to start as you mean to go on. This is very difficult for young lawyers who feel a certain powerlessness in regard to senior lawyers and the firm's exacting demands. But you are simply fooling yourself if you think that you can begin by working fifteen hours a day for seven days a week and then, once you have established yourself, ease back. If you set a reasonable standard that you will be able to sustain over the years, you are more likely to have a happier and more satisfying life.

Over the past few years, the prospects for young lawyers have been relatively bright; the effects of the mid-1990s recession have largely passed. Indeed, some predict that there is a shortage of lawyers and therefore a greater demand for their services. Relying on sophisticated economic projections, some commentators suggest that the levelled-off supply of lawyers has fallen below the number required to meet the increasing demand for legal services. Recent evidence confirms that there has been a rise in legal salaries and that the decreases of a few years ago were simply a market response or "correction" to the boom of the 1980s when there was a shortage of lawyers. Isolating the fact that there is a strong connection between the demand for legal services and the national Gross Domestic Product (GDP), table 3 tracks the annual growth rates in supply of lawyers and GDP from 1972 to 1995.

Table 3 Lawyers in Private Practice

Year	Members of Law Society	Number	% of total	Average annual increase %	Warranted growth rate %/year	Real GDP average annual growth rate
1972	7,610	7,078	93	—	—	—
1976	10,572	8,850	84	6.3	7.4	4.9
1981	15,011	10,803	72	4.4	4.5	3.0
1986	18,588	13,037	70	4.1	6.3	4.2
1991	23,469	15,435	66	3.7	2.6	1.7
1995	27,096	16,420	61	1.6	3.8	2.5
2000	30,741	—	—	1.5	3.8	2.5

On these figures, the bottom line seems to be much healthier than many prognosticators suggested a few years back. Indeed, it might well be the case that those who graduate in the next few years will be well placed to enter an expanding profession. Of course, the question whether this results in a better distribution of legal services or a further concentration at the high-end of the market is an entirely different matter.

What lawyers earn seems to fascinate everyone, including law students. It is difficult to give any hard-and-fast answer. The fact that there is no one kind of lawyer means that there is no one common scale: the range stretches from the single practitioner eking out a living in a remote community to the managing partner of a downtown mega-firm. According to a recent survey in *Canadian Lawyer* (June 1999), average starting salaries for associate lawyers were between $30,000 and $62,000 in the more cosmopolitan urban areas, with annual bonuses of about $4000, and between $24,000 and $50,000 in less populated regions. After a couple of years' experience, these figures rose by about 20 percent. However, it should be noted that, in order to achieve those figures, both associates and partners are on average expected to bill annually about 1500 hours. Allowing for holidays and weekends, it means that lawyers probably work an average week of 50 hours, on the basis that 1 billable hour can take up to 1 1/2 hours to fill. In the larger cosmopolitan firms, this can be much higher for young associates.

In a survey done in *Canadian Lawyer* a few years before (and there is little reason to think that much has changed), associates were asked about job satisfaction. The results were obviously mixed, but the general message is that, while many feel they made the right career choice in law and in being at their particular firm, there are a significant number who have some real misgivings and regrets — long hours, last-minute demands, competitive rivalry, etc. The following questions and answers make for interesting reading:

1. Do you feel you've made a mistake in entering law?
   How Everyone Answered It:
   Never 27%
   Sometimes 57%
   Frequently 13%
   Definitely 2%

   How Men Answered It:
   Never 28%
   Sometimes 57%
   Frequently 11%
   Definitely 2%

   How Women Answered It:
   Never 23%
   Sometimes 56%
   Frequently 16%
   Definitely 3%

2. Are annual billing targets in your firm unreasonably high?
   Yes 23%

3. Is the quality of work suffering because of pressure to meet targets?
   Yes 19%

4. Is the quality of life suffering because of pressure to meet targets?
   Yes 43%

5. Do you have confidence in the management of your firm?
   Yes 85%

6. Do partners treat associates as professional equals?
   Yes 76%

7. Are you personally satisfied with your firm?
   Yes 89%

8. Would you recommend your firm to others entering law?
   Yes 85%

Like people, law firms come in all shapes and sizes. The large firms pay well and are an entrée to the establishment, but they demand long hours, tend to concentrate on corporate-commercial matters, and are bureaucratic in structure. The medium-size firms pay a little less and are less part of the power circuit, but they offer the possibility of more hands-on experience and quicker advancement to positions of responsibility. While the small firms pay less and have fewer support staff, they require much less specialization (except for the boutique firms), allow for greater client contact, and are less impersonal in style. Also, there are one-person practices. Although some people thrive on the independence, it is obviously not for everyone: the hours are long, the responsibility is large, and the work is isolated. Nevertheless, a growing number of lawyers, often with one or two friends, are prepared to give the life of the (almost) single practitioner a go.

Of course, law firms are not the only way to have a legal career. Although they tend to hire few articling students, large corporations often have in-house law departments. The financial benefits are not always as high as in large law firms, but there is a much less competitive atmosphere and the pace of work is more even. The government is also a major employer of lawyers, involving a wide variety of work (criminal, commercial relations, health, child protection, etc.), and the working environment is less frenzied than in a law firm. However, the salary is not as good as in the private sector and, with fiscal cutbacks, there are fewer jobs than previously. Finally, there are many non-governmental organizations that employ lawyers, including unions, clinics, municipalities, banks, transit authorities, media organizations, and public advocacy agencies; the work is challenging and, although the financial rewards may be relatively small, job satisfaction is often high.

BEING PROFESSIONAL

Law and lawyering seem full of oxymorons. In the popular imagination, the most prominent of these is the notion of "legal ethics." For many, it is a contradiction in terms to talk about lawyering and ethical standards of behaviour in one and the same breath: lawyers are on a par with pariahs, not paragons. Indeed, some go so far as to suggest that to be a lawyer is to vacate the ordinary domain of ethical judgment and to inhabit a perverse world of normative disingenuity. Yet, in spite of (or, perhaps, because of) this common understanding, it is imperative for students to appreciate that it need not be this way and that it is possible to be a lawyer and be ethical. As the legal profession's status grows in terms of power and influence in public and private life, there is a strong need to construct a re-visioning of ethical lawyering that is consonant with the profession's contemporary socioeconomic organization and political responsibilities in a society that still, at least nominally, pays lip-service to the ideals of democratic governance and accountability. This challenge is particularly acute in the provision of available and appropriate legal representation to the least advantaged and most disenfranchised in society.

The traditional image of the ethical lawyer has remained largely static and unchanged for many decades. Caricatured as "hired guns," the traditional image of lawyering is centred on the idea that lawyers are supertechnocrats; they possess a special set of talents and techniques that they deploy for the advantage of the people who hire them. They regard themselves as being neutral on the substance and form of the law, and see their task as applying the law, perhaps criticizing it, but most certainly not making it. The lawyer-as-hired-hand's commitment is to the legal system, which must be accepted as given. Almost indifferent to who their clients are, lawyers think of themselves as more chosen than choosing. The relationship between lawyer and client is built upon trust and respect: clients are to trust lawyers to act in the clients' best interests and, in return, lawyers will respect the clients' autonomy. It is not for lawyers to impinge upon the clients' autonomy, but to act on behalf of the clients to realize their interests and inspirations. Indeed, clients tend to be fungible. While it is recognized that richer and poorer clients will have different problems because of their relative wealth, and that the appropriate strategies to be followed will be tailored to the particular client's needs and demands, the lawyer-as-hired-hand treats all clients exactly the same: they are each citizens who have had their rights infringed and want relief or vindication. Insofar as lawyer and clients are from different cultures and classes, lawyers are expected to bridge the gap by personal empathy and professional solidarity.

The fact that this traditional image still has great currency in the legal profession has much to do with the equally traditional theory of law from which it draws its shape and justification. For better or for worse, the hallmark of good lawyers is considered to be found in their cultivation of rule-craft — the ability and possibility of identifying the extant rules of the legal system and applying them to particular situations. As such, the image of the lawyer-as-hired-hand embraces the idea that the law has a life of its own and is not influenced by the lawyers or legal officials who engage in the system. In this sense, any legal practice that craves and expects professional recognition must be seen to take law seriously in the sense that it pursues clients' interests through the extant rules, procedures, and venues of law: overt politicization is severely frowned upon. It is a proud, unapologetic, and defiant defence of the Rule of Law. As should be obvious, the traditional understanding of legal ethics has remained largely immune to the insights and ideas of new thinking about law and lawyering (see chapter 2).

As attractive and comforting as this image of the lawyer-as-hired-hand may be to legal practitioners, its problems are manifest and manifold. It fails theoretically, empirically, and ideologically and ought to be treated sceptically by law students:

- It is based upon a formalistic theory of law that is largely discredited and defunct as a serious attempt to understand law and its operation; almost all jurists of any credibility or respectability accept that the law is not as objective, stable, or determinate as the image of lawyer-as-hired-hand maintains or requires. The law never simply *is*, and lawyering is never completely the passive and technical involvement in that *is*. Choice and responsibility for the choices made are part and parcel of lawyering.

- It describes a version of legal practice that no longer has any empirical validity or historical accuracy, if it ever did have. It is fairly obvious that lawyers pick their clients indirectly through the fees that they charge. It is not that lawyers openly pick between competing clients for their services, but that only certain kinds of clients come in to certain kinds of law offices: Imasco is not shopping around at the local mall for an affordable or available lawyer. Not only is access to legal services obviously disparate, but the needs of the poor require a very different kind of lawyering. Treating all clients the same will do little to alleviate the situation of poorer people.

- The insistence that lawyering is a neutral exercise that does not implicate lawyers in any political process or demand a commitment to any particular ideology is as weak as it is wilful. Such an image is a profoundly conservative and crude understanding of what it is to engage in the business of courts, legislatures, and the like: it accepts and works within the bounds of the status quo. Lawyers tend to confuse legal justice with social fairness. Indeed, the power and prestige of lawyers flows from their professional allegiance to the state's official laws and existing institutions; lawyers are the enlisted custodians of the status quo.

As well as being a very misleading account of lawyering, the image of lawyer-as-hired-hand is an impoverished vision of the part that lawyers can and do have in the establishment of a substantively just society. Of course, dissatisfaction with the dubious assumptions and limited aspirations of the traditional image has led to a call for alternative visions of lawyering which strive to redeem the ideal of lawyering as a noble profession and which place the needs of popular justice above the demands of institutional allegiance. There are many emerging responses to this important challenge. Most remain fairly incremental in their reform suggestions, but others demand a much more rigorous rethink of the lawyers' collective and personal responsibilities.

The first imperative is that, if legal practice is to be transformative, it must first transform legal practice itself. At present, lawyering does not so much march to the beat of the clients' drum, but to the organizational imperatives of the legal profession. This is effected in myriad ways and demands a robust exploration of the means for their transformation — loss of monopoly and self-regulation, and socialized legal services. Nevertheless, there are three primary obstacles to the realization of a truly radical legal practice: lawyers are trained to see law and its institutions as just and necessary structures; there is a professional discipline of political neutrality; and the social organization of the profession and its continuing lack of real diversity in membership marginalize any alternative or challenging modes of lawyering. Any transformation will require changes not only in the legal profession but also in the way that legal education is carried out; law schools and the professoriate must accept their share of the blame for the profession's continuing state of affairs.

As part of this overhaul, a very important initiative would be to institutionalize and accelerate the diversification of the legal profession. Instead of paying lip-service to the idea, there must be aggressive and sustained efforts to open up the legal profession to the many different groups that presently face significant barriers to entry. Indeed, some of those changes have already taken place, and it is for the profession's ruling bodies and establishment to recognize and accommodate to that fact. However, in spite of the diversity in forms of business organization and delivery of legal services, the legal profession is still a bastion of privilege and elitism that is largely populated and dominated by white, middle-aged men of old European stock. In the same way that the cultural and ethnic diversity of Canada has changed, so must the legal profession reorganize itself to reflect this postmodern fact of social living. Effective transformation will occur only when that group is willing or obliged to relinquish its hold on power. The only real changes in the system will come when the composition, demographics, and life-experience of lawyers change, and their different view of what it is to be a lawyer displaces or transforms the regnant images that have been nurtured by the dominant group in society and falsely heralded as neutral in operation and design. To pretend that legal regulation or instruction can be based on anything but plural and multiple visions of legal practice is to flout social reality.

On the personal front, the most effective change would be to urge lawyers to take personal responsibility for what they say and do in their professional capacities. By rejecting the hackneyed and unsustainable notion of an entirely differentiated role, lawyers might begin to gain the respect of the public and themselves. In the same Quintilian way that "good oratory is a good person speaking well," so good lawyering is a good person acting well. As trivial and trite as this may seem, it is the best advice that can be given to the fledgling lawyer, and the most compelling injunction to the jaded lawyer. It offers no magical guide to any specific or conflicted situation, because there is none to be given. It is for each person to arrive at an informed and conscientious decision in accordance with his or her own political and moral lights. The objective is not to chastise lawyers simply because they are corporate lawyers, or because they represent rapists and bigots: it is to encourage lawyers to take responsibility for the clients they take, the causes they fight for, and the tactics they use. In doing so, however, lawyers will ensure that those moral and political lights are always brought into play and are themselves open to debate and reconsideration. An enforced and impersonal orthodoxy is not the goal, but rather a respectful and responsible heterodoxy.

The directive to lawyers to take responsibility for what they do (and, as importantly, what they do not do) ought not to be viewed as an excuse to ignore the needs of clients, or to take control of a legal case in the same way that some critics open-ly defend and some traditionalists covertly effect. The recommendation is that a lawyer is to be neither the client's unquestioning servant nor know-all master. Instead, lawyers and clients are to work towards a non-hierarchical relationship that is premised on the fact that they both have something to contribute — the lawyer's insider knowledge and the client's outsider perspective — to the joint enterprise in which they are both equally, if differently, engaged. An important distinction here is that between lawyers' personal set of substantive values and the more general con-straints of their moral convictions. Lawyers ought not to foist their own values on the client, nor will they work with clients in ways that offend their own moral con-victions. The lawyer-client relationship will be mutually respectful and engaged.

Also, in assuming responsibility, it is important that lawyers look beyond their dealings with their own clients. Part of any mature understanding of what amounts to responsible behaviour will include in its moral almanac the belief that one should do as little harm as possible. Although it will make life much more complicated, it is incumbent on modern lawyers to weigh the effects of their actions on other people and the harm that will ensue. Society has a stake in the legal profession's actions, and this reality should be accepted by lawyers. Sadly, law schools tend to ignore or down-play this important ethical dimension in the training of lawyers. Consequently, it is all the more essential that law students take time to reflect upon their professional role and responsibilities. Otherwise, you will simply back into an ethical stance whose dictates and consequences you will neither appreciate nor respect. Also, because you are backing into it, you are more likely to trip over and hurt yourself.

CONCLUSION

Some readers will feel that I have been very down on the profession. However, I still believe that, if there is to be change, it must come as much through the legal profes-sion as in spite of it. It is those committed and concerned members of the profession who will have to bear the lion's share of the responsibility for pulling it out of its sheepish situation. In order to do that, lawyers must be prepared to abandon affec-tation and to speak "truth to power." Rather than keep snug in power's comfortable privileges, you must risk the anger and rejection of the establishment. The profession must serve citizens at large, and not members themselves. In doing so, lawyers will accept such an obligation as a matter of civic trust, and not as an exceptional act of charity or a good business move. The last thing that lawyers need to do is to retrieve a vision of lawyering that draws on the aristocratic language of *noblesse oblige*.

As much as a democratic society demands modern lawyers, a modern society needs democratic lawyers. When you enter the profession, you will find that there is not a series of hard truths out there to which lawyers can cling to through thick and thin in the vain hope that it will relieve them of the professional and personal burden of taking responsibility for their lawyering activities. There are simply diffi-cult choices and different visions of what we can be as lawyers, and through which we can try to vindicate ourselves and our actions as citizens in a dangerous world. As an incorrigible romantic, I ask you to take seriously Tennyson's Ulyssean incite-ment to moral redemption:

Come, my friends,
'Tis not too late to seek a newer world . . .
Though much is taken, much abides; and though
We are not now that strength which in old days
Moved earth and heaven, that which we are, we are,
One equal temper of heroic hearts,
Made weak by time and fate, but strong in will
To strive, to seek, to find, and not to yield.

FURTHER READINGS

Abel, R. *Lawyers in Society: The Common Law World*. Oxford: Oxford University Press, 1988.

Cain, M. & C. Harrington. *Lawyers in a Postmodern World: Translation and Transgression*. New York: New York University Press, 1994.

Hutchinson, A. *Legal Ethics and Professional Responsibility*. Toronto: Irwin Law, 1999.

The Law Students' Guide to Articling and Summer Positions in Canada. Toronto: Emond Montgomery, 1993.

"Legal Profession Symposium" (1995) 33 Alberta L. Rev.

McLaughlin, P. *Welcome to Reality: A New Lawyer's Guide to Success*. Toronto: CCH Canadian Ltd., 2000.

Stager, D.A. & H.W. Arthurs. *Lawyers in Canada*. Toronto: University of Toronto Press, 1990.

APPENDIX A

Long Legal Memorandum

MEMORANDUM

TO: Wallace Wright   DATE: February 16, 1996

FROM: Student   CLIENT: Lance Fritz

RE: PRELIMINARY RESEARCH: Cause of Action and Class Proceedings

---

Pursuant to your request, I have prepared a memo regarding the preliminary research into a cause of action in product liability and negligence founded upon duty to warn and informed consent as it pertains to our client's claim against the Canadian Dental Association. I have researched the relevant case law in this area which define the common law principles of tortious injury claims. The relevant legislation for defective products liability is the Ontario *Sale of Goods Act*, R.S.O. 1990, c. S.1, s.15. Secondly, as per your request I have investigated the feasibility of commencing a class proceeding on behalf of all those who have suffered from mercury poisoning from dental amalgams. In Ontario, the relevant legislation is found in the *Class Proceedings Act, 1992*, S.O. 1992, c. 6 (the Act), and the Rules of Civil Procedure, R.R.O. 1990 Reg. 194, R. 12. In the United States, the regulations regarding class proceedings are found in the Federal Rules of Civil Procedure (U.S.), Rule 23, Class Actions.

THE FACTS

Our client. Lance Fritz suffered from chronic fatigue syndrome since 1992. After drastic dietary changes and consultations with various doctors which proved to be unsuccessful, Mr. Fritz began to research mercury poisoning leaking from mercury amalgam dental fillings. Mercury comprises 35 to 50% of silver amalgam fillings, and mercury vapours slowly leaking from these compounds are poisonous.[1] Despite opposition by the Canadian Dental Association, numerous international studies have identified the harmful effects of amalgam fillings to people with sensitivities to mercury. These effects include brain, kidney, and heart damage, weakened immune systems, increased antibiotic resistance and disorders such as Alzheimers, multiple sclerosis, leukemia, chronic fatigue syndrome, and epilepsy.[2]

The Canadian Dental Association (CDA) claims that mercury amalgams have been used for over 150 years, and when mercury is combined with other metals it is harmless.[3] Mercury amalgams are also more durable and cheaper than gold or porcelain alternatives.[4] However, Sweden has banned the use of amalgam fillings, Germany has issued advisory warnings, the U.S. Food and Drug Association has never certified amalgams, and in 1995 Health Canada issued a report recommending a limit to the number of mercury fillings dentists should use.[5]

Mr. Fritz believes that his chronic fatigue syndrome is a result of mercury amalgams and is interested in their removal and replacement. He also feels that due to the reticence of the Canadian Dental Association to investigate and warn both dentists and the public of the dangers, there are likely other Canadians suffering from mercury associated problems.

A) CAUSE OF ACTION - PRODUCT LIABILITY, DUTY TO WARN, INFORMED CONSENT

The Issues

In Canada product liability and the duty to warn of a risk associated with a product are assessed according to the principles of negligence with the exception of a product's implied warranty of fitness as regulated in s.15 of the *Sale of Goods Act* (see Appendix A). Courts cannot apply doctrines of strict liability on manufacturers of defective products as American courts have the liberty to do. At issue are the legal tests applicable to satisfy the necessary tort principles of duty of care, standard of care, causation, and remoteness of damages as developed in the common law. Does our client's situation meet these tests?

i)   Does the CDA owe a duty of care to ensure the quality and safety of dental materials, and if a risk is discovered, is there a duty to warn or an obligation to obtain informed consent? Is this duty owed as an entity similar to a manufacturer, a learned intermediary, a dentist, or a regulatory agency?

ii)   If a duty is owed, has the CDA failed to meet the requisite standard of care?

iii)   If a duty is owed, and the standard of care is inadequate, is there a sufficient causal link between our client's injuries, mercury amalgam fillings, and the actions or omissions of the CDA?

iv)   Could the injury incurred by our client have been reasonably foreseen, thus negating a CDA claim of remoteness of damages?

v)   What is the extent of the damages claimed by our client, and are these damages recoverable?

Preliminary Conclusions

In relying on the negligence principles outlined in the common law, it is likely that our client can assert a cause of action in products liability, and a stronger cause of action for failure to warn. However, a major weakness lies in pursuing the liability of the CDA rather than a commercial manufacturer of mercury amalgams or Mr. Fritz's dentist. The case law strongly supports the liability of a manufacturer who provides inherently dangerous goods, not fit for purpose and/or fails to warn of the risks, and the liability of a physician who fails to obtain informed consent before commencing a procedure. However, the CDA is neither a manufacturer, nor a seller, nor a physician, thus there is a lack of precedent to support our case. While it may be found that someone owed a duty of care to Mr. Fritz, and that this duty was breached, it is unlikely that the tenuous link between our client's condition and the CDA will render a judgment of liability in our favour.

Analysis of Cause of Action

i) *Duty of Care* - In order to hold the CDA liable for Mr. Fritz's condition, it must be established that the CDA owes a duty of care to our client either as an entity comparable to a manufacturer or as a medical caregiver

Manufacturer's Duty of Care:

It is well established in the common law that a manufacturer owes a duty to a consumer to exercise reasonable care in ensuring the quality of a product (*Donoghue v. Stevenson*,[6] *Anns v. London*[7]). As well as ensuring quality, manufacturers also owe a common law duty to warn of risks inherent in the use of their products that would not otherwise be known to ordinary consumers (*Lambert v. Lastoplex Chemicals Co. Ltd.*[8]). Furthermore, this is an ongoing duty to warn as soon as a risk becomes known or apparent to the manufacturer, (*Hollis v. Dow Corning Corp.*,[9] *Rivtow Marine v. Washington Iron Works*[10]). Knowledge of a risk creates a duty to warn the consumer directly, as well as intermediary handlers such as doctors (*Buchan v. Ortho-pharmaceutical (Canada) Ltd.*[11]).

To claim that a duty is owed by the CDA under these principles, we must assimilate the role of the CDA to that of a manufacturer, seller or supplier. To do so we must show that the CDA has a substantial degree of control over the mercury amalgams before they reach the consumers (patients).[12] According to the CDA Statement on Dental Amalgam, the federal government is responsible for ensuring the safety of dental materials.[13] The CDA Position on Silver Dental Amalgam, "bases its position on the existing scientific consensus on which government approval is based, and from the range of relevant scientific literature as distinct from individual and sometimes conflicting studies."[14]

As the CDA does not play a regulatory or statutory role in researching or approving the fitness of mercury amalgams, there cannot be a claim of liability from this aspect. Also, in *Mahoney v. R.*[15] a Federal Court found that a federal ministry's failure to fulfill a statutory mandate in creating and enforcing safety regulations regarding product liability is not a valid cause of action. There cannot be a "spillover" of products liability from the manufacturers to hold a non-manufacturer vicariously liable. In our case a court may also hold that there isn't a valid cause of action against the CDA.

Perhaps a better strategy is to name the actual manufacturers of mercury amalgams as defendants in a products liability or duty to warn suit. Under a products liability cause of action, the *Sale of Goods Act* imposes a duty upon sellers with a special skill or judgment over the buyer to supply goods with an "implied condition that the goods will be reasonably fit for [the relied upon] purpose." [16] In Mr. Fritz's case, it may be questionable whether mercury is reasonably fit for the purpose of implantation into the human body, particularly when the manufacturer is in a better position to know of the fitness of this purpose.

Based on recent Canadian case law, it also may be easier to find a manufacturer of mercury amalgams liable for failing to warn than it would be to find the CDA liable. In both *Hollis, supra* and *Buchan, supra*, the manufacturers of harmful medical products that failed to warn of risks were found liable for the subsequent injuries of patients.

Learned Intermediary's Duty of Care:

In *Hollis, supra* the defendant manufacturer attempted to discharge the duty to warn on a doctor as a technically skilled intermediary with supervisory responsibility and direct access to the consumer. However, Justice LaForest held that the learned intermediary rule is only applicable when the intermediary's knowledge approximates that of the manufacturer. Thus, a manufacturer of mercury amalgams can only discharge the duty to warn if the CDA has the same knowledge of the risks as the manufacturer. The CDA can escape liability by proving that they are not an intermediary between the manufacturer and the dentist, and that the manufacturer did not provide information of any known or suspected risks in mercury amalgams that the CDA could otherwise be expected to know.

Physician's Duty of Care:

An alternative route is to claim that the CDA owes a duty of care to dental patients based on its authoritative position in a physician-patient relationship. The Supreme Court of Canada has held that doctors owe a duty to disclose material risks inherent in a procedure that a reasonable patient would want to know (*Reibl* v. *Hughes*[17]). To establish this duty we must show that there is a material risk expressed as either a low occurrence of a serious consequence or a high occurrence of a minor consequence (*Reibl, supra*).

Even if the risk is small it can only be neglected if there is a reasonable excuse. In *Overseas Tankship, (U.K.)* v. *Miller Steamship Co.*,[18] Lord Reid stated that even if the probability of risk is low, it should not be ignored if the burden of reducing or eliminating the risk is not unreasonable. Thus, we must argue that fulfilling a duty to warn of risks associated with mercury would be a reasonable burden in comparison to the consequences. However, evidence must be presented to persuade the court to accept mercury poisoning as a sufficient risk requiring disclosure, particularly to patients with sensitivities to mercury.

It is worth noting that patients have a right to be informed specifically. A defendant cannot rely on the promulgation of information through the media or in medical journals (*Buchan, supra*). As well as a duty to warn of risk, physicians have an obligation to obtain the informed consent of a patient unless the patient expressly wishes not to be informed (*Hopp* v. *Lepp*[19]). Unless a patient is knowledgeable of a risk he or she cannot be said to have given consent to voluntarily assume the risk, thus shifting liability from the physician (*Lambert, supra*).

As our client was not informed of the risks associated with mercury amalgams, he also did not give his informed consent to the procedure. Although this is a solid cause of action, perhaps again we are not focusing on the correct defendant. It would be easier to establish a breach of duty to warn and the obligation to obtain consent owed by Mr. Fritz's dentist as a joint and severally liable defendant. Then it is up to the dentist and the CDA to divide the onus of responsibility to warn patients.

ii) *Standard of Care* - If it can be found that the CDA owes a duty to our client in either products liability or duty to warn, then the next issue is whether a requisite standard of care was breached. The standard of care for products liability "is the duty to use reasonable care in the circumstances" (*Phillips* v. *Ford Motor Co. of Canada Ltd.,*[20]). However, in *Buchan, supra* it was stated that where a product is 'inherently dangerous' such as mercury, there is a higher standard of care owed by those with a duty to warn, particularly to susceptible users. It was found that the standard in the pharmaceutical industry moves away from the 'reasonableness' required in *Phillips, supra* to one that "may be so high it approximates to or almost becomes strict liability" *Buchan, supra*). Thus, if the CDA or a mercury amalgam manufacturer is found to owe a duty in products liability, standard of care owed to warn patients of the risks associated with mercury is high. As our client was not warned at all, the defendant(s) would fail this burden.

If we proceed in the alternative in claiming a duty is owed by virtue of a physician-patient relationship, the standard of care owed is also one of reasonableness. In *Haughian* v. *Paine,*[21] the court held that a doctor owed a duty not only to warn of small risks, but also to disclose alternatives to the procedure as a standard in the profession. Again our client was not warned of any risks, nor the probability of these risks, nor was he told of alternatives to mercury amalgams (i.e., gold or porcelain fillings, no fillings). The court must find that the degree of risk involved would make it reasonable to require warnings and that the warning given is reasonable according to common standards within the profession. Only then would the CDA and/or Mr. Fritz's dentist fail to meet the requisite standard of care owed by a duty to warn and obtain informed consent. The question of whether the risk is substantial enough would rest on the persuasiveness of our experts and evidence.

iii) *Causation* - In order for our client to recoup his losses, we must establish a link between chronic fatigue syndrome, mercury amalgams, and the CDA. With the scientific and empirical evidence gathered from various journals and medical experts, a court must first accept on a balance of probabilities that a causal link exists between chronic fatigue syndrome and mercury poisoning. Secondly, a court must find that an act or omission by the defendant(s) in either manufacturing mercury amalgams or failing to warn of their risks is the cause of our client's condition.

In *Snell* v. *Farrell*[22] the Supreme Court of Canada outlined the test for the necessary degree of correlation between the defendant's actions and the plaintiff's injuries sufficient to infer causation in medical cases. It must be shown that the defendant's negligence in failing to warn *significantly increased the probability* of the plaintiff's injury occurring, barring the defendants' evidence to the contrary. The defendant(s) may also attempt to prove that the injury has an alternative cause. This may pose a problem for Mr. Fritz as the exact cause of chronic fatigue syndrome is not conclusively known, and it may in fact have other causes. We can take advantage of a relaxed burden of proof as we must only show a significant increase of risk on a balance of probabilities (*Snell, supra*), but we must also be prepared to rebut the suggestion of other causes.

A plaintiff must also prove that had the duty to warn not been breached, the injury would likely not have occurred (*Reibl, supra*). In other words, we must show that if our client had been informed of the risk by the defendants, he would not have consented to the procedure. In medical negligence cases, this test is whether a reasonable, fully informed patient would agree to the procedure (*Hollis, supra*). In *Buchan, supra* the test used was whether there was a reasonable likelihood on a balance of probabilities that a reasonable, fully informed patient would refuse the procedure. Although both of these tests are intended to be objective, the result is a subjective decision on the part of the court as to what a person in our client's situation is likely to do.

The issue of causation is likely to create difficulties if a class action is brought forward. To hold the defendants liable for failure to warn the representative plaintiff must prove that every class member: 1) has an injury caused by mercury amalgams, 2) was not informed of the risk by the defendant(s), and 3) would not have consented if fully informed. The problem of individual proof of causation and the defendant's right to discovery resulted in a denial of class certification in *Abdool* v. *Anaheim Management Ltd.*[23] These issues will be further discussed in Part B in an analysis of an identifiable class for certification.

iv) *Remoteness* - The general test for determining whether damages are too remote from the acts or omissions of the defendant is found in *The Wagon Mound No. 2*. As mentioned earlier, if there was a risk of injury occurring because of the defendant's negligence in products liability or failure to warn, and there is no valid justification for taking this risk, then the injury is deemed to be foreseeable. In the absence of intervening causes, the reasonable foreseeability of an injury will negate a defendant's claim of remoteness. The onus of proving an intervening cause is placed on the defendant. As long as a duty of care breach of a standard of care, and causation is established there does not seem to be a formidable barrier in claiming the proximity of damages.

v) *Damages* - Before deciding whether to proceed by means of a class action it is advisable to seek additional information as to the type of loss incurred by our client. If the damages are substantial such as loss of work, medical expenses, and pain and suffering, then it may be worth it to proceed individually. It is also important to note that damages incurred from inferior products have not traditionally been recoverable in Canada (*Rivtow Marine, supra*). However, a recent Supreme Court of Canada decision in *Winnipeg Condominium Corp.* v. *Bird Construction Co.*[24] allowed recovery for economic loss due to inferior products if there is a threat or existence of physical harm. Alternately, I cannot foresee any difficulties in recovering valid damages if failure to warn is tried as a cause of action, but whether it is economically feasible for our client requires further information.

B) FEASIBILITY OF A CLASS PROCEEDING

The Issues

i) Do the facts of our client's case meet the criteria necessary for certification as set out in section five of the Act (see Appendix A)?

    A) Are there any issues that may be hindering class certification that are barred from consideration according to section six of the Act (see Appendix B)?

    B) What is the likelihood of receiving approval for a certified national class?

Preliminary Conclusions

Subject to the inclusion of other defendants to ensure certification will not fail due to a tenuous cause of action, our client's situation seems to fulfill the necessary criteria for class certification. Any issues that may weigh against our case, such as individual differences in causation and damages, are protected from a bar to certification by section-six. Lastly, as long as an Ontario court would not be considered unreasonable in assuming jurisdiction over a national class, and extra-provincial plaintiffs can enforce judgments rendered under the Act, there are few legal barriers to the certification of a national class. There is recent case law and considerable public policies that supports an argument for national class certification in Mr. Fritz's case.

Analysis of Class Proceeding Issues

In Ontario, class proceedings are governed by the *Class Proceedings Act, 1992* (the Act), and Rule 12 in the *Rules of Civil Procedure*. The general policies desired by the legislators of these statutes are objectives of improved access to Justice, increased judicial economies of scale, and the deterrence of actual and potential wrongdoers. These policies were defined by the court in *Abdool, supra* and have played a role in certification decision making since 1992. Generally, it has been held that the courts should err in favour of allowing the class to proceed in order to uphold the social policies behind the legislation (*Bendall* v. *McGhan*[25]). While social policies are at the root of the Act, section five outlines the specific criteria necessary to bring a class action to trial.

5.1(a) Cause of Action- A class must plead a valid cause of action in order to be certified. However, the merits of the action are not to be assessed by the courts, nor should evidence be introduced to support a cause of action *(Abdool, supra)*.

In Peiat v. N the test of an invalid action was one which was "plain and obvious" to the court that it could not succeed. It is also necessary that a valid cause of action be claimed against each defendant (*Abdool, supra*), although it is not necessary for the causes of action to be the same for every defendant or claimed by the same plaintiffs (*Bendall, supra*).

As a claim both in products liability against a manufacturer or negligence in failure to warn against a manufacturer or physician are valid causes of action, it is likely that a court would not deny our client class certification. However, a class proceeding against the CDA as the sole defendant may pose greater problems in certification as it may be obvious that the CDA's alleged duty of care is weak.

5.1(b) Identifiable Class - the Act states that a certified class proceeding must consist of at least two or more persons. Although there are no specified limits as to class size the court will consider the policy implications of certifying a very small or very large class. If a class is too small, a class action is not necessarily the preferable procedure (see 5. 1 (d) below) and can be subject to decertification (*Bendall, supra*). If the class is too large, it may be feasible to break the class down into subclasses to determine common issues according to judicial efficiency and manageability. In section 5.(3) the party requesting certification must file an affidavit of the best available information as to the number of members in the class (see Appendix C). This requirement is subject to section 6(4) which does not allow a bar to certification if the number or identity of class members is not known (see Appendix B).

Applied to our case, the exact number of claimants is not known. The CDA estimates that 3% of the population with fillings are sensitive to mercury amalgams.[27] However, it is not known how many of these people have displayed or fear injurious symptoms, were not warned, and would have refused the procedure if informed of the risks. It may be safe to assume that there is more than one other person besides our client but evidence is needed to avoid a denial of certification or future decertification on this basis. To ensure manageability there could be a division of this potentially large class into sub-classes of those with injuries and those without manifest injuries from mercury amalgams, as long as all members received the fillings without a warning. In *Nantais* v. *Telectronics Proprietary Ltd.*[28], the court held that even those members that had not yet suffered physical damages from a defective pacemaker part should not be barred from inclusion in the class at the certification level.

5.1(c) Common Issues - While the wording of section five requires the class only to "raise common issues," the courts have been inconsistent in determining what a common issue is and what weight it should bear. For example, in *Bendall, supra* Justice Montgomery found that common issues do not have to predominate individual differences, unlike class proceedings in the United States.[29] Yet, in *Sutherland* v. *Canadian Red Cross Society*[30] the same judge found that at least 366 people in Ontario infected with HIV after a blood transfusion did not raise enough common issues to transcend individual differences. However, the recent case of *Maxwell* v. *MLG Ventures Ltd.*[31] attempted to minimize problems associated with the differences of class members by requiring that the individual knowledge of every class member be submitted by written affidavits.

In a motion for certification in our case, we must show that common issues exist among all members of the class. Although all members would share the common issue of an implanted mercury amalgam this alone is probably not enough to certify on its own. It would be best to minimize the differences within the class by defining which cause of action and which defendant to pursue. For example, limit the class to those with sensitivities to mercury, or those that received the amalgam materials from the same manufacturer, or those with dentists that failed to warn, or even only those that were treated by Mr. Fritz's dentist.

It is also important to note that many differences that may stem from individual damage assessments, remedies and issues not shared between all sub-classes, are not to stand as a barrier to certification according to section 6 of the Act (s. 6(l), (3),(5)). However, in *Abdool, supra* the trial judge found that the existence of four out of the five grounds referred to in this section played a role in denying certification. The number of differences among members that would require individual discovery and assessment would defeat any judicial economies in proceeding with a class action. This decision was upheld in the Ontario Divisional Court, the highest appellate court to render judgment on a certification motion.

Therefore, although it is sufficient for our client to proceed with a common issue, the differences in causation (i.e. who would have refused treatment if adequately warned) and damages may swing the balance against certification. As Watson notes, "at least at this stage, the outcome of certification motions may depend on who is the judge and it may well be too early to make generalizations about the jurisprudence on certification.[32]

5.1(d) Preferable Procedure - This section closely considers the social policies outlined in *Abdool,supra*, specifically access to justice, judicial economy, and behaviour modification. In *Abdool, supra* it was found that a class action is not a preferable procedure where none of these three objectives are met. Access to justice was an important issue in the court's decision to grant certification in *Bendall, supra*, noting that there were a large number of women that would otherwise not be able to afford the costs of litigation. Secondly, is the judicial economy of processing one (albeit complicated) claim as opposed to a multiplicity of individual claims. Judicial economy is a strong argument in favour of class certification when there are a number of common issues to be decided. This creation of a judicial economy of scale was noted in the successful certification of *Pepiatt, supra.* Thirdly, the threat of class actions by smaller plaintiffs provides an incentive for defendants to modify their behaviour both before and during a trial.

These policy arguments seem to work in favour of certification for our case. As the damages incurred from mercury amalgams may range greatly it may not be financially feasible for potential plaintiffs to litigate individually. This cost consideration is an effective barrier to justice that should be taken into account for a socially meritous claim. Secondly, despite differences within the class it is possible to determine a common issue of liability for either products liability or failure to warn in the interests of judicial economy. The court can determine the necessary principles to establish liability and then assess each member for specific details, rather than proceed in a number of different courts that may provide inconsistent decisions. This approach was approved in *Nantais, supra.* Third, a threat of a class action may prod the defendant(s) to change their standard of procedure in either manufacturing an inherently dangerous product or failing to warn. Cases such as this would encourage more research into the risks to public health and the dissemination of public information regarding the risks of mercury amalgams.

5.1(e) Representative Plaintiff - The Act states that only one plaintiff may represent the interests of the class. The criteria requires that the representative fairly and adequately can represent the class, has a workable strategy to advance the proceeding and notify members, and does not have a conflict of interests with others in the class. Section 5(2) requires that the representative plaintiff also represents the interests of a sub-class according to the above conditions (see Appendix D). Unlike the United States, a representative plaintiff need not be 'typical' of class members (*Abdool, supra*) as long as he or she possesses 'adequate knowledge' of the class interests (*Maxwell, supra*). This rule was slightly altered in *Sutherland, supra* in denying certification because the representative did not display all of the characteristics of members of the class, but this ruling has not seemed to be followed in subsequent cases.

In order to proceed with a class certification to litigate the mercury amalgam issue as a question of liability, we must canvass potential class members and find an adequate representative. It is likely that Mr. Fritz would volunteer as he has taken the initiative in pursuing this claim. I cannot foresee any problems should Mr. Fritz become a class representative that would be sufficient to deny certification as long as differences in the type of injury and remedies sought can be individually assessed after the common issue of liability is processed. Also, depending on the existence of a sub-class, such as one consisting of those that have not displayed any manifest injuries, there may be a need to persuade the court that someone claiming physical injuries can adequately represent those with only a fear of injury. However, there is a precedent in *Nantais, supra* that included plaintiffs without manifest physical injuries and their families as full members of the class without the use of a sub-class.

ii) Feasibility of a National Class Certification

While a national class may give more credence to a claim, generate further judicial economies, and avoid nationally inconsistent decisions, it also has its shortcomings. Of primary importance in considering the merits of a national class are the jurisdictional limitations of the courts in which a motion for certification is requested and a trial is conducted, particularly their ability to enforce an out-of-province decision. It is helpful that even in the relatively new area of class proceedings both *Bendall, supra* and *Nantais, supra* received certification to commence a national class proceeding.

The Supreme Court of Canada has visited the issue of extra-provincial plaintiffs and the recognition to be given by the courts of one province to the decisions of another (*Morguard Investments Ltd.* v. *De Savoye*,[33]). In *Morguard, supra* the court followed the American constitutional doctrine of "full faith and credit" of the judgments of one court to another as long as there were reasonable grounds for assuming jurisdiction.

In *Nantais, supra* the court also considered the impact of a national class on a defendant. It was held that the overriding concern was to ensure that the common issue of liability was decided consistently and applicable to all Canadian plaintiffs in such a way that the social policies behind class proceedings were met.

Supplemented by *Morguard, supra* (which has been followed in 27 cases), *Bendall, supra* and *Nantais, supra* bode well for a motion for class certification on behalf of patients with mercury amalgam fillings. While it is likely that a national class would proceed as long as the criteria set out in section five of the Act is met, we must discuss the extra costs and responsibilities this would place on the representative plaintiff. For example, there is an extra burden of informing all class members of information regarding the proceedings and settlement offers, as well as providing members with an opportunity to opt out of the proceedings. The larger and more geographically diverse the class, the greater the burden on the representative.

CONCLUSIONS

Based on the above analysis of class proceedings, it is likely that there is sufficient legislative and judicial weight to support a successful motion to certify a class action in Mr. Fritz's case. As stated in the cause of action analysis, the weakness in our client's case lies in naming the CDA as the sole defendant. To increase the odds of generating a successful cause of action both in a certification motion and at trial, a defendant with a more direct duty of care such as a manufacturer or a dentist should be named to any civil proceeding commenced on behalf of a plaintiff suffering from mercury poisoning from dental amalgams.

While the above information is not exhaustive I hope it has provided a satisfactory overview of the preliminary research for this case. Please feel free to contact me should you require any further assistance with this file.

SOURCES CITED AND CONSULTED

Canadian Dental Association Statement on Dental Amalgams, approved by the CDA Board of Governors 1986, amended in 1995, faxed from Public Relations Dept. from head office in Ottawa.

Cochrane, Michael. "Steps in a Proceeding," in *Class Actions*. Aurora: Canada Law Book, 1993, (pp. 88-102, LRW teaching materials).

Mandel, Lawrence H. "The Plaintiff's Perspective in Products Liability Actions," in *Recent Trends and Developments in Products Liability*. Toronto: Insight, 1985, pp. Tab II.

McGowan, Michael. "A Comparison to Rule 23 of the U.S. Federal Rules of Civil Procedure," in *Certification of Class Actions in Ontario*, 16 C.P.C. (3d) 172 (QL).

Smith, Robert and Katherine M. Gower. "The Legal Ground Rules," in *Recent Trends in Products Liability*. Toronto: Insight, 1985, pp. Tab I.

Solomon, Robert M. and Bruce P. Feldthusen. *Cases and Materials on the Law of Torts*. 3rd ed. Toronto: Thompson Professional Publishing Canada, 1991.

Watson, Garry D. "A 'Stocktaking' of Class Proceedings in Ontario: Is The Price Wrong?", draft in Civil Procedure 1, Supplementary Materials 1996, p. 68.

Watson, Garry D. et al. *Civil Litigation: Cases and Materials*. 4th ed. Toronto: Emond Montgomery Publications Ltd., 1991.

APPENDIX A

Sale of Goods Act, R.S.O. 1990, c. S.1, s.15.

15. Subject to this Act and any statute in that behalf, there is no implied warranty or particular purpose of goods supplied under a contract of sale, except as follows:

> 1. Where the buyer, expressly or by implication, makes known to the seller the particular purpose for which the goods are required so as to show that the buyer relies on the seller's skill or judgement, and the goods are of a description that it is in the course of the seller's business to supply (whether the seller is the manufacturer or not), there is an implied condition that the goods will be reasonably fit for such purpose,

APPENDIX B

Class Proceedings Act, 1992, S.O. 1992, c. 6.

Certification
5. —(1) The court shall certify a class proceeding on a motion under section 2, 3, or 4 if,
(a) the pleadings or the notice of application discloses a cause of action;
(b) there is an identifiable class of two or more persons that would be represented by the representative plaintiff or defendant;
(c) the claims or defences of the class members raise common issues;
(d) a class proceeding would be the preferable procedure for the resolution of the common issues; and
(e) there is a representative plaintiff or defendant who,

> (i) would fairly and adequately represent the interests of the class,
> (ii) has produced a plan for the proceeding that sets out a workable method of advancing the proceeding on behalf of the class and of notifying class members of the proceeding, and
> (iii) does not have, on the common issues for the class, an interest in conflict with the interests of other class members.

Certain matters not bar to certification
6. — The court shall not refuse to certify a proceeding as a class proceeding solely on any of the following grounds:
1. The relief claimed includes a claim for damages that would require individual assessment after determination of the common issues.
2. The relief claimed relates to separate contracts involving different class members.
3. Different remedies are sought for different class members.
4. The number of class members or the identity of each class member is not known.

5. The class includes a subclass whose members have claims or defences that raise common issues not shared by all class members.

APPENDIX C

Class Proceedings Act, 1992, S.O. 1992, c. 6. s. 5(3).

Evidence as to size of class
5. (3) Each party to a motion for certification shall, in an affidavit filed for use on the motion, provide the party's best information on the numer of members in the class.

APPENDIX D

Class Proceedings Act, 1992, S.O. 1992, c. 6, s. 5(2).

Certification, subclass protection
5.(2) Despite subsection (1), where a class includes a subclass whose members have claims or defences that raise common issues not shared by all the class members so that, in the opinion of the court, the protection of the interests of the subclass members requires that they be separately represented, the court shall not certify the class proceeding unless there is a representative plaintiff or defendant who,

(a) would fairly and adequately represent the interest of the subclass;

(b) has produced a plan for the proceeding that sets out a workable method of advancing the proceeding on behalf of the subclass and of notifying subclass members of the proceeding; and

(c) does not have, on the common issues for the subclass, an interest in conflict with the interests of other subclass members.

ENDNOTES

[1] "Teeth Fillings May Be Poisoning You," in *Toronto Star*, December 27, 1990, p. 13.

[2] *Australasian Society of Oral Medicine and Toxicology*, and "Mercury Filling Linked with Alzheimers" in *BC Herald*, May 21, 1991.

[3] "Teeth Fillings May be Poisoning You," p.13.

[4] "Mercury Fillings Should be Limited, Says Official," in *Global Mail*, March 15, 1995.

[5] *Ibid.*, and *Australasian Society of Oral Medicine and Toxicology*.

[6] *Donoghue* v. *Stevenson*, [1932] A.C. 562.

[7] *Anns* v. *London Borough of Merton*, [1977] 2 All E.R. 492.

[8] *Lambert* v. *Lastoplex Chemicals Co.*, [1972] S.C.R. 569, 25 D.L.R. (3d) (S.C.C.).

[9] *Hollis* v. *Dow Corning Corp.*, [1995] S.C.J. No. 104 (QL).

[10] *Rivtow Marine* v. *Washington Iron Works* (1973), 40 D.L.R. (3d) 530 (S.C.C.).

[11] *Buchan* v. *Ortho-Pharmaceutical (Canada) Ltd.* (1986), 54 O.R. (2d) 92 (Ont. C.A.).

[12] Robert Smith and Katherine M. Gower, "The Legal Ground Rules", in *Recent Trends and Developments in Products Liability*, 1985, p.7.

[13] Canadian Dental Association Statement on Dental Amalgam, approved by the CDA Board of Governors in 1986, and amended in 1995. Public relations fax from Ottawa Head Office.

[14] *Ibid.*

[15] *Mahoney* v. *R.* (1986), 38 C.C.L.T. 21.

[16] *Sale of Goods Act*, R.S.O. 1990, c. S.1, s. 15.

[17] *Reibl* v. *Hughes* (1980), 114 D.L.R. (3d) 1, [1980] 2 S.C.R. 880, 14 C.C.L.T. 1, 33 N.R. 361, 5 A.C.W.S. (2d) 259.

[18] *Overseas Tankship (U.K.) Ltd.* v. *Miller Steamship Co. Pty.*, [1967] 1 A.C. 617, [1966] 2 All E.R. 709 (P.C.) (The Wagon Mound No.2).

[19] *Hopp* v. *Lepp* (1980), 112 D.L.R. (3d) 67 (S.C.C.).

[20] *Phillips* v. *Ford Motor Co. of Canada Ltd.*, [1971] 2 O.R. 637, 18 D.L.R. (3d) 641 (Ont. C.A.).

[21] *Haughian* v. *Paine* (1987), 40 C.C.L.T. 13 (Sask. C.A.).

[22] *Snell* v. *Farrell* (1990), 72 D.L.R. (4th) 289 (S.C.C.).

[23] *Abdool* v. *Anaheim Management Ltd.*, [1995] 21 O.R. (3d) 453.

[24] *Winnipeg Condominium Corp.* v. *Bird Construction Co. Ltd.*, [1995] 1 S.C.R. 85 (S.C.C.).

[25] *Bendall* v. *McGhan* (1993), 14 O.R. (3d) 734.

[26] *Peppiatt* v. *Nicol* (1993), 16 O.R. (3d) 133, 20 C.P.C. (3d) 272 (Gen.Div.).

[27] Canadian Dental Association Statement on Dental Amalgam, facts from 1991.

[28] *Nantais* v. *Telectronics Proprietary (Canada) Ltd.*, [1995] O.J. No. 2592(QL).

[29] McGowan, Michael. "A Comparison to Rule 23 of the U.S. Federal Rules of Civil Procedure," *Certification of Class Actions in Ontario*, 16 C.P.C. (3d) 172 (QL).

[30] *Sutherland* v. *Canadian Red Cross Society* (1994), 17 O.R. (3d) 645.

[31] *Maxwell* v. *MLG Ventures Ltd.*, [1995] O.J. No. 1136 (QL).

[32] Watson, Garry D. "A Stocktaking of Class Proceedings in Ontario: Is the price wrong?" draft in Civil Procedure I Supplementary Materials 1996, p. 75.

[33] *Morguard Investments Ltd.* v. *De Savoye*, [1990] 3 S.C.R. 1077 (S.C.C.).

TABLE OF CASES

Abdool v. *Anaheim Management Ltd.*, [1995] 21 O.R. (3d) 453

Anns v. *London Borough of Merton*, [1977] 2 All E.R. 492

Bendall v. *McGhan* (1993) 14 O.R. (3d) 734

Buchan v. *Ortho-pharmaceutical (Canada) Ltd.* (1986), 54 O.R. (2d) 92 (Ont. C.A.)

Donoghue v. *Stevenson*, [1932] A.C. 562

Haughian v. *Paine* (1987), 40 C.C.L.T. 13 (Sask. C.A.)

Hollis v. *Dow Corning Corp.*, [1995] S.C.J. No. 104 (QL)

Hopp v. *Lepp* (1980), 112 D.L.R. (3d) 67 (S.C.C.)

Lambert v. *Lastoplex Chemicals Co.*, [1972] S.C.R. 569, 25 D.L.R. (3d)

Mahoney v. *R.* (1986), 38 C.C.L.T. 21

Maxwell v. *MLG Ventures Ltd.*, [1995] O.J. No. 1136 (QL)

Morguard Investments Ltd. v. *DeSavoye*, [1990] 3 S.C.R. 1077 (S.C.C.)

Murphy v. *St. Catharines General Hospital*, [1964] 1 O.R. 637, 18 D.L.R. (3d) 641

Nantais v. *Teletronics Proprietary (Canada) Ltd.*, [1995] O.J. No. 2592 (QL)

Overseas Tankship (U.K.) Ltd. v. *Miller Steamship Co. Pty.*, [1967] 1 A.C. 617, [1966] 2 All E.R. 709 (P.C.) (The Wagon Mound No. 2)

Peppiatt v. *Nicol* (1993), 16 O.R. (3d) 133, 20 C.P.C. (3d) 272 (Gen Div.)

Phillips et al. v. *Ford Motor Co. of Canada Ltd. et al.*, [1971] 2 O.R. 637, 18 D.L.R. (3d) 641 (C.A.)

Reibl v. *Hughes* (1980), 114 D.L.R. (3d) 1, [1980] 2 S.C.R. 880, 14 C.C.L.T. 1, 33 N.R. 361

Rivtow Marine v. *Washington Iron Works* (1973), 40 D.L.R. (3d) 530 (S.C.C.)

Rogers Broadcasting v. *Alexander* (1994), 25 C.P.C. (3d) 159

Snell v. *Farrell* (1990), 72 D.L.R. (4th) 289 (S.C.C.)

Sutherland v. *Canadian Red Cross* (1994), 17 O.R. (3d) 645

Winnipeg Condominiums Corp. v. *Bird Construction Co. Ltd.*, [1995] 1 S.C.R. 85

TABLE OF LEGISLATION

Class Proceedings Act, 1992, S.O. 1992, c. 6.

Rules of Civil Procedure, R.R.O. 1990, Reg. 194, R. 12.

Sale of Goods Act, R.S.O. 1990, c. S.1, s. 15.

U.S. Federal Rules of Civil Procedure, Federal Rule 23, Class Actions.

APPENDIX B

Short Legal Memorandum

MEMORANDUM

DATE: November 22, 1993

RE: Sleepwalking and the Non-insane Automatism Defence

I. INTRODUCTION:

You have asked me to prepare a memo on the issue of sleepwalking as it relates to the defence of non-insane automatism. Our client has come to us for advice on his options pursuant to his involvement in a double murder. In researching the issues involved, I have looked primarily at Canadian and British jurisprudence and have considered both common law and statute law in my analysis. In particular, I have looked at the *Criminal Code* and its treatment of "mental disorder" and "insanity."

FACTS:

Our client has been charged with two counts of second degree murder[4] arising out of the deaths of a Mississauga couple. He claims he does not know these people and that he has never before driven to the location where the murders took place. After falling asleep around 2:00 a.m., our client remembers nothing except returning home with blood all over his hands and clothing, and having a vague notion that he was involved in a tragic incident. At that point he called the police. His only statement to the police was that he thought "something terrible had happened."

Our client has been experiencing a great deal of financial, marital and work-related stress. He has never before exhibited symptoms of a sleep disorder, but the doctor who examined him says that his family has a long history of somnambulism and sleep associated disorders.

---

[4] *Criminal Code*, s. 229, s. 231(7)

ISSUES:

1. Is "non-insane automatism" a valid defence to the crime of second degree murder?
2. Is sleepwalking properly classified as non-insane automatism, or is it considered to be a "mental disorder" for the purposes of s. 16 of the *Criminal Code*?
3. What is the likely verdict arising from a successful defence of non-insane automatism?

CONCLUSION

A survey of primarily Canadian and British jurisprudence suggests that a defence of non-insane automatism results in absolute acquittal, whereas insane automatism (insanity) generally results in a verdict of not guilty by reason of insanity. The Canadian *Criminal Code* provides a defence of "mental disorder" in s. 16; however, this would seem to apply only to cases of insane automatism. At issue, then, is whether sleepwalking is considered to be non-insane automatism or insane automatism.

1. Yes, "non-insane automatism is a valid defence to the crime of second degree murder.
2. Yes, sleepwalking is properly classified as non-insane automatism. It does not fall within the classification of "mental disorder" for the purposes of the *Criminal Code*.
3. The likely verdict arising from a successful defence of non-insane automatism is an unqualified acquittal.

ANALYSIS

I. *Relevant Statutes:* Of Primary Concern is the Canadian *Criminal Code*, s.16.

The statute of primary concern in this case is the Canadian *Criminal Code*.[5] S. 16(1) of the Code provides a defence of mental disorder:

> No person is criminally responsible for an act committed or an omission made while suffering from a mental disorder that rendered the person incapable of appreciating the nature and quality of the act or omission or of knowing that it was wrong.

"Mental disorder" is defined as "...a disease of the mind" in s.2 of the *Criminal Code*.[6]

---

[5] R.S.C. 1985, c. C-46.

[6] While there is no other Canadian statute which is directly relevant to the issue at hand, it might be noted that the Ontario *Mental Health Act*, R.S.O. 1990, c. M-7, s. 1 also defines a mental disorder as any disease or disability of the mind. In addition, the Ontario *Mental Incompetency Act*, R.S.O. 1990, c. M-9, which provides for the custody of mentally incompetent persons and the management of their estates, defines a "mentally incompetent person" as one who suffers from some kind of disease of the mind(s. 1). From these two Ontario statutes, it is clear that "mental disorder" means "a disease of the mind."

The definition of "mental disorder" is important since, as will be shown later, the courts tend to place a great deal of emphasis on whether or not sleepwalking should be classified as a "disease of the mind." From the above-mentioned statues, we can feel confident that s. 16 of the *Criminal Code* equates "mental disorder" with a "disease of the mind."

In Britain, automatism is described as a state in which there is a complete absence of choice and control over one's acts. The law provides a defence of automatism specifically in cases of sleepwalking. *Halsbury's Laws of England* states: "[a] person does not incur criminal liability for acts done in a state of automatism, as when in his sleep he kills someone…."[7]

The authoritative rule in *M'Naghten's Case*[8] describes *insanity* as existing in circumstances where there is a complete absence of control by reason of a *disease of the mind*.[9] It should be noted, however, that in Britain, automatism and insanity are distinguished by the trial judge as a matter of law. While the accused has the burden to prove insanity, it is the prosecution who must negative the defence of automatism.[10]

II. CASE LAW

1. *Non-insane Automatism is Automatism which is Not Caused by a Disease of the Mind*

It is generally agreed, at least in the Canadian, British and American jurisdictions, that automatism is a state in which a person acts involuntarily, without choice or control. In the United States, automatism is subsumed under the defence of diminished capacity. There, the courts have said that a person should not be held responsible for acts s/he commits while unconscious"[11] or which are completely beyond their knowledge and control."[12]

In both Canada and Britain, insane automatism is distinguished from non-insane automatism. Adopting the reasoning of Martin, J.A. from the Ontario Court of Appeal, the Supreme Court of Canada made this distinction clear in *R. v. Rabey*."[13] Insane automatism is automatism caused by a "disease of the mind." Martin, J.A. held that a "disease of the mind" is a legal term, making it a question of law for the trial judge to determine which mental states constitute a disease of the mind. Generally he said, any state of automatism arising from *internal* factors (i.e. some subjective condition or weakness internal to the accused, such as his/her psychological or emotional make-up) shall be deemed to be a "disease of the mind."

Non-insane automatism, on the other hand, is automatism which is *not* caused by a disease of the mind; it is automatism which occurs with a perfectly healthy

---

[7] *Halsbury's Laws of England*, vol. 11(1) (4th edition re-issue), para. 6.

[8] (1843), 10 Cl. & Fin. 200, [1843-60] All E.R. 229 (H.L.).

[9] Adopted as law in Britain. See *Halsbury's Laws*, *supra*, para. 31.

[10] *Ibid*, para. 7.

[11] *State v. Massey*, 747 P. 2d 802 (Kan. 1987)

[12] *Sellers v. State*, 809 P. 2d 676 (Okla. Crim. App.1991).

[13] [1980] 2 S.C.R. 513, 114 D.L.R. (3d) 193, 15 C.R. (3d) 225 [hereinafter *Rabey* cited to C.R.].

mind. At p. 233, the Supreme Court of Canada upheld Martin, J.A.'s distinction that any state of automatism arising from *external* factors, such as a blow to the head, shall qualify as non-insane automatism.

The Supreme Court also said these two defences must differ in their application. Insane automatism is normally subsumed under the defence of insanity (i.e. mental disorder, s. 16), which leads to a special verdict of not guilty by reason of insanity. After this verdict, the accused may be indefinitely confined to a psychiatric institution. Non-insane automatism, on the other hand, leads to an absolute acquittal. Similar to the law in Britain, the onus of proof is on the Crown to prove the existence of a voluntary act (i.e. absence of automatism) beyond a reasonable doubt."[14]

The defence of non-insane automatism has been recognized in numerous cases and several jurisdictions involving crimes such as murder,[15] attempted murder,[16] manslaughter,[17] criminal negligence causing death,[18] rape,[19] and assault[20] and fraud.[21] The defence has variously been referred to (and successfully applied) as non-insane automatism or simply "automatism", "automation",[22] "an unconscious condition",[23] and, in the United States, as "diminished capacity."

In answer to the first issue raised in this memo, non-insane automatism is a valid defence to an indictable offence, including the crime of second degree murder.

2. *Sleepwalking is Non-insane Automatism*

If non-insane automatism is a valid defence, the question now becomes whether sleepwalking is considered to fall within that category or whether it is considered to be a "disease of the mind", under s. 16 of the *Code* and hence within the classification of *insane* automatism.

This question has been considered by several superior courts in Canada, Britain and the United States. The short answer to the question is that sleepwalking *does* fall within the category of non-insane automatism. Perhaps the strongest authority for this proposition is the 1992 unanimous Supreme Court of Canada decision in *R. v. Parks.*"[24] The facts in this case are strikingly similar to those in Mr. Rigby's case: the

---

[14] *Ibid*, at 226. This finding was also made by La Forest in *R. v. Parks* (1992), 140 N.R. 161, 75 C.C.C. (3d) 287 (S.C.C.) [hereinafter *Parks* cited to N.R.].

[15] See *Bleta v. The Queen*, [1964] S.C.R. 561, 48 D.L.R. (2d) 139; *R. v. Hartridge* (1966), 57 D.L.R. (2d) 332, 48 CR 389 (Sask. C.A.); *R. v. Cusack* (1971), 3 C.C.C. (2d) 527 (P.E.I.S.C.); *R. v. Parks, supra*, note 11; *HM Advocate v. Fraser* (1978), 4 Couper 70 (H.C. Scot.) [hereinafter *Fraser*]; *Bratty v. Attorney-General for Northern Ireland*, [1961] 3 All E.R. 523, [1963] A.C. 386 (H.L.) [hereinafter *Bratty* cited to All E.R.]; *State v. Massey*, 747 P. 2d 802 (Kan. 1987); *Sellers v. State* 809 P. 2d 676 (Okla. Crim. App. 1991).

[16] See *R. v. O'Brien*, [1966] 3 C.C.C. 288 (N.B.C.A.); *R. v. Parks, supra*, note 11; *People v. Dunigan*, 421 N.E. 2d 1319 (Ill. App. 1981).

[17] See *R. v. K.*, [1971] 2 O.R. 401 (H.C).

[18] See *R. v. Cullum* (I 973), 14 C.C.C. (2d) 294 (Ont. Co. Ct.).

[19] See *People v. Dunigan, supra*, note 13.

[20] See *R. v. Rabey, supra* note 10; *R. v. Burgess*, [1991] 2 All E.R. 769 (C.A.); *People v. Grant*, 377 N.E. 2d 4 (Ill. 1978).

[21] See *State v. Orth*, 359 S.E. 2d 136 (W. Va.1987).

[22] See *Bleta v. The Queen, supra*, note 15.

[23] See *R. v. Minor* (1955), 21C.R. 377 (Sask. C.A.).

[24] *Supra*, note 14.

accused, while in a somnambulistic state, drove 23 km on a multi-lane high-speed highway to the home of his in-laws, where he murdered them with a tire iron taken from his car and a knife retrieved from the victims' kitchen. He then drove to a police station where he reported that be had just killed two people. He allegedly recalled little of the event.

The main issue in *Parks* was the same as the question raised above, that is whether sleepwalking is included in the definition of non-insane automatism. At the Ontario Court of Appeal, Galligan, J.A. said the evidence did not suggest that the accused suffered from any "disease of the mind," but rather that his faculties were merely impaired under the normal conditions of sleep. Sleepwalking, it was held, is a disorder of sleep which occurs *during* sleep; however, the impairment of the accused did not suffer from a "disease of the mind;" he only experienced an episode of non-insane automatism.[25]

This reasoning was later upheld on appeal to the Supreme Court of Canada. In addition, La Forest, J. applied the distinction outlined by Martin, J.A. in *Rabey* to conclude that the particular amalgam of factors that cause somnambulism are external factors and, therefore, somnambulism properly falls within the category of non-insane automatism.[26]

In the English case of *Bratty*,[27] the House of Lords was called upon to decide whether psychomotor epilepsy, which caused the accused to experience periods of "blackness," should be classified as automatism or insanity. The court held that a rejection of the insanity defence does not preclude the application of the automatism defence. As Viscount Kilmuir, L.C. said, at p. 528: "For example, it may be alleged that the accused had a blow on the head after which he acted without being conscious of what he was doing, *or was a sleepwalker*" {emphasis mine}. Although any mention of sleepwalking as falling within the category of [non-insane] automatism was *obiter dicta* in that case, the fact that it came from a court as high as the House of Lords is persuasive authority.

In the Scottish case of *HM Advocate* v. *Fraser*,[28] the High Court of Scotland allowed a defence of somnambulism for the crime of murder. In that case, the accused, while asleep, had picked up his 18 month old son out of its crib and threw him on the floor. The baby died. The court held that the accused's act occurred in an unconscious state and thus found him to be absolved of criminal responsibility. The verdict was absolute acquittal.

American jurisprudence is somewhat divided on the issue of sleepwalking and the non-insane automatism [diminished capacity] defence. Although not every state recognizes the defence of diminished capacity, sleepwalking *has* been recognized (albeit in *obiter dicta*) by at least one superior court. In *People* v. *Grant*,[29] the Illinois Supreme Court held that a person is *not* criminally responsible for acts committed in a state of automatism, whether those acts are of a simple or complex nature. While the accused

---

[25] *R.* v. *Parks* (1990), 78 C.R. (3d) 1, 56 C.C.C. (3d) 449 (Ont. C.A.) [cited to C.R.], at 19.

[26] *R.* v. *Parks* (S.C.C.), *supra* note 11, at 173.

[27] *Supra*, note 12.

[28] *Supra*, note 12.

[29] *Supra*, note 17.

in that case was charged with assaulting a police officer during an epileptic seizure, the court did say, at page 8, that "[s]uch involuntary acts may include those committed during convulsions, sleep, unconsciousness, hypnosis or seizures."

On the authority of decisions such as *Parks*, *Bratty*, *Fraser* and *Grant*, I would suggest that sleepwalking is properly classified as non-insane automatism.

3. *For Sleepwalking and the Defence of Non-insane Automatism: The Likely Verdict is Unqualified Acquittal*

From the discussion of the non-insane automatism defence (*supra*, pp. 3-5) and from cases like *Parks* and *Fraser*, it seems the likely verdict arising from a successful application of this defence is an unqualified acquittal. The only exception might be where the court interprets the evidence as suggesting the accused suffered from a "disease of the mind" ("mental disorder" under s. 16 of the *Code*). In such circumstances, the likely verdict is "not guilty" by reason of insanity.

This exception accurately describes the outcome in *R. v. Burgess*[30] where the British Court of Appeal elected *not* to accept the defence of non-insane automatism by reason of sleepwalking. The Court believed, instead, that the evidence pointed to more than non-insane automatism; that it, in fact, amounted to insanity under the *M'Naghten* Rules. The accused was subsequently found not guilty by reason of insanity and detained in a secure hospital.

In this case, the court's interpretation of the evidence was pivotal in arriving at a verdict of insanity. This kind of interpretation poses the greatest problem when dealing with the issue of sleepwalking as it relates to the defence of non-insane automatism. This, and related problems will be discussed next.

III. PROBLEM:

The factor which poses the greatest problem to a successful application of the defence of non-insane automatism in a case involving sleepwalking is the court's interpretation of the evidence. Although both the Ontario Court of Appeal and the Supreme Court of Canada believed the facts in *Parks* suggested the accused suffered from non-insane automatism and not a "disease of the mind," Lamer, C.J.C. added the following qualifier at p. 205: "This is not to say that sleepwalking could never be a disease of the mind, in another case on different evidence." I suggest, however, that the facts in Mr. Rigby's case are so close to those in *Parks* that the court is likely to interpret his condition as non-insane automatism as well, rather than a "disease of the mind."

The British case of *R. v. Burgess* was one example where the court believed the medical evidence amounted to insanity rather than non-insane automatism. The court decided not to follow the Ontario Court of Appeal's decision in *Parks*, relying instead on medical evidence which suggested that sleepwalking *is* a mental disorder or "disease of the mind." On the other hand, Lamer C.J.C. pointed out, distinguishing the *Burgess* decision from *Parks*, that in *Burgess*, there was medical evidence

---

[30] *Supra*, note 17.

to suggest that the accused's act was liable to recur and that it may have been dissociative (i.e. resulting from factors internal to the accused, such as psychological or emotional distress). The Supreme Court had already acknowledged that the ordinary stresses and disappointments of life are a subjective condition or weakness, *internal* to the accused, and shall be deemed to constitute a "disease of the mind;"[31] however, such circumstances were not believed to exist in *Parks*.

In the case at hand, the Crown may argue that the financial, marital and work-related stresses suffered by Mr. Rigby at the time of the offence were the causes of his sleepwalking. While such factors are clearly, within the category of "internal" factors described by Martin, J.A. in *Rabey*, and referred to in *Burgess*, the court may not consider them to be the cause of Mr. Rigby's sleepwalking (as the Supreme Court of Canada decided in *Parks*). Even if Mr. Rigby's sleepwalking was caused by internal factors, his mental impairment is likely to be considered to have been caused by the normal condition of sleep. Under strikingly similar facts in *Parks*, the Supreme Court held that an accused person is not considered to be suffering from a disease of the mind if his/her acts arise from an otherwise normal condition such as sleep.[32]

As for the American jurisdiction, the case law on the defence of non-insane automatism [diminished capacity] is relatively inconclusive. There are numerous states where this defence is not even recognized.[33] On the other hand, however, there are several states which *do* recognize such a defence, including one whose Supreme Court (albeit in *obiter*) classified sleepwalking as being included in the defence of automatism.[34]

In short, the greatest barrier to a successful application of the defence of non-insane automatism arising out of sleepwalking lies in the interpretation of the medical evidence. If the court is persuaded that Mr. Rigby's stress was the cause of his sleepwalking, it may decide that he was suffering from a disease of the mind at the time of the act. If the court follows the recent Supreme Court of Canada decision in *Parks*, however, Mr. Rigby's sleepwalking is likely to be considered to have been caused by the normal condition of sleep, in which case a defence of non-insane automatism will apply.

---

[31] *R. v. Rabey*, *supra*, at 233.

[32] It is interesting to note that the British Court of Appeal in *Burgess* considered the Ontario Court of Appeal's decision in *Parks* and decided not to follow it. When *Parks* was appealed to the Supreme Court of Canada, however, *Burgess* was distinguished. From this, it might be argued that the Supreme Court of Canada's decision is a more persuasive authority since it is a relatively higher court in its respective jurisdiction. It should further be noted that *Parks* has been judicially considered in another Canadian high court; it was applied in *R. v. Tasse* (May 31, 1993), Doc. CA014860 (B.C.C.A.).

[33] For examples of states which do not recognize the defence of diminished capacity, see *Chestnut v. State*, 538 So. 2d 820 (Fla. 1989); *State v. Butler*, 563 So. 2d 976 (Ia. App. 1990); *Hightower v. State*, 386 S.E. 2d 509 (Ga. 1989); *State v. Huertas*, 553 N.E. 2d 1058 (Ohio 1990); *State v. Torkelson*, 404 N.W. 2d 352 (Minn. App. 1987); *State v. Chapman*, 451 N.W. 2d 263 (Neb. 1990).

[34] See *People v. Grant*, *supra*, note 17.

TABLE OF CASES

Bleta v. *The Queen*, [1964] S.C.R. 561, 48 D.L.R. (2d) 139.

Bratty v. *Attorney-General for Northern Ireland*, [1961] 3 AII E.R. 523, [1963] A.C. 386 (H.L.).

HM Advocate v. *Fraser* (1878) 4 Couper 70 (H.C. Scot.).

M'Naghten's Case (1843), 10 Cl. & Fin. 200, [1843-60] All E.R. 229 (H.L.).

People v. *Dunigan*, 421 N.E. 2d 1319 (Ill. App. 1981).

People v. *Grant*, 377 N.E. 2d 4 (Ill. 1978).

R. v. *Baker* (1970), 1 C.C.C. 203 (N.S. Co. Ct.).

R. v. *Berger* (1975), 27 C.C.C. (2d) 357 (B.C.C.A.).

R. v. *Burgess*, [1991] 2 All E.R. 769 (C.A.).

R. v. *Cullum* (1973), 14 C.C.C. (2d) 294 (Ont. Co. Ct.)

R. v. *Cusack* (1971), 3 C.C.C. (2d) 527 (P.E.I.S.C.).

R. v. *Hartridge* (1966), 57 D.L.R. (2d) 332, 48 C.R. 389 (Sask. C.A.).

R. v. *K.* [1971] 2 O.R. 401 (H.C.).

R. v. *Minor* (1955), 21 C.R. 377 (Sask. C.A.).

R. v. *O'Brien* (1966), 56 D.L.R. (2d) 65, 3 C.C.C. 288 (N.B.C.A.).

R. v. *Parks* (1992), 140 N.R. 161, 75 C.C.C. (3d) 287 (S.C.C.) affirming (1990), 78 C.R. (3d) 1, 56 C.C.C. (3d) 449 (Ont. C.A.).

R. v. *Rabey*, [1980] 2 S.C.R. 513, 114 D.L.R. (3d) 193, 15 C.R. (3d) 225.

R. v. *Tasse* (May 31, 1993), Doc. CA014860 (B.C.C.A.).

APPENDIX C
Model Factum

IN THE HIGH COURT OF THE DOMINION OF CANADA
(On Appeal from the Ontario Court of Appeal)

BETWEEN:

ORGANIZATION OF ABORIGINAL WOMEN
(OAW)

Appellant

-AND-

HER MAJESTY THE QUEEN IN RIGHT OF ONTARIO

Respondent

FACTUM OF THE APPELLANT
ORGANIZATION OF ABORIGINAL WOMEN

Counsel for the Appellant

Team #1
Wilson Moot 2000

PART 1: STATEMENT OF FACTS

1. The Appellant, the Organization of Aboriginal Women (the "OAW"), is a national non-profit organization which was incorporated in 1977. Its members are Aboriginal women who self-identify as Aboriginal and have provided proof of Aboriginal ancestry. The OAW's membership includes Métis, status, and non-status Indian women.

Official Problem at 2.

2. The Respondent is the Assembly of Ontario's First Nations (the "AOFN"), an organization representing 132 band councils in Ontario. The bands represented by the AOFN are comprised mainly of Indians registered under the *Indian Act* (often referred to as "status Indians") and all of them have reserve land bases. Under the provisions of the *Indian Act*, each band council represented by the AOFN controls access to residency on their respective reserves.

Official Problem at 1, 2.

Indian Act, R.S.C. 1985, c. I-5, s. 81(1) [hereinafter the *Indian Act*].

3. The Appellant appeals from a decision of the Ontario Court of Appeal reversing a decision of the Ontario Superior Court which found that Ontario's Casino Program violated the Appellant's section 15 rights and is not justifiable under section 1 of the *Canadian Charter of Rights and Freedoms.*

Casino Corporation Ontario Act, per Official Problem [hereinafter the Act].

Canadian Charter of Rights and Freedoms, ss. 1, 15, Part I of the *Constitution Act, 1982*, being Schedule B to the *Canada Act 1982* (U.K.), 1982 c.11, s. 2(a) [hereinafter the *Charter*].

4. The Casino Program is a provincial program instituted in Ontario to assist on-reserve Aboriginal communities. The Program was the result of exclusive negotiations between the Ontario Government and the AOFN. Pursuant to those negotiations, it was agreed that a Casino would be located on one of the bands' reserves and that the net revenues from the Casino would be distributed to and between the 132 bands in the province. In September 1994, a selection committee of the AOFN and the Ontario Government announced that a First Nations Reserve in northern Ontario had been chosen as the site for the new Casino.

Official Problem at 1.

5. Under the provisions of the Program, Casino profits will be provided through the First Nations Fund to band councils, who can then spend the money on reserves for the benefit of the communities residing thereon. In addition, the band councils are themselves actual beneficiaries of the Program.

Official Problem at 2-4.

6. No equivalent to the Casino Program exists to benefit Aboriginal women as a group who are not band members. This is so despite the fact that Aboriginal women suffer marked disadvantage. The OAW's non-status and Métis members belong to a severely disadvantaged group within Canadian society. Furthermore, many of its status Indian members have been subject to historical neglect and disadvantage imposed by provisions of the *Indian Act.*

Indian Act, supra.

7. Recognizing this, the OAW sought the inclusion of off-reserve Aboriginal women as negotiating partners and beneficiaries in the Casino Program. Despite this expression of interest, the Ontario Government has steadfastly refused to include the OAW in any aspect of the Program.

Official Problem at 1-4.

JUDICIAL HISTORY

8. The OAW brought an application in the Ontario Superior Court seeking a declaration that the Casino Program violates its members' equality rights under section 15 of the *Charter*, and a declaration that it is entitled to a share of the Casino's future profits. The Attorney General of Ontario was the Respondent.

Official Problem at 2.

9. The Government of Ontario has stated that its object in excluding the AOW is to benefit communities of on-reserve Aboriginal people by distributing the funds of the Casino Program to band councils. The Government further attempted to justify its choice of beneficiary by stating that it was simply utilizing an accepted statutory definition found in the *Indian Act.*

Indian Act, supra at s. 2.

Official Problem at 2-3.

10. Mr. Justice Perrin of the Ontario Superior Court held that Ontario's Casino Program was not authorized by section 15(2) of the *Charter*. His Lordship agreed that section 15(2) should not be seen as an exception or defence to a breach of section 15(1) of the *Charter*. He noted the inherent danger that a broad reading of section 15(2) of the *Charter* would leave the courts powerless to protect those groups with the weakest lobbies and least access to government, or those labelled as "problems." If all that is required of a program in order to comply with section 15 is that the purpose of the impugned program be designed to benefit a disadvantaged group, groups with the strongest lobbies and most access to government will be the groups that most often benefit from these programs.

Official Problem at 3-4.

11.   Mr. Justice Perrin also found that the Casino Program violated the Appellant's section 15(1) rights. His Lordship stated that Ontario's decision to benefit band councils was especially unfair to Aboriginal women who are doubly disadvantaged by virtue of both their race and gender.

12.   In overturning the trial decision, the Ontario Court of Appeal did not dispute the findings of fact made by Mr. Justice Perrin. However, the Court held that the Casino Program was a valid expression of affirmative action under section 15(2) of the *Charter*. According to Mr. Justice Morin any program which has an ameliorative purpose and is targeted at a disadvantaged group complies with section 15(2) and is thereby consistent with the *Charter*.

Official Problem at 5.

PART II: STATEMENT OF ISSUES

13.   The High Court of the Dominion of Canada has granted leave to appeal on the following two questions:
   (1) Does the exclusion of the Appellant from participating in negotiations and sharing in the proceeds from the Casino violate section 15 of the *Charter*?
   (2) If the answer to question (1) above is yes, is the violation justified under section 1 of the *Charter*?

PART III: APPELLANT'S ARGUMENTS

ISSUE 1: THE EXCLUSION OF THE APPELLANT FROM PARTICIPATING IN THE CASINO PROGRAM VIOLATES SECTION 15 OF THE *CHARTER*

A. The Ontario Court of Appeal erred in its interpretation of section 15(2) of the *Charter*.

14.   The Appellant submits that the Ontario Court of Appeal erred in its interpretation of section 15(2) of the *Charter*. While noting that section 15(2) is an enhancement to the equality guarantee in section 15(1), Mr. Justice Morin applied a broadly articulated two stage test focusing exclusively on the ameliorative object of the Casino Program. This interpretation effectively renders section 15(2) an exception to the guarantee of equality under section 15(1) undermining the *Charter* guarantee of substantive equality.

Official Problem at 5

i) Section 15(2) is an enhancement rather than an exception to the equality guarantee under section 15(1).

15.   It is submitted that section 15(2) was intended to enhance the guarantee of equality in section 15(1). Any interpretation of section 15(2) as an exception to those guarantees is thus incorrect in law. It is a settled principle that section 15(1) guarantees substantive rather than mere formal equality. Furthermore, the promotion of substantive equality necessitates that where pre-existing discrimination has resulted in disadvantage or vulnerability, differential treatment is sometimes required to ameliorate the offending conditions.

> *Andrews* v. *Law Society of British Columbia*, [1989] 1 S.C.R. 143 at 171 per Wilson J. [hereinafter *Andrews*].

16. Accordingly, the inclusion of section 15(2) in the *Charter* explicitly recognizes that affirmative action programs which confer ameliorative benefits upon members of disadvantaged groups will not be subject to claims of "reverse discrimination" under section 15(1) by members of a more advantaged group. To ensure the guarantees in section 15(1) are not undermined however, section 15(2) should be viewed as limited to this purpose.

> *R.* v. *Hess*, [1990] 2 S.C.R. 906 at 945-46 per McLachlin J. [hereinafter *Hess*], citing *Re MacVicar and Superintendent of Family and Child Services* (1986), 34 D.L.R. (4th) 488 (B.C.S.C.) at 502-503, per Huddart L.J.S.C.

17.   Section 15(2) was not intended, however, to shield from judicial scrutiny all programs which are properly characterized as affirmative action under section 15(2). As Madam Justice McLachlin noted in *Hess*, such an expensive interpretation "threatens to circumvent the purpose of section 1."

> *Hess, supra* at 946 per McLachlin J.

18.   Implicit in this understanding of section 15(2) is the recognition that government programs which have an ameliorative object may nonetheless be discriminatory. Failure to scrutinize such a program gives rise to the immediate risk that it may create or aggravate inequality for some individuals, even as it purports to alleviate it for others. This result is utterly discordant with a purposive interpretation of section 15.

ii) The Court of Appeal's interpretation of section 15(2) exempts government measures from the appropriate judicial scrutiny.

19.   The Appellant submits that in imposing the two-stage analysis under section 15(2) which focuses on the Casino Program's ameliorative purpose and target group, the Court of Appeal circumvented a proper analysis of the Program under section 15(1).

> Official Problem at 5.

20.   The Supreme Court of Canada has held that the fundamental purpose of section 15(1) of the *Charter* is to protect and promote essential human dignity by preventing the imposition of discriminatory laws or measures and to promote a society in which all Canadians are worthy of equal recognition and value. Accordingly, the court has developed a highly contextualized method of analysis to recognize those laws and measures which offend that purpose.

> *Egan* v. *Canada*, [1995] 2 S.C.R. 513 at 543 per L'Heureux-Dubé J.
> *Vriend* v. *Alberta*, [1998] 1 S.C.R. 493 at 535 per Cory J.

> *Law* v. *Canada (Minister of Employment and Immigration)*, [1999] 1 S.C.R. 497 at 529 per Iacobucci J. [hereinafter *Law*].

21.   Moreover, the Supreme Court of Canada has consistently upheld the principle that a law or measure need not be discriminatory in its purpose to be found a violation of section 15(1), but that adverse effect discrimination will equally attract attention under the *Charter*. The Ontario Court of Appeal has also recognized in relation to section 15(2) ameliorative programs that even where the substance of a program is authorized under the section, some feature of the program may nonetheless be discriminatory.

> *Andrews, supra* at 174 per McIntyre J.

> *Lovelace* v. *Ontario* (1997), 33 O.R. (3d) 735 at 755 (C.A.).

22.   In the present case, by assessing only the government's assertion of the Program's ameliorative object in relation to on-reserve Aboriginal communities, the Court of Appeal ignored the possibility that the Program may discriminate against the OAW in effect. In light of the pervasiveness and subtlety of many forms of discrimination, and the contextualized analysis developed by the Supreme Court of Canada to recognize and combat them, it is inappropriate to allow any government program to escape scrutiny under section 15(1) solely by virtue of its ameliorative purpose in relation to a disadvantaged group.

23.   The risk of tautological reasoning is inherent in this approach, leaving the government free to take measures which, while ameliorative to the target group, nonetheless discriminate in effect. It affords an exception to the guarantee of substantive equality in section 15(1) and, as noted by Mr. Justice Simonsen in *Apsit* v. *Manitoba Human Rights Commission*, if such an approach were permitted, "the equality guarantees in s. 15(1) would become a hollow shell."

> *Apsit* v. *Manitoba Human Rights Commission*, [1988] 1 W.W.R. 629 at 634 (Man. Q.B.) [hereinafter *Apsit*].

B. The Casino Program is not authorized by section 15(2) of the *Charter*.

24.   Further and in the alternative, the Appellant submits that the Court of Appeal erred in holding that the Casino Program is a valid affirmative action program within the meaning of section 15(2) of the *Charter*. Section 15(2) should be read narrowly in order to interpret and apply section 15 purposively and in a manner which promotes equality and protects from discrimination. Its application should be ameliorative in effect and purpose and be limited only to those programs benefiting groups which are disadvantaged as compared to the group to which the claimant belongs. The Casino Program meets neither of these criteria.

i) The disadvantage of on-reserve Aboriginal communities should be measured against that of the Appellant.

25.   A program grounded under section 15(2) is only consistent with the purposes of section 15 to the extent that it promotes substantive equality by addressing pre-existing inequality. An ameliorative program which discriminates between disadvantaged groups, thereby creating inequality, is therefore not a *bona fide* section 15(2) affirmative action program.

26.   As noted by Mr. Justice Perrin at the trial level, there is an inherent danger in allowing governments to define the disadvantage of the beneficiary group in the abstract. This approach gives rise to the real possibility that disadvantaged groups are distinguished on a discriminatory basis as to which are worthy of assistance. This danger becomes even more apparent where excluded groups share substantially the same disadvantage, in cause or effect, with those deemed eligible for benefit.

Official Problem at 3.

27.   It is submitted that where the claimant's disadvantage is equal to or greater than that of the beneficiary group and, moreover, is substantially the same in character or cause, the exclusion of the claimant from an affirmative action program *prima facie* gives rise to the possibility that the government's choice of beneficiary was discriminatory. Under these circumstances it is more consistent with the overall purpose of section 15 of the *Charter* that the program be subjected to the same rigorous scrutiny under section 15(1) as would any other government measure.

28.   This approach protects the government's freedom to take affirmative action consistent with the promotion of substantive equality. Through the proper operation of section 15(2), claimants in a comparatively advantaged position would be unable to demonstrate discrimination, as would those who are disadvantaged but whose disadvantage is objectively determined to be of a sufficiently distinct character in cause or effect. However, claimants who experience equal or greater disadvantage of substantially the same character as the beneficiary group would not be barred from attempting to demonstrate that the program in question is in some way discriminatory.

29.   Rather than engaging the court in an unproductive exercise to determine which group is more disadvantaged, this approach imports a contextual analysis to the distinction between those programs which genuinely accord with the purpose of section 15(2) and those which do not. This in turn leaves the government free to set priorities as to how and when various disadvantaged groups will be targeted as beneficiaries while avoiding the otherwise apparent danger of gross unfairness amounting to discrimination.

R. v. Willocks (1995), 22 O.R. (3d) 552 at 571 (Gen. Div.) per Watt J.

30.   In the case at bar, it is submitted that the OAW suffers disadvantage which is equal to or greater than that experienced by the Casino Program's intended beneficiaries, on-reserve Aboriginal communities. At trial, Mr. Justice Perrin noted that Aboriginal women are "doubly disadvantaged by virtue of their race and gender." Moreover, he held as a finding of fact that "Aboriginal women who are not eligible to register under the *Indian Act* are, as a whole, a severely disadvantaged group within Canadian society." In addition, the Appellant's disadvantage is substantially the same as that experienced by the intended beneficiaries. Aboriginal women suffer economic, social and cultural deprivation, owing largely to the intersection of their ethnic identity and gender and patterns of historical discrimination based thereupon.

Official Problem at 3.

ii) The Casino Program is not demonstrably ameliorative in effect.

31.   It is submitted that to be considered a *bona fide* affirmative action program under section 15(2) of the *Charter*, the program in question must be ameliorative in effect as well as purpose. Exclusive reliance upon an ameliorative object baldly asserted by the government would seriously undermine the purpose of section 15. In order to ensure that discriminatory measures are not thus shielded by section 15(2), Mr. Justice Simonsen noted in *Apsit* that "there must be a real nexus between the object of the program as declared by the government and its form and implementation."

Apsit, supra at 642 per Simonsen J.

32.   In the case at bar it is submitted that such a nexus is manifestly absent. At trial, Mr. Justice Perrin acknowledged that under section 15(2) an affirmative action program must be assessed not only by its stated purpose, but by whether or not it actually achieves that purpose as well. Furthermore, it was held as a finding of fact that the Casino Program actually benefits band councils, despite the government's assertion that the intention of the Program is to benefit on-reserve Aboriginal communities.

Official Problem at 4.

C. The Casino Program violates the Appellant's equality rights under section 15(1) of the *Charter*.

33. The Appellant submits that the Court of Appeal erred in finding that the Ontario Government's Casino Program did not violate the Appellant's equality rights under section 15(1) of the *Charter*.

34. In *Law*, the Supreme Court of Canada synthesized its earlier jurisprudence regarding section 15(1) of the *Charter* and outlined the analytical framework within which alleged breaches of the equality guarantee are to be assessed. According to this framework, a tribunal is called upon to examine:

A. whether a law, in purpose or effect: (i) draws a formal distinction between the claimant and others on the basis of one or more personal characteristics, or (ii) fails to take into account the claimant's already disadvantaged position within Canadian society;

B. whether one or more enumerated or analogous grounds of discrimination are the basis for the differential treatment; and

C. whether the law in question has a purpose or effect that is discriminatory within the meaning of the equality guarantee.

The second and third branches of the analysis are determinative of whether or not the differential treatment in question is discriminatory.

Law, supra at 532-540 per Iacobucci J.

35. The Supreme Court in *Law* held that the core value enshrined in section 15(1) was the protection and promotion of human dignity. Accordingly, an infringement of section 15(1) exists if it can be established that, from the perspective of a reasonable person in circumstances similar to the claimant, the imposition of differential treatment has the effect of demeaning his or her dignity.

Law, supra at 533-534 per Iacobucci J.

36. Under the analysis outlined in *Law* the Casino Program violates the Appellant's section 15(1) *Charter* rights. Furthermore, even if it is found that the Program has an ameliorative purpose, it nonetheless constitutes adverse effect discrimination against the Appellant.

i) The Casino Program imposes differential treatment upon the Appellant in effect.

37. The Appellant submits that the Casino Program imposes differential treatment upon the OAW in effect with respect to participation in the negotiation for and sharing of the Program's revenues. It is further submitted that the design and implementation of the Program utterly fail to take into account the Appellant's already disadvantaged position within Canadian society.

38. The Supreme Court has held that discrimination can arise both from the adverse effects of rules of general application as well as from, express distinctions flowing from the distribution of benefits. A facially neutral law or measure therefore violates section 15 of the *Charter* where it imposes discriminatory differential treatment in effect.

Eldridge v. *British Columbia (Attorney General)*, [1997] 3 S.C.R. 624 at 670 per LaForest J. [hereinafter *Eldridge*].

Brooks v. *Canada Safeway Ltd.*, [1989] 1 S.C.R. 1219 at 1242 per Dickson C.J. [hereinafter *Brooks*].

39. The Casino Program, while facially neutral as to gender, nonetheless imposes differential treatment upon the Appellant amounting to discrimination on the basis of sex. The intentional exclusion from the Program of off-reserve Aboriginal communities, as well as the status of band councils as administrators and beneficiaries of Casino revenues, render benefits under the Program contingent upon residing on-reserve or access to band council largesse. This effectively imposes differential treatment upon Aboriginal women.

a) The inability to reside on a reserve disproportionately affects Aboriginal women.

40. Despite the repeal of those provisions of the Indian Act which were directly discriminatory towards Aboriginal women, a legacy of discrimination remains. While the forcible loss of status under the old provisions often entailed a corollary loss of the right to reside on a reserve or benefit from band funds, the 1985 amendments failed to restore these rights. Band membership and the ability to reside on a reserve is within the exclusive jurisdiction of band councils to decide. Furthermore, despite the fact that 75% of status Indians residing off-reserve are women, as are nearly three-quarters of those who have applied to regain status since the passage of Bill C-31, band councils have maintained restrictive residency policies owing to concerns about overcrowding and disruption. These policies therefore have a disproportionate impact on Aboriginal women.

Indian Act, supra at s. 81(1).

Official Problem at 4.

Royal Commission on Aboriginal Peoples, Perspectives and Realities (Ottawa: Minister of Supplies and Services Canada, 1996), vol. 4 at 36 [hereinafter *RCAP*].

41. Because federal funding to each band council is contingent upon the number of on-reserve status Indians only, access to any reserve by non-status Indians would represent a net loss in revenue for the band council and a significant strain on its fiscal resources. This is a significant disincentive for any band council to permit non-status Indians or Métis to reside upon its reserve. Given the finding at trial that

status Indians are generally provided with more financial and social benefits than those who are non-status, and moreover that non-status and Métis women as a group are severely disadvantaged, the practical inability to gain access to reserve residency and the corollary benefits provided through the Casino Program has a significantly more severe impact on these groups.

RCAP, supra at 49-50.

Official Problem at 3-4.

b) The administration of Casino revenues by band councils is detrimental to Aboriginal women.

42.   Under the Casino Program, band councils are designated to receive and administer Casino revenues on their respective reserves. Moreover, it was a finding of fact at trial that the band councils themselves are the primary beneficiaries of the Program. The Appellant submits that this central feature of the Casino Program places Aboriginal women at a distinct disadvantage.

Official Problem at 2, 4.

43.   There is strong evidence to support the contention by many Aboriginal women that their interests are not sufficiently represented or addressed within the current band council structure. As one manifestation of this disadvantage, Aboriginal females who do reside on-reserve are significantly more likely to leave and take up residence elsewhere than their male counterparts. Furthermore, unlike males, they are more likely to do so for gender-related reasons:

> Many Aboriginal women have no option, therefore, but to live in urban areas even though they would prefer to live in their community of origin. Their options are circumscribed by abuse, loss of status, or the fact that their needs and perspectives are not taken into account.

RCAP, supra at 573-574.

44.   Recognizing this, the *RCAP* has acknowledged the crucial importance of separate organizations comprised of and responsive to Aboriginal women alone. It has recommended that the Federal Government provide funding directly to such organizations, both on and off-reserve, to ensure the full participation of Aboriginal women in the process of nation building, health care delivery and other important facets of Aboriginal community development.

RCAP, supra at 53, 71.

45.   The Supreme Court held in *M. v. H.* that in assessing the nature of the "benefit" denied a broad view should be taken, encompassing not only an economic benefit but also access to a process that could confer an economic or other benefit.

Accordingly, both the Government's choice to negotiate exclusively with the AOFN and the role of band councils as beneficiaries and administrators of Casino revenues is inherently disadvantageous to the interests of Aboriginal women. The Government's initial exclusion of the Appellant is compounded by the unlikelihood in deciding who may or may not reside upon reserves, and as a consequence to whom the benefits of the Casino Program will accrue, that band councils are capable of affording the needs of Aboriginal women their due consideration.

M. v. *H.*, [1999] 2 S.C.R. 3 at 53, per Cory J.

ii) The differential treatment is imposed in effect upon an enumerated ground.

46.   It is submitted that the differential treatment imposed upon the OAW by the Casino Program is based upon the enumerated ground of sex.

47.   Discrimination based upon an enumerated ground may affect only a subgroup of the relevant group, in this case, a subgroup of Aboriginal women. The fact that those Aboriginal women who reside on-reserve have ostensibly been included within the ambit of the Casino Program is therefore no bar to a claim of gender-based discrimination by the Appellant.

Battlefords and District Co-operative v. *Gibbs*, [1996] 3 S.C.R. 566 at 583-584 per Sopinka J.

Brooks, supra at 1247 per Dickson C.J.

iii) The differential treatment imposed upon the Appellant is discriminatory in effect.

48.   The Appellant submits that the effect of the differential treatment imposed upon Aboriginal women residing off-reserve is discriminatory. Submission of the Casino Program to the contextual analysis prescribed under the third branch of the analysis in *Law* leads to a finding that the Program violates the Appellant's section 15(1) *Charter* rights in effect.

Law, supra at 522 per Iacobucci J.

a) The OAW has significant pre-existing disadvantage.

49.   The Supreme Court of Canada has held that the establishment by the claimant of pre-existing disadvantage, vulnerability, stereotyping or prejudice is likely the most compelling factor favoring a finding that differential treatment under the impugned legislation or measure is discriminatory. The importance of these factors derives from the likelihood that the claimant has already been subject to unfair treatment or a lack of equal concern and that further differential treatment will have a more severe impact upon them as a result.

Law, supra at 534 per Iacobucci J.

50. The Appellant's pre-existing disadvantage is a matter of record. At trial, Mr. Justice Perrin found that as a group, Aboriginal women are doubly disadvantaged by virtue of their race and gender and yet no equivalent to the Casino Program was provided to Aboriginal women who are not band members. Moreover, the continuing legacy of discriminatory treatment under the law and the lack of adequate representation within their own conununities have left Aboriginal women acutely vulnerable. The Casino Program's inclusion of band councils with reserve land bases and consequent exclusion of off-reserve Aboriginal women has only served to aggravate this vulnerability and disadvantage. Furthermore, it serves to perpetuate the stereotype recognized by the Supreme Court in *Corbière* v. *Canada (Minister of Indian and Northern Affairs)* that only those residing on reserves are seen as "truly Aboriginal."

> *Corbière* v. *Canada (Minister of Indian and Northern Affairs)*, [1999] 2 S.C.R. 203 at 258 per L'Heureux-Dubé J. [hereinafter *Corbière*]

b) There is a close relationship between gender and the OAW's circumstances.

51. The Supreme Court in *Law* held that this stage of the discrimination analysis gives rise to the need to examine whether or not the impugned legislation or measure takes into account the actual needs, capacity or circumstances of the claimant. At the same time, the analysis must remain focused upon the central question of whether, from the claimant's perspective, the differential treatment in question has the effect of violating human dignity.

> *Law, supra* at 537 per Iacobucci J.

52. The Ontario Government's decision to provide a benefit to on-reserve Aboriginal communities and band councils effectively imposed differential treatment upon off-reserve Aboriginal women on the basis of their sex. Given that the needs and circumstances experienced by Aboriginal women are linked directly to their gender as well as their race, the exclusion of the OAW can only be viewed as suggesting that off-reserve Aboriginal women are less deserving and worthy of recognition as Aboriginal males who reside on-reserve.

c) The Casino Program is an underinclusive ameliorative program.

53. The ameliorative purpose or effect of the legislation or measure at issue is an additional pertinent factor in assessing whether or not discrimination has taken place. Ameliorative legislation which accords with the purpose of section 15(1) will rarely violate the human dignity of a more advantaged claimant. However, underinclusive legislation which excludes from its scope members of a historically disadvantaged group will rarely escape the charge of discrimination.

> *Law, supra* at 539 per Iacobucci J.

54. It is submitted that the Casino Program constitutes an underinclusive ameliorative program which, in excluding the OAW, discriminates against an historically disadvantaged community.

The OAW experience much of the same disadvantage as the intended beneficiary, only more acutely by virtue of gender. The Casino Program's distinctly discriminatory effect upon the Appellant serves only to aggravate that disadvantage. As such, the Program is in complete discord with the purposes of section 15(1).

d) The Casino Program affects a vital interest.

55.   The last contextual factor outlined by the Supreme Court in *Law* is the nature and scope of the interest affected by the legislation or program. In general, the more significant the interest affected, the more likely it is that differential treatment affecting this interest will be discriminatory.

> *Corbière, supra* at 272 per L'Heureux-Dubé J.

56.   As noted, Aboriginal women are doubly disadvantaged by virtue of both their race and their gender. Their denial of access to purportedly ameliorative funding represents therefore a significant infringement on the economic, social and cultural interests of one of the most disadvantaged segments of the Aboriginal population. Furthermore, their outright exclusion from the process through which access to funds is determined, as well as the denial of funds itself, is highly detrimental to the crucial interest of Aboriginal women in attaining a proper position of equality within their own community and Canadian society as a whole.

57. In summary, the Appellant submits that under the analysis prescribed by law, a reasonable person in the circumstances of the claimant will ascertain that the Casino Program's exclusion of off-reserve Aboriginal women fundamentally demeans the human dignity of the Appellant.

ISSUE 2: THE CASINO PROGRAM IS DISCRIMINATORY AND CANNOT BE SAVED BY SECTION 1 OF THE *CHARTER*.

[paras, 58–94 omitted]

PART IV: ORDER SOUGHT

95.   The Appellant respectfully submits that this appeal be allowed and that the questions in this appeal be answered as follows:
(1) Does the exclusion of the Appellant from participating in negotiations and sharing in the proceeds from the Casino violate section 15 of the Charter?

Yes

(2) Is the violation justified under section 1 of the Charter?

No

REMEDY

96. If the decision by the Casino Corporation to exclude the OAW is not pre-scribed by law the Appellant requests that the court read down the authority of the Casino Corporation so as to require it to include the OAW in the Program unless the legislature otherwise provides.

97. If the decision is prescribed by law the Appellant requests that the court extend or read into the purpose of the Program the amelioration of the OAW there-by severing the exclusion. Such an extension does not require a "marked change to the thrust of the original program."

Schachter, supra at 718 per Lamer C.J.

98. Striking down the legislation would be contrary to the spirit of the *Charter* as it would result in the Government being unable to remedy inequity through the Program. It is inconceivable that a beneficial Program be abandoned outright rather than modified to ensure compliance with the *Charter*.

ALL OF WHICH IS RESPECTFULLY SUBMITTED.

Dated at this 15 day of February, 2000.

TEAM: 2
COUNSEL FOR THE APPELLANT

APPENDIX A: TABLE OF AUTHORITIES

1. LEGISLATION

Canada Corporations Act, R.S.C. 1970, c. C-32 Part II as am.
Canadian Charter of Rights and Freedoms, ss. 1, 15(l), 15(2), Part I of the
Constitution Act, 1982, being Schedule B to the *Canada Act 1982*, c. 11.
Indian Act, R.S.C. 1985, c. I-5, s. 81(1).
Saskatchewan Gaming Corporation Act, R.S.S. 1994, c. S-18.2, s. 30(b).

2. CASE LAW

Andrews v. *Law Society of British Columbia*, [1989] 1 S.C.R. 143.
Apsit v. *Manitoba Human Rights Commission*, [1988] 1 W.W.R. 629 (Man. Q.B.).
Battlefords and District Co-operative v. *Gibbs*, [1996] 3 S.C.R. 566.
Brooks v. *Canada Safeway Ltd.*,[1989] 1 S.C.R. 1219.
Corbière v. *Canada (Minister of Indian and Northern Affairs)*, [1999] 2 S.C.R. 203.
Egan v. *Canada*, [1995] 2 S.C.R. 513.
Eldridge v. *British Columbia (Attorney General)*, [1997] 3 S.C.R. 624.
Law v. *Canada (Minister of Employment and Immigration)*, [1999] 1 S.C.R. 497.
Lovelace v. *Ontario* (1997), 33 O.R. (3d) 735.(C.A.).
M. v. *H.*, [1999] 2 S.C.R. 3.
R. v. *Edwards Books and Art Ltd.*, [1986] 2 S.C.R. 713.
R. v. *Hess*, [1990] 2 S.C.R. 906.
R. v. *Oakes*, [1986] 1 S.C.R. 103.
RJR-MacDonald v. *A-G Canada*, [1995] 3 S.C.R. 199.
Reference re Education Act of Ontario and Minority Language Education Rights (1984),
10 D.L.R. (4th) 491 (O.C.A.).
Reference Re MacVicar and Superintendent of Family and Child Services (1986), 34
D.L.R. (4th) 488 (B.C.S.C.).
Reference re ss. 193 and 195.1(1)(c) Criminal Code of Canada, [1990] 1 S.C.R. 1123.
Reference re Secession of Quebec, [1998] 2 S.C.R. 217.
Schachter v. *Canada*, [1992] 2 S.C.R. 679.
Singh v. *Minister of Employment and Immigration*, [1985] 1 S.C.R. 177.
Slaight Communications v. *Davidson*, [1989] 1 S.C.R. 1038.
Thomson Newspapers v. *Canada*, [1998] 1 S.C.R. 877.
Vriend v. *Alberta*, [1998] 1 S.C.R. 493.
R. v. *Willocks* (1995), 22 O.R. (3d) 552 (Gen. Div.).

3. SECONDARY MATERIALS

Bourgeois, D.J., *The Law of Charitable and Non-profit Organzations*, 2nd edition,
(Toronto: Butterworths, 1995).
Hogg, P.W. *Constitutional Law of Canada* (4th ed., loose-leaf, supp. to 1997)
(Scarborough: Carswell).
Royal Commission on Aboriginal Peoples, Perspectives and Realities, vol. 4 (Ottawa:
Minister of Supplies and Services Canada, 1996).

IN THE HIGH COURT OF THE DOMINION OF CANADA
(Appeal from the Ontario Court of Appeal)

BETWEEN:

ORGANIZATION OF ABORIGINAL WOMEN
(OAW)

Appellant

-AND-

HER MAJESTY THE QUEEN IN RIGHT OF ONTARIO

Respondent

FACTUM OF THE RESPONDENT
ORGANIZATION OF ABORIGINAL WOMEN

Counsel for the Respondent

Team #2
Wilson Moot 2000

PART I: STATEMENT OF FACTS

1. The Respondent is the Attorney-General of Ontario.

2. The Appellant is the Organization of Aboriginal Women (OAW), an organization which claims to represent status Indian women, non-status Aboriginal women and Métis women across Canada. The OAW is a national, non-profit organization that was incorporated in 1977.

3. The Casino Program is an Ontario Government initiative to assist Aboriginal people who live on-reserve to set up a casino on reserve land. The Casino Program was implemented after three years of negotiations between the Ontario Government and the Assembly of Ontario's First Nations (AOFN), an organization that addresses the interests of 132 band councils in Ontario.

4. The AOFN has an accountable political structure that democratically represents its 132 band councils. The band councils also have political structures that represent their respective members. The 132 bands are comprised mostly, but not exclusively, of Indians registered under the *Indian Act* (often referred to as "status Indians"), and all of them have reserve land bases

Official Problem at 1, 2.

Indian Act, R.S.C. 1985, c. I-5.

5. The negotiations resulted in an agreement between Ontario and the AOFN that the Casino's net revenues would be distributed to the 132 bands in the province through a First Nations Fund. The exact distribution will be determined in future negotiations between Ontario and band representatives.

6. The province's legislation governing regulation of casinos is the *Casino Corporation of Ontario Act*, which the province amended in 1995 to allow payments to be made pursuant to approved agreements regarding the Casino.

Official Problem at 1.

Casino Corporation of Ontario Act. The Respondents are assuming this *Act* is different from the *Ontario Casino Corporation Act*, R.S.O. 1996, c. 26, s. 5.

7. The Appellant is seeking a share in the Casino Program's proceeds and inclusion in the Program's ongoing negotiations. The Respondent has restricted negotiations and proceeds to the AOFN, which represents the legitimate recipients of the Program's profits, namely, on-reserve Aboriginal communities.

8. The Appellant brought an application in the Ontario Superior Court against the Attorney-General of Ontario, seeking a declaration that the Casino Program violates its members' equality rights under section 15 of the *Canadian Charter of Rights and Freedoms*. In addition, the Appellant sought a declaration that its members are entitled to a share of the Casino's future profits.

Canadian Charter of Rights and Freedoms, ss. 1, 15, Part I of the *Constitution Act, 1982,* being Schedule B to the *Canada Act, 1982* (U.K.), 1982 c. II, [hereinafter *Charter*].

Section 15(1) of the *Charter* guarantees

Equality before and under the law and equal protection and benefit of law - Every individual is equal before and under the law and has the right to the equal protection and equal benefit of the law without discrimination and, in particular, without discrimination based on race, national or ethnic origin, colour, religion, sex, age or mental or physical disability.

Section 15(2) of the *Charter* guarantees

Affirmative Action programs - Subsection (1) does not preclude any law, program or activity that has as its object, the amelioration of the conditions of disadvantaged individuals or groups including those that are disadvantaged because of race, national or ethnic origin, colour, religion, sex, age or mental or physical disability.

DECISION OF THE ONTARIO SUPERIOR COURT

9. Mr. Justice Perrin of the Ontario Superior Court held that the Casino Program was not authorized by section 15(2) of the *Charter* and that the Program violated the OAW's section 15(1) equality rights.

10.   The Court ruled that the Program unfairly benefited band councils to the detriment of Aboriginal people and, particularly, Aboriginal women. Mr. Justice Perrin found that the distinction between "status" and "non-status" with regards to First Nations Fund eligibility was likely an analogous ground of discrimination under section 15(1).

Official Problem at 3.

11.   Mr. Justice Perrin held that there should be limits to the government's discretion under section 15(2), as groups with access to government stand to benefit from section 15(2) programs to the disadvantage of groups without such access. His Lordship consequently decided that, under Section 15(2), one needs to examine the purpose of an affirmative action program and whether the program actually achieves the intended purpose.

Official Problem at 3.

12.   Mr. Justice Perrin determined that the Casino Program was intended to benefit Aboriginal communities in Ontario, and that the Program was underinclusive by

not benefiting the Appellant. His Lordship also found that the dignity of Aboriginal women in Ontario was offended because the Casino Program excluded a larger number of status Indian women than status Indian men from its reaches.

Official Problem at 4.

DECISION OF THE ONTARIO COURT OF APPEAL

13.   The Province and the AOFN appealed the decision of Mr. Justice Perrin to the Ontario Court of Appeal. The Ontario Court of Appeal overturned the decision and upheld the Casino Program as a legitimate affirmative action program within the meaning of section 15(2) of the *Charter*.

14.   Madam Justice Morin, writing for a unanimous Court of Appeal, stated that section 15(2) was an enhancement of the equality rights of section 15(1) and should therefore be interpreted broadly, and liberally.

Official Problem at 5.

15.   The Court of Appeal held that "section 15(2) requires governments to target disadvantaged groups, and also requires that the object or purpose of the program is to ameliorate the conditions of the targeted group." Once those conditions are satisfied, a program is a valid expression of affirmative action according to the principles of equality in the *Charter*.

Official Problem at 5.

16.   In granting the Ontario Government's appeal, Madam Justice Morin stated that governments have significant discretion to enact affirmative action programs without the hindrance of *Charter* challenges, as:

> [it] would be a perverse exercise for the court to try and ascertain which group is the most disadvantaged in this case and in others like it. Governments, who have no specific statutory obligation to set up affirmative action programs, should not be called on to defend such a program every time another group who believes it is or actually is more disadvantaged wants to be included.

Official Problem at 5.

PART II: STATEMENT OF ISSUES

17.   The High Court of the Dominion of Canada has granted leave to appeal on the following two questions:

1. Does the exclusion of the Appellant from participating in negotiations and sharing in the proceeds from the Casino Program violate section 15 of the *Charter*?

2. If the answer to question 1 above is yes, is the violation justified under section 1 of the *Charter*?

PART III: THE RESPONDENT'S ARGUMENTS

ISSUE 1: THE EXCLUSION OF THE APPELLANT FROM PARTICIPATING IN NEGOTIATIONS AND SHARING IN THE PROCEEDS FROM THE CASINO PROGRAM DOES NOT VIOLATE SECTION 15 OF THE *CHARTER*.

A. Section 15(2) should be interpreted as an enhancement of the equality rights under section 15 and should be interpreted in a broad and permissive manner.

i) Section 15(2) is an enhancement of the equality rights of section 15.

18.   It is respectfully submitted that the Casino Program, as an affirmative action initiative, is a legitimate expression of the equality rights guaranteed under section 15(2) of the *Charter* and therefore does not violate section 15 of the *Charter*.

19.   Canadian jurisprudence has not adequately examined the relationship between sections 15(1) and 15(2) of the *Charter*. There exists an underlying tension between section 15(1) as a guarantee of equal rights and benefits to all, and section 15(2) as a means to provide rights and benefits to certain disadvantaged groups to the exclusion of others.

Ferrell v. *Ontario* (*Attorney General*) (1999), 42 O.R. (3d) 97 at 110 (C.A.).

Lovelace v. *Ontario* (1997), 33 O.R. (3d) 735 (C.A) at 752 [hereinafter *Lovelace*].

20.   This tension is relieved through the treatment of section 15(2) as an enhancement of, and not an exception to, the equality guarantees of section 15(1). By their nature, affirmative action programs are exclusionary. However, they are not discriminatory, as they are singular attempts to overcome disadvantage, thus contributing to the overarching guarantee of equality in Canadian society.

21.   This interpretation of section 15 as a holistic guarantee of equality is best expressed in *Lovelace*, where the unanimous Court of Appeal stated that an analysis of discrimination is done on the following basis:

> Section 15(2) enhances this concept of equality by recognizing that achieving equality may require positive action by government to improve the conditions of historically disadvantaged individuals and groups in Canadian society. We therefore read sections 15(1) and (2) of the *Charter* together to embrace this one consistent concept of equality. Treating section 15(2) as an exception or defence to section 15(1) is antithetical to this concept.

Lovelace, supra at 752.

ii) Section 15(2) should be interpreted in a broad and permissive manner.

22.   In order to ensure the realization of equality through section 15(2) affirmative action programs, the programs should be assessed in light of their positive contribution to equality as a whole. This contribution merits a broad and permissive approach when these programs are challenged as discriminatory.

23.   There are great risks involved in subjecting affirmative action programs and their eligibility requirements to a high level of judicial scrutiny. American jurisprudence has indicated that an approach of "strict scrutiny," where affirmative action programs must serve compelling state interests and must be narrowly tailored to the purpose of the programs, has led to a substantial diminution of such beneficial programs. This approach is contrary to Parliament's recognition of section 15(2) as a legitimate means for bolstering equality for disadvantaged groups.

> Peirce, M. "A Progressive Interpretation of Subsection 15(2) of the Charter" (1993) 57 Saskatchewan Law Journal 263 at 265-272.

> McLachlin, Madame Justice B. "The Evolution of Equality" (July 1996) 54 The Advocate Part IV 559 at 563–564.

24.   It is in the best interest of promoting equality that governments are given every incentive to continue to implement affirmative action programs. Government action in this area should be encouraged rather than "chilled" by subjecting such programs to an unnecessarily high level of judicial scrutiny. As the unanimous Ontario Court of Appeal opined in *Lovelace*:

> Governments should therefore, be able to rely on section 15(2) to provide benefits to a specific disadvantaged group and should not have to justify excluding other disadvantaged groups even if those other groups suffer similar disadvantage. To hold that an affirmative action program violates section 15 because it excludes disadvantaged groups or individuals that were never the object of the program would undermine the effectiveness of section 15(2) and the ability of governments to redress disadvantage.

> *Lovelace, supra* at 757.

25.   Focused affirmative action programs which involve the distribution of fixed government resources should not be broadened in near-sighted attempts to alleviate the varied conditions of all those who are disadvantaged. Governments, which are under no positive obligation under Canadian law to enact ameliorative legislation, will be hesitant to institute such programs for fear of having to enact responses to all social ills.

> *Egan* v. *Canada*, [1995] 2 S.C.R. 513 at 596 per Iacobucci J. [hereinafter *Egan*].

> *Symes* v. *Canada*, [1993] 4 S.C.R. 695 at 760 per Iacobucci J.

26.   These programs may not be in the financial position to have their recipient groups broadened beyond their originally planned target groups, and the government may as a cautionary measure decline from participating in such programs as a result. Furthermore, over-scrutinizing the government's choice of recipients of a section 15(2) program will likely dissuade the government from implementing such programs, for fear of litigation from "would-be" recipients.

27.   Disadvantaged communities, such as on-reserve Aboriginal communities, will be less likely to propose affirmative action initiatives if they are forced by the courts to share benefits with other disadvantaged communities.

28.   The AOFN instigated the Casino Program and has exerted significant effort in the negotiation, establishment and operation of the Program. This Program has allowed the AOFN to improve its community without resorting to government dependency or other paternalistic "benevolent" measures. If the AOFN is forced to redistribute funds to groups that did not exert similar effort, then the impetus for self-improvement is strongly diminished. The AOFN's future ideas for an ameliorative program would be tainted by the threat of external parties usurping proceeds and benefits.

29.   The addition of further disadvantaged groups to affirmative action programs has significant detrimental impact on the effectiveness of these programs. This is particularly true when the program involves the cooperation of the government and disadvantaged groups, such as the Casino Program. The Program is not a broad spending initiative, as in *Eldridge* v. *British Columbia* (*Attorney-General*), or a general recognition of the rights of disadvantaged groups, as in *Vriend* v. *Alberta*. The Program only has a fixed amount of monies that can be distributed among specific recipients.

Vriend v. *Alberta*, [1998] 1 S.C.R. 493 [hereinafter *Vriend*].

Eldridge v. *British Columbia* (*Attorney-General*), [1997] 3 S.C.R. 624.

30.   It is incoherent to force the government to contribute additional revenue to a program that is a profit-making venture. The Program's fixed revenue means that adding further disadvantaged recipients will result in each recipient receiving a smaller amount. A reduction in proceeds to each group will lead to a drastically diluted program that may not be able to accomplish the ameliorative goals for which it was established.

31.   It is not in the spirit of equality to have a competition of "neediest" groups. It is impossible to compare the disadvantage of different groups in society when the disadvantages being compared arise out of wholly distinct economic, historical, social and political circumstances. The objectives of targeted affirmative action programs must be recognized and it is necessary to avoid condemning these programs as under-inclusive without examining the reasons for excluding certain disadvantaged groups.

Lovelace, supra at 760.

B. Challenges to affirmative action programs should be analyzed under a unique section 15(2) test, and this test should be liberally construed.

32.   Canadian jurisprudence has recognized a myriad of deference levels given to section 15(2) programs. Some courts base the legitimacy of these programs merely on the government's stated purpose and target group. In contrast, other courts have required further examination into whether the program meets its intended purpose. Some have gone as far as only protecting affirmative action programs from challenges by advantaged groups and have refused to protect these programs from any disadvantaged groups.

> *Ontario Human Rights Commission* v. *Ontario* (1994), 117 D.L.R. (4th) 297 at 303 (C.A.) per Houlden J.A.

> *Lovelace, supra* at 754.

> *R.* v. *Willocks* (1995), 22 O.R. (3d) 552 (Ont.Ct.GD) at 570.

33.   The Respondent submits that the appropriate test is in fact a compromise between these extremes. It is necessary to recognize the need for a liberal interpretation of section 15(2), while paying heed to the concerns that these programs may not be fairly benefiting disadvantaged groups.

34.   It is submitted that the appropriate test for determining whether a program is discriminatory under section 15(2) requires the following: a) objective proof of the purpose, and b) an examination of whether the program is underinclusive. To achieve these goals, the correct test, as outlined in *Lovelace* is as follows:
   a) Does the program have as its purpose the amelioration of conditions of a particular disadvantaged group?
   b) If yes, does the excluded group fall within the objectively determined purpose of the program? (If the answer to this is no, then there is no violation.)
   c) If the program is not authorized, a contextual approach to section 15(1) applies. In other words, is the exclusion of the group discriminatory within the meaning of section 15(1), taking into.account the particular context of the program? (If the answer to this question is no, then there is no violation, and the program is not discriminatory.)

> *Lovelace, supra* at 758.

C. The Casino Program is not discriminatory under the section 15(2) test.

35.   It is submitted that the Casino Program is not discriminatory under the section 15(2) test because it has as its purose the amelioration of a specific disadvantaged group, and the excluded group does not fall within that objectively determined purpose.

i) The purpose of the Casino Program is the amelioration of the conditions of a specific disadvantaged group.

36.　It is submitted that the objective of the Casino Program is to ameliorate the unique social, political, and economic disadvantages of Aboriginal on-reserve communities through a self-managed Casino gambling program and funding system.

Official Problem at 2, 3.

37.　Reserve communities are severely lacking in social programs in comparison to off-reserve communities. These communities have also expressed demands for self-government through reserve-based programs, with Casino gambling as a specific and historic exercise of these demands.

Lovelace, supra at 761, 763.

Official Problem at 2, 3.

38.　Reserve communities are also subject to restrictions on economic development as a result of the operation of the *Indian Act.* As outlined in the *Royal Commission on Aboriginal Peoples*, "the effect of these (property-based) *Indian Act* provisions has been to reduce access to financing for economic development significantly," and "the *Indian Act* removed Indian lands and property from the Canadian economic realm and set them aside in enclaves."

Royal Commission on Aboriginal Peoples, *Report of the Royal Commission on Aboriginal Peoples* (Ottawa: Minister of Supply and Services Canada, 1996) Vol. 2, Part 2, at 809, 812 [hereinafter *RCAP*].

39.　The Casino Program will provide substantial social programs for these communities while allowing then to develop their land bases. More importantly, the Program allows these goals to be achieved under a framework that realizes the interest of self-government and self-reliance.

40.　Ontario has a long-standing policy of encouraging targeted affirmative action programs for Aboriginal communities. The 1985 *Ontario Native Affairs Policy Framework* indicates that the government takes "a pro-active and developmental approach to Native affairs, based upon the goal of assisting Native people to become more self-reliant and less dependent on government services." The Framework promotes initiatives that support self-determination, enhance self-reliance and "provide specific services to meet the needs *of Native people* and support the protection of their cultures." Ontario's 1989 *Guidelines for the Negotiation of Aboriginal Self-Government* indicate that Ontario was guided by the objectives of "accountability of aboriginal institutions to community members consistent with the requirements of the *Charter* and applicable provincial legislation."

Ontario Native Affairs Directorate, *Ontario's Corporate Native Affairs Policy Framework*, (Toronto: Queen's Park, 1985) 1 [emphasis added].

Ontario Native Affairs Directorate, *Guidelines for the Negotiation of Aboriginal Self-Government* (Toronto: Queen's Park, 1989) 2.

41.   The Respondent submits that the Ontario Court of Appeal was correct in finding that Mr. Justice Perrin erred in concluding that the Casino Program benefited band councils. The band councils, as democratically elected, politically accountable bodies, are conduits to the on-reserve communities but are not the recipients *per se.*

42.   Furthermore, it is not "First Nations" in a broad sense that are intended to be benefited by this program. The term "First Nations Fund" does not connote all Aboriginals, but rather refers to the reserve communities. The *RCAP* has recognized that the term "First Nation" can mean "a single local community of Indian people living on its own territorial base, often a reserve governed by the *Indian Act.*" Ontario has used this context in formulating the First Nations Fund. The Fund targets a collection of single local communities with territorial bases, namely on-reserve communities.

RCAP, supra at Vol. 2, Part I at 157.

ii) The OAW does not fall within the objectively determined purpose of the Program, as it was defined, and therefore there is no violation of section 15(2).

43.   The OAW and on-reserve Aboriginal communities do not suffer the same disadvantages, and therefore the OAW is not within the objective purpose of the Casino Program. First, the OAW has no expressed or historic interest in casino gambling as an expression of self-government. Second, it does not suffer the same reserve-based economic development difficulties. Third, the OAW has not provided evidence that it is a financially and politically accountable body. Finally, the Appellant has access to a variety of provincially funded programs, to which the Respondent does not.

iii) If the Court finds the OAW is within the purposes of the Program, its exclusion is still not discriminatory, based on a modified analysis of section 15(1).

44.   If this Court finds that the Appellant is within the objectively-determined purpose of the Casino Program, the Respondent submits that the Program is still not discriminatory based on a modified analysis of section 15(1).

D. The Casino Program is not discriminatory under a section 15(1) test.

45.   If this Court finds that the Casino Program is not a legitimate affirmative action program, it is submitted that the Program is not discriminatory under section 15(1) of the *Charter.*

46.   The Respondent submits that this analysis is the same whether it is used as the third step of the section 15(2) test set out above, or whether it is used as the only test, resulting from this Court's refusal to give merit to a section 15(2) argument. In the case of the latter, it is submitted that the context in which this analysis occurs, i.e., an affirmative action program, is of the utmost significance and should therefore be recognized when proceeding through the test.

47.   The prime objective of section 15 is the preservation and promotion of human dignity. Mr. Justice McIntyre in *Andrews* v. *Law Society of British Columbia* stated that the purpose of section 15 is to promote a society "in which all are secure in the knowledge that they are recognized at law as human beings equally deserving of concern, respect and consideration." This purpose has been echoed in subsequent Supreme Court jurisprudence.

Andrews v. *Law Society of British Columbia*, [1998] 1 S.C.R. 143 at 171.

Egan, supra at 519 per L'Heureux-Dubé J.

Vriend, supra at 535.

48.   Mr. Justice Iacobucci restated this position in *Law* v. *Canada* and added insight through his definition of "human dignity":
Human dignity is harmed by unfair treatment premised upon personal traits or circumstances which do not relate to individual needs, capacities or merits. It is enhanced by laws which are sensitive to the needs, capacities, and merits of different individuals, taking into account the context underlying their differences. Human dignity ... rather concerns the manner in which a person legitimately feels when confronted with a particular law."

Law v. *Canada*, [1999] 1 S.C.R. 497 at 530 [hereinafter *Law*].

49.   The Respondent submits that the dignity of the Appellant is in no way harmed by the Casino Program, and therefore cannot be in violation of section 15 of the *Charter*. The Program has taken into account the needs, capacities and merits of the Appellant, and has found that in the context of the specific objective set out for the Program, the Appellant does not fit the criteria.

50.   This case is distinguishable from others where human dignity actually was in jeopardy of being offended. In *Corbière* v. *Canada*, for example, the right to vote was at issue. This affects the ability to fully participate in society by effectively silencing the voice and opinions of some of the communities' members. This constitutes an infringement of one's dignity. Such an issue touches the very essence of what it means to be a respected and worthwhile individual in society.

Corbière v. *Canada* (*Minister of Indian and Northern Affairs*), [1999] 2 S.C.R. 203 at 269 per L'Heureux-Dubé J. [hereinafter Corbière].

51. The Respondent submits that this is not a case where the dignity of the members of the OAW is in jeopardy. There is no evidence to show that the OAW contested its exclusion from negotiations about or participation in the Program, which were ongoing for a number of years. There is no evidence to suggest that the OAW felt in any way prejudiced when confronted by this well-advertised and media-exposed Program. There is only evidence that the OAW raised this claim as a result of its exclusion as a beneficiary of the First Nations Fund. This is a case about monetary beneficiaries, and nothing more.

52. While there is varying jurisprudence concerning the appropriate test to be used to determine whether discrimination exists under section 15(1) of the *Charter*, Mr. Justice Iacobucci in *Law* put it into concise terms as follows:

> a) Does the impugned law draw a formal distinction between the claimant and others on the basis of one or more personal characteristics, or fail to take into account the claimant's already disadvantaged position within Canadian society?
> b) Is the claimant subject to differential treatment based on one or more enumerated and analogous grounds?
> C) Is that distinction discriminatory?

Law, supra at 524.

i) The distinction drawn is not based on the Appellant's personal characteristics.

53. Affirmative action programs in their essence are programs aimed at specific individuals suffering particular disadvantage. It is these individuals, in this case on-reserve Aboriginal communities, who are being distinguished from the rest of society. The distinction drawn is not based on the Appellant's personal characteristics any more than all other Ontarians who are excluded from this Program.

54. Further, the Program does not fail to take into account the historically disadvantaged position of the Appellant. The Respondent recognizes that the OAW are historically disadvantaged, but this disadvantage cannot be appropriately addressed by the unique nature of the Casino Program.

ii) The Appellant is subject to differential treatment based on a specific set of criteria within the objective of the Program, not on enumerated or analogous grounds.

55. Under the Casino Program, the Appellant and all other Ontarians are subject to differential treatment based on a wide variety of characteristics, including accountability, access to reserve land, self-government concerns, historic interest in gambling and reserve-based need regarding economic and social development. These characteristics are unique to reserve residence and are not enumerated or analogous grounds.

56.   The Supreme Court of Canada has not recognized reserve residence as an enumerated or analogous ground. The Supreme Court had the opportunity to do so in *Corbière*, but instead restricted its judgment to allowing only "off-reserve band member status" as an analogous ground.

iii)   The distinction is not discriminatory based on a number of contextual factors.

57.   In determining whether or not discrimination exists in the case of an alleged affirmative action program, contextual factors must also be taken into consideration. While not an exhaustive list, the following, established by Mr. Justice Iacobucci in *Law*, provides a guideline of factors to be considered:

Law, supra at 534-540.

a) Pre-existing disadvantage.

58.   While the Appellant may be a historically disadvantaged group, this should be given little weight in the present circumstances, where merit and capacity to participate in the Program were the sole criteria for eligibility. Merit and capacity were based on an examination of the parties' accountable government, reserve land, long-term interest in casino gambling, and labour and participation in the early planning and negotiation stages.

59.   If the Court finds it necessary to take into account the Appellant's pre-existing disadvantage, it is useful to compare this disadvantage with that suffered by on-reserve Aboriginal communities.

60.   The Appellant is not a "discrete and insular minority," which is a significant indicator of pre-existing disadvantage. Only 48.5% of status Indians live on-reserve, while 51.5% live off-reserve. The status women, Métis, and non-status women who are challenging the Casino Program may, in fact, outnumber the actual recipients of the Program.

Official Problem at 4.

Corbière, supra at 258 per L'Heureux-Dubé J.

b) Relationship between grounds and claimant's characteristics or circumstances

61.   Legislation that takes into account the needs, capacity or circumstances of the claimant and others with similar traits will be less likely to have negative effects on human dignity.

Law, supra at 539.

62. The OAW is a broad coalition of interests that has no accountable governmental structure. The Appellant expressed neither an interest in casino gambling nor self-government. It has no distinct land base that would allow for future on-site casinos. The exclusion on which the claim is based has clearly taken into account the needs, capacity and circumstances of the Appellant.

c) Ameliorative purpose or effects

63. Mr. Justice Sopinka in *Eaton v. Brant County Board of Education* stated "the purpose of section 15(1) of the *Charter* is not only to prevent discrimination by attribution of stereotypical characteristics to individuals, but also to ameliorate the position of groups within Canadian society who have suffered disadvantage by exclusion from mainstream society."

Eaton v. Brant County Board of Education, [1997] 1 S.C.R. 241 at 266.

64. The Casino Program is an ameliorative initiative that will have a substantial positive effect on the targeted on-reserve Aboriginal communities in Ontario. These communities have suffered exclusion from mainstream society and the Program is a calculated and measured attempt to remedy that exclusion.

d) Nature of Interest Affected

65. In considering this factor, Mr. Justice Iacobucci in *Law* advises that we ask the question whether "the distinction restricts access to a fundamental social institution" or affects a "basic aspect of full membership in Canadian society," or "constitute[s] a complete non-recognition of a particular group."

Law, supra at 540.

66. The Casino Program in question is not a fundamental social institution, but rather an affirmative action program designed to benefit a particular group in society. The exclusion of the OAW in no way restricts it from participating fully in Canadian society. As with other Ontarians, the OAW is merely restricted from a program targeted at one sector of society. It is in no way restricted from participating in any other provincial programs which may include it in their target group.

67. Finally, the exclusion of the Appellant from this particular Casino Program does not constitute complete non-recognition. Members of the OAW are not precluded from accessing different social programs, as off-reserve Aboriginal women, nor are they prevented from instigating their own ameliorative programs in conjunction with the Government.

ISSUE 2: THE EXCLUSION OF THE APPELLANT FROM THE CASINO PROGRAM IS JUSTIFIED UNDER SECTION 1 OF THE *CHARTER*.

[paras. 68–104 omitted]

PART IV: ORDER SOUGHT

105. The Respondent respectfully submits that this appeal be dismissed and that the questions in this appeal be answered as follows:

1. Does the exclusion of the Appellant from participating in negotiations and sharing in the proceeds from the Casino Program violate section 15 of the *Charter*?

No.

2. If the answer to question 1 above is yes, is the violation justified under section 1 of the *Charter*?

Yes.

ALL OF WHICH IS RESPECTFULLY SUBMITTED
Dated at Toronto, this 15th day of February, 1999
COUNSEL FOR THE RESPONDENT
TEAM 2

PART V: APPENDIX

TABLE OF AUTHORITIES

1. LEGISLATION

Canadian Charter of Rights and Freedoms, ss.1, 15, Part I of the *Constitution Act, 1982*, being Schedule B to the *Canada Act, 1982* (U.K.), 1982, c. II.
Indian Act, R.S.C. 1985, c. I-5.
Ontario Casino Corporation Act, R.S.O. 1996 c. 26, s. 5.

2. CASE LAW

Andrews v. *Law Society of British Columbia*, [1989] 1 S.C.R. 143.
Corbière v. *Canada (Minister of Indian and Northern Afairs)*, [1992] 2 S.C.R. 203 at 269.
Dagenais v .*Canadian Broadcasting Corp.*, [1994] 3 S.C.R. 835.
Eaton v. *Brant County Board of Education*, [1997] 1 S.C.R. 241.
Edwards Books and Art v. *The Queen* (1986), 35 D.L.R. (4th) 1 (S.C.C.).
Egan v. *Canada*, [1995] 2 S.C.R. 513.
Eldridge v. *British Columbia (Attorney-General)*, [1997] 3 S.C.R. 624.
Ferrell v. *Ontario (Attorney General)* (1999), 42 O.R. (3d) 97 at 110 (C.A.).
Irwin Toy Ltd. v. *Quebec (AG)* (1989), 58 D.L.R. (4th) 577 (S.C.C.).
Law v. *Canada*, [1999] 1 S.C.R. 497.
Lovelace v. *Ontario* (1997), 33 O.R. (3d) 735 (C.A.).
McKinney v. *University of Guelph* (1990), 76 D.L.R. (4th) 545 (S.C.C.).
Ontario Human Rights Commission v. *Ontario* (1994), 117 D.L.R. (4th) 297 (C.A.).
R. v. *Oakes* (1996), 26 D.L.R. (4th) 200 (S.C.C.).
R. v. *Willocks* (1995), 22 O.R. (3d) 552 (Ont.Ct.GD).
Reference Re Secession of Quebec, [1998] 2 S.C.R. 217.
RJR MacDonald Inc. v. *Canada (Attorney General)*, [1995] 3 S.C.R. 199.
Symes v. *Canada*, [1993] 4 S.C.R. 695.
Thomson Newspapers Co. v. *Canada (Attorney General)* (1998), 159 D.L.R. (4th) 385 (S.C.C.).
Vriend v. *Alberta*, [1998] 1 S.C.R. 493.

3. SECONDARY MATERIALS

Hogg, P.W. *Constitutional Law of Canada, 1998* (student edition), (Scarborough: Carswell, 1998).
McLachlin, Madam Justice B., "The Evolution of Equality" (July 1996) 54 The Advocate Part IV 559.
Ontario Native Affairs Directorate, *Guidelines for the Negotiation of Aboriginal Self-Government* (Toronto: Queen's Park, 1989).
Ontario Native Affairs Directorate, *Ontario's Corporate Native Affairs Policy Framework* (Toronto: Queen's Park, 1985).
Ontario Native Affairs Secretariat, *Aboriginal Policy Framework* (1999), online: Government of Ontario <http.//www.nativeaffairs.jus.gov.on.ca/english/goals.htm, http://www.nativeaffairs.jus.gov.on.ca/english/self-rel.htm> (date accessed: 13 February 2000).

Ontario Native Affairs Secretariat, *Aboriginal Policy Framework* (1999), online: Government of Ontario (date accessed: 13 February 2000).

Peirce, M., "A Progressive Interpretation of Subsection 15(2) of the *Charter*," (1993) 57 Saskatchewan Law Journal 263.

Royal Commission on Aboriginal Peoples, *Report of the Royal Commission on Aboriginal Peoples* (Ottawa: Minister of Supply and Services, 1996).

Model Examinations

QUESTION:

Ding Dong operate the main phone service in Downsvoid, a mid-sized community in Northern Ontario. A worker at their headquarters negligently causes the electrical power supply to Ding Dong and the surrounding industrial area to be shut down; this puts the whole telephone service in Downsvoid out of action. Power is not restored for two days to the industrial area and the telephone service is out for three days throughout Downsvoid. A variety of effects results from this — a local taxi-cab company that relies almost exclusively on phone orders is unable to operate for three days; a couple of people die as a result of the emergency telephone service being out of service and ambulances arriving too late to provide timely care; a neighbouring plastics factory is not only shut down for three days, but its machines are so damaged from being halted in mid-production that they have to be scrapped and it takes two weeks for replacements to be obtained; and a set of traffic lights in a neighbouring street fails to work and an accident results. Determine the relevant tortious rights and responsibilities of the various parties. In so doing, what effect would it have on your answer if: (A) it was the custom among about half of the local telephone service providers across Canada to have an emergency back-up electrical supply; (B) there was a clause on the back of the monthly bill that Ding Dong sent to all its subscribers which stated that "any liability resulting from the negligent operation of the telephone service is limited to the cost of each subscriber's monthly bill"; and (C) an hour after the shut-down of power and the telephone service, Ding Dong issued a press release on radio and TV that negligently advised everyone that power and telephone services would be restored within a couple of hours.

ANSWER:

Before we assess the fundamental issue of how Ding Dong (hereinafter "DD") and/or his employee could be liable, we have to first establish there are three potential sources of liability: vicarious liability for the negligent act, breach of the standard of care based on custom, and negligent misrepresentation relating to a misleading press release.

The first thrust of liability pertains to the doctrine of vicarious liability and whether the employee or DD should be held liable for the negligent act of cutting the power to the local area. As stated in *London Drugs*, an employer will be held strictly liable for the actions of his employees when three criteria have been fulfilled: (1) and employee has committed a tort: (2) the person shown committing the tort is an employee; and (3) the tort committed was done during the course of employment. Perhaps the biggest factual contention will relate to whether the act of negligence was committed during the course of "employment." In other words, was the act in question an unauthorized or an authorized act? If the act is found to be unauthorized, then the employee alone, as per *Lister*, will be held liable for the negligent act of cutting power. If not, and the negligent act was committed during the course of "employment," DD will be held responsible for the consequences of negligently cutting power.

The second thrust of the liability relates to DD's breach of the duty of care with regard to providing telephone services. In particular, not having an emergency back-up supply. As per *Trimarco*, to establish a custom a plaintiff must: (1) present evidence of a general practice: and (2) have that evidence satisfy a standard of reasonable prudence. The ultimate threshold being that an assumed custom need not be universal, only well defined in the same calling. A plaintiff relying on this claim would argue that half the industry having back-ups warrants the assumption of a custom and/or a reasonable expectation. However, using *T.J. Hooper*, DD could counter that just because a portion of the industry had back-ups that does not mean that there was a custom and that a standard had been breached. Nonetheless, a plaintiff could also retort with *Hooper* by arguing that such a precaution was so imperative that its universal disregard would not excuse for omission.

The final thrust of liability pertains to DD's negligent misstatement on the restoration of power and telephone services. To pursue a successful claim, a plaintiff would have to establish a "special relationship" (*Hedley Byrne* and *Cognos*), that the statements were inaccurate or misleading, that making the statements demonstrated a failure to exercise due care, and lastly that there was detrimental reliance. If these criteria are fulfilled, a claim of negligent misrepresentation can be established.

An auxiliary issue pertains to whether DD can shield itself from liability as it pertains to the negligent act of the cutting power, the breach of standard of care relating to telephone services, and lastly with regard to negligent misrepresentation. With regard to the loss of power, DD would be hard pressed to argue that a contractual clause relating to telephone services governs negligence pertaining to loss of local power (*BG Checo*). However, DD could use *BG Checo* to its advantage by arguing that the clause does negate liability on an issue such as the breach of the standard of care relating to phone services. Nevertheless, on the issue of negligent misstatements it would again be difficult to argue that the exemption clause dealt with the specific subject of negligent misrepresentation.

FACTORY

The plastics factory (hereinafter "PF") would attempt to recover their economic losses related to the loss of power from either the negligent employee and/or DD—

pending a ruling on vicarious liability. The dominant issue being: was the economic loss pure or consequential? As per *Spartan Steel*, PF would argue that it can recover damages and lost profits that are consequential to damage directly inflicted on profit producing property. Based on this rule, PF would claim damages and lost profit for the two weeks it was without its machines (profiting producing property).

ACCIDENT VICTIMS

Similar to the factory, the traffic accident victims would also try to recover damages from either the employee and/or DD, however in this case the issue would be: was the defendant liable for injuries relating to power being cut to the traffic light? Using *Dorset*, the victims could argue that the loss of power to the traffic light does not break the chain of causation from the original wrongdoing because it was something "very likely to happen" as a result of negligently cutting power to the immediate area. However, using *Lamb*, either defendant could argue that the condition of the traffic light really is a matter to be governed by the question of whose job was it to ensure safety at the traffic light (policy)? However, we should not forget that the drivers could have contributed to their injuries by way of either not driving by the objective standard and/or not wearing a seatbelt (*Roberts/Froom*).

TAXI COMPANY

Distinguished from both the factory and the traffic accident, the taxi company would aim to recover its economic losses from DD from a claim of breach of duty of care. If a breach of custom were successfully proved, the defendant could argue that the company's losses was not from personal injury or property damage and hence was not recoverable because it was a "pure economic loss." However, the plaintiff could retort that DD could be held liable if it was in the "reasonable contemplation" of the defendant that the plaintiffs were likely to suffer economic losses as a result of the loss of telephone services (*Caltex*). However, using *Norsk*, DD could retort that although the taxi company's dependency on the phones was analogous to that of CN's on the bridge, the extension of recovery to this type of loss would produce floodgate claims against essential utilities.

AMBULANCE

There are two potential ways that the estates of those who died as a result of the late ambulances could claim damages for death. The plaintiffs could either argue breach of the standard of care of negligent misrepresentation. With the former, the issue exposes how values can condition the test of reasonable foreseeability. In order to prevent liability, DD could argue that even if there was a breach in the standard of care resulting in a paralyzed emergency system, one could have reasonably foreseen delayed ambulances and not death as a consequence (*Wagon Mound #1*). On the flip-side, the estates could argue that injuries are reasonably foreseeable if the emergency system does not operate and hence one is not required to foresee the extent or precise circumstances of injury (*Leech*, *Hughes*). Ultimately, the facts and liability will be interpreted based on how one phrases the question.

Lastly, using *Cognos*, one might try to claim damages for personal injury resulting from negligent misrepresentation. Whereby, as a custodian of emergency telephone services (*Spring*) one could argue that DD was in a "special relationship" with the public and failed to exercise reasonable care when it misled the public as to the reliability of that system. Moreover, referring to *Haig*, one could also argue that the deceased were certainly among the limited class expected to rely on this information.

QUESTION

(a) Is the decision in *Las Vegas Strip Ltd.* (Watson et al.., *Casebook* 5th ed. 1999 p. 494) a good one?

(b) There is a fire at a large shopping mall and this causes extensive damage. Property Inc., the owner of the building, brought an action against the 3 tenants in whose shops the fire allegedly started. One of the tenants, Episodes Bookstore, was found liable in negligence for starting the fire: the other tenants were found not liable. Now, the other 12 tenants bring an action against the same 3 tenants who also include Property Inc. as a third party. Three motions are brought:

(i) by Property Inc. to dismiss the third party proceeding against it;
(ii) by the 12 plaintiff tenants against Episodes Bookstore to have its statement of defence. denying liability struck out; and
(iii) by the other 2 defendant tenants for orders dismissing the plaintiffs' claims against them.

How would you dispose of these three motions?
[Students had 1.5 hours to provide an answer and a word limit of around 1250]

ANSWER:

As Justice Sharpe identified in his decision and Watson also notes in his article, *res judicata* exists to protect the public interest in finality of litigation and the private interest in being protected from repeat litigation. *Grandview* indicates that this principle not only applies to what courts actually decided upon, but also "to every point which properly belonged to the subject of litigation and which the parties, exercising reasonable diligence, might have brought forward at that time." The *Restatement* suggests that this "subject of litigation" is increasingly understood as the "transaction" uniting the plaintiff and the defendant. The decisions of *Cahoon* and *Cox* denote that this understanding is also the predominant approach in Canada. Indeed, Pinos suggests that the concept of "cause of action" as it applies to *res judicata* should be supplanted with that of "matter" or "transaction."

In *Las Vegas*, the matter, as Sharpe defined it, was whether LasVegas had a legal right to carry on its operation. Clearly, as one defines the matter more broadly, the chance of attracting the bar of *res judicata* increases; but Sharpe, in distinguishing the facts before him from those of *Greymac* and considering the view in *Grandview* on this point, appears to have characterized the matter appropriately.

As challenging the constitutionality of legislation is (and was in the mid 1990s) commonly referred to as "the last defence of all scoundrels," there can be little doubt that the status of the by-law "properly belonged to the subject of litigation" in the first action of Las Vegas, thereby attracting the application of *res judicata*. Moreover, given the evidence before Sharpe, it was clearly open for him to determine that Hilmy, Khan, and Sohmer were merely the privies of Las Vegas, thereby precluding their actions. His further finding in *obitur*, however, that Sohmer's action would have constituted an abuse of process even if she was not a Las Vegas privy, likely goes too far. *At most*, it appears that even if it may be said that Sohmer should have litigated her action with Las Vegas in the first action, she should simply be forced to pay solicitor and client costs, as *Germscheid* suggests; not have her claimed barred altogether.

Cleary, however, suggests that dismissing an action on grounds endorsed by *Grandview* and *Las Vegas* is too severe a penalty. Although he wrote before the case was decided, Cleary favours applying the approach of *Germscheid* to circumstances where plaintiffs should have brought a particular cause of action in their first action against the same defendant. Indeed, there may be compelling reasons to adopt this approach given the facts of *Las Vegas*. For example, the public's interest in determining the constitutionality of legislation should be considered, the plaintiff's change of lawyers may have been a complicating factor (although Sharpe dismisses this point), and the plaintiff's attempt to have their pleadings read liberally by the Court of Appeal in their first action was refused. Indeed, courts' broad-based approach to the abuse of process doctrine, as evident in *Vos*, may leave room for Cleary's approach. Nevertheless, *Las Vegas* remains a "good" decision as it appropriately applies the existing principle of *res judicata*; a principle also founded on important policy considerations.

(5)(b)(i)

The issue here is whether the three tenants rightly include Property *as a third party* to this proceeding. Because the facts stipulate that Property is to be added as "a third party," I assume that compulsory joinder under Rule 5.03 is not at issue.

Rule 29.01 indicates that a defendant may commence a third party claim against a person who a) may be liable to the defendant for all or part of the plaintiff's claim, b) may be liable to the defendant for an independent claim, or c) the third party should be bound by the determination of an issue arising between the plaintiff and the defendant. This rule is subject to Rule 29.09, which stipulates that the plaintiff is not to be prejudiced by the inclusion of the third party.

Carswell further indicates that the "primary consideration here is that all parties involved in the same factual situation have their rights determined without a multiplicity of proceedings." Moreover, *Hannah* suggests that courts consider whether or not the addition of the third party will constitute an inconvenience.

Given the facts, it appears possible that Property, as it is the owner of the building at issue, may be liable to either the plaintiff or the defendants as its negligence in caring for the building *could* have been a contributing factor to the fire; thereby meeting the requirements of Rule 29.01 and *Carswell*. Also, there does not appear to be any issue of inconvenience to the plaintiff or the court; thereby passing the scrutiny of Rule 29.09 and *Hannah*.

However, given the *Las Vegas* case, if the defendants wanted to bring a claim against Property, they should have done so in the first action. Accordingly, I would grant Property's motion on the grounds that cause of action estoppel would prevent the defendants from forwarding any claim against Property.

(5)(b)(ii)

As *Park Lane* suggests, in the United States, the issue here would be termed as whether or not the plaintiffs may apply the doctrine of offensive non-mutual issue estoppel against Episodes. In Canada, however, the issue would be phrased as whether or not Episodes' defence in this action (given the judgement against it in the first action) would constitute an abuse of process.

Because the plaintiffs in this action did not litigate their claim alongside Property and, given the requirements of Rule 5.02, the facts leave room to suggest that such a strategy may have been appropriate. Hence, the plaintiffs may be found to be "wait and see plaintiffs" and, accordingly, their action may itself be found to constitute an abuse of process.

Bomac indicates that in such circumstances, "wait and see plaintiffs" will be bound by the result of the first action; *regardless* of whether or not the decision is favourable to their position. Moreover, *Germscheid* denotes that, to deter the phenomenon of "wait and see plaintiffs," plaintiffs may bring their action but must pay solicitor and client costs.

Accordingly, given *Bomac*, I would grant the plaintiffs' motion as permitting Episodes to forward its defence a second time would constitute an abuse of process. However, *if* it were found that the plaintiffs could have easily joined Property in the earlier action, I would order them to pay solicitor and client costs.

(5)(b)(iii)

The issue here is whether the plaintiffs have rightly claimed against the other two defendants.

Although the facts do not explicitly suggest that this is the case, if any of the plaintiffs constituted privies of Property, I would dismiss the claims of those plaintiffs on the grounds of cause of action estoppel as justice Sharpe dismissed Sohmer's action in *Las Vegas*.

Moreover, given *Bomac*, if the first action found that the other two defendants where not liable (as the facts leave room for one to infer), I would also grant the defendants' motion to avoid an abuse of process.

I should note that my rulings are consistent with those of the judge who presided over a very similar set of facts in *Nigro*.

INDEX

Marquis Book Printing Inc.

Québec, Canada

2008